The Agricultural Economy
of Northeast Brazil

A WORLD BANK RESEARCH PUBLICATION

The Agricultural Economy of Northeast Brazil

Gary P. Kutcher and Pasquale L. Scandizzo

PUBLISHED FOR THE WORLD BANK
The Johns Hopkins University Press
BALTIMORE AND LONDON

Library of Congress Cataloging in Publication Data

Kutcher, Gary P., 1944–
    The agricultural economy of northeast Brazil.
    (A World bank research publication)
    Bibliography: p. 259
    Includes index.
    1. Agricultural—Economic aspects—Brazil, Northeast.
I. Scandizzo, Pasquale L.   II. Title.   III. Series.
HD1872.K87   338.1'0981'3   81-47615
ISBN 0-8018-2581-4   AACR2

Contents

Tables

Figures

Map

Abbreviations

ANCAR	Associacao Nordestina de Credito e Assistencia Rural (National Agricultural Extension and Credit Agency)
BB	Banco do Brasil (Bank of Brazil)
BNB	Banco do Nordeste do Brasil (Bank of Northeast Brazil)
CEPA	Comissao Estadual de Planejamento Agricola (State Agricultural Planning Commissions)
CHESF	Sao Francisco Hydroelectric Company
CVSF	Sao Francisco Valley Commission
DNOCS	Departamento Nacional de Obras Contra as Secas (National Department of Works against the Droughts)
EMBRAPA	Empresa Brasileira de Pesquisa Agropecuaria (Brazilian Agricultural Research Company)
ENDEF	Estudo Nacional da Despesa Familiar (National Study of Family Expenditures)
FUNRURAL	Fundo de Assistencia ao Trabalhador Rural (Assistance Fund for Rural Workers)
GERAN	Grupo de Estudo para a Reorganizacao da Industria Acucareira (Study Group for the Reorganization of the Sugar Industry)
GTDN	Grupo de Trabalho para o Desenvolvimento do Nordeste (Working Group for the Development of the Northeast)
IBGE	Instituto Brasileiro de Geografia e Estatistica (Brazilian Institute of Geography and Statistics)
IBRA	Instituto Brasileiro de Reforma Agraria (Brazilian Institute for Agrarian Reform)
IPEA	Instituto de Planejamento Economico e Social (Institute of Economic and Social Planning)
INCRA	Instituto Nacional de Colonizacao e Reforma Agraria (National Institute of Colonization and Agrarian Reform)

INDA   Instituto Nacional de Desenvolvimento Agricola
                (National Institute for Agricultural Development)
POLONORDESTE   Programa de Desenvolvimento de Areas Integradas do
                Nordeste
                (Development Program for Integrated Areas in the
                Northeast)
PROTERRA   Programa de Redistribuicao de Terras e de Estimulo a
                Agro-Industria do Norte e do Nordeste
                (Program for Land Redistribution and Stimulation of
                Agro-Industry in the Northeast)
SUDAM   Superintendencia para o Desenvolvimento da
                Amazonia
                (Superintendency for the Development of the Amazon
                Region)
SUDENE   Superintendencia do Desenvolvimento do Nordeste
                (Northeast Development Superintendency)
SUPLAN   Superintendencia do Desenvolvimento do Plano de
                Obras do Governo
                (State Superintendency of Works)
34/18   Article 34/18, which instituted a tax credit scheme to
                induce industrial investment in the Northeast

Preface

The research reported in this study began in 1973. In that year, Robert McNamara's Nairobi speech signaled a broadening of emphasis in World Bank policies and operations toward a direct concern with the problems of poverty and the distribution of the benefits of growth. This change of emphasis had particular ramifications for Bank activities in Brazil, one of its principal borrowers. The Brazilian "economic miracle" of the 1950s and 1960s, in which World Bank financing had played a not insignificant role, had left conditions in the Northeast virtually unchanged. Despite several massive developmental efforts, this tradition-bound, predominantly rural region of 30 million people remained the largest concentration of poverty in the Western hemisphere.

A team from the World Bank's Development Research Center visited Brazil several times in late 1972 and 1973 to identify researchable questions about the Northeast. The team assumed that the Northeast "problem" was not confined to any single sector, and accordingly a study of the agricultural economy was only one component of the multisectoral Brazil Regional Studies Project that was originally formulated. Once the agricultural component had been embarked upon, however, the issues to be confronted proved so complex that the research on other sectors was not pursued.

At the outset information about Northeastern agriculture was so scarce that even the most obvious developmental questions could not be adequately addressed. Earlier students of Northeastern problems, most notably the Working Group for the Development of the Northeast (GTDN), led by Celso Furtado, had not been deterred by this situation. The Northeast Development Superintendency (SUDENE), the regional authority first directed by Furtado, had long had an agricultural survey planned and budgeted, but it was never carried out, reportedly for lack of technical assistance.[1] The result of this mutual interest in data collection was a survey of 8,000 farms conducted jointly by SUDENE and the World Bank in late 1973 and early 1974.

The present study is only one attempt to analyze the data from that survey and is by no means comprehensive. No panacea for the rural

---

1. Entitled "The Typical Size of the Unit of Production in the Northeast" ("tamanho tipico"), this survey was authorized during Furtado's term as superintendent of SUDENE.

Northeast emerges; no single policy prescription; no lending program. It is hoped, however, that the presentation of detailed data on the characteristics of the agricultural economy and the application of new analytical tools to identify some of the causal influences at work will help shed light on the sorts of measures required to stimulate agriculture and reduce the extent of poverty in the Northeast.

The views and conclusions presented in this study are our sole responsibility and are not to be attributed to SUDENE, the World Bank, or any organization or individual. We acknowledge our gratitude for the guidance, assistance, and support of the following: Peter B. Clark, who conceived and directed the project in its early stages and without whose relentless efforts the study would not have commenced; Arlindo da Costa Lima, our research counterpart in SUDENE, without whose expertise on Northeastern agriculture and immense energy the study would have also come to naught, and his colleagues, Alfredo Arruda Branco and Joaquim Veloso Maranhao; Yony Sampaio, Quirino Paris, Lee Bettis, and Daniel Loucks, who assisted in the early analytical stages; and Maria Helena de Castro Silva, Vinh Le-Si, and Scott Sirles, who provided expert research assistance, toiling long hours on computers in both Washington and Recife. Various stages of the manuscript were typed by Miriam Bailey, Maria McReynolds, Thelma Rapatan, Wendy Shinn, Leela Thampy, and Elizabeth Trask. Various drafts benefited from the comments of Jock Anderson, Bela Balassa, Wilfred Candler, Wellington Dantas, John Duloy, Antonio Giles, Vander Gontijo, Peter Hazell, Constantino Lluch, Gerald O'Mara, Roger Norton, Guy Pfeffermann, T. N. Srinivasan, and two anonymous reviewers. Rachel Weaving and Vivianne Lake edited the manuscript, and Barbara Palmer prepared it for publication. Chris Jerome corrected proof of the book, Pensri Kimpitak prepared the figures, and Ralph Ward and James Silvan indexed the text. The map was compiled by Julio Ruiz and drawn by Larry A. Bowring under the supervision of the World Bank's Cartography Division. The authors, of course, remain solely responsible for any errors contained herein.

More important than all of us are the nearly 8,000 farmers, administrators, and sharecroppers who freely gave their time and answers to the survey, and we wish to salute them; their only remuneration was the promise that the survey results would be used to study means of improving the lot of the Nordestino. If we have failed, our apologies are to them, their workers, and their would-be workers.

The Agricultural Economy
of Northeast Brazil

1

Introduction and Summary

The Northeast "problem" is one of massive economic and social disparity, compounded by an apparent intractability. For over a century, the plight of the Northeast has been a source of embarrassment to Brazilians, of unrelenting frustration to politicians, and an enigma to economic planners. More recently, the problem has become a major concern of other Western Hemisphere governments and international organizations, because it exemplifies the extreme case of a large and persistent pocket of poverty in an otherwise dynamic, rapidly developing country.

Since World War II, Brazil's growth and development have often been termed a "miracle." An agrarian, coastal economy has been transformed into a thriving, industrialized, geographically dispersed economic power. Per capita incomes have recently surpassed US$1,780 (1979) because growth rates in the industrial sectors often exceeded 10 percent. Population has more than doubled since 1945, and its concentration in urban areas has increased from 35 percent to over 60 percent.[1]

Industry, population, and wealth, however, have remained concentrated in the Center-South, and the available evidence suggests that this concentration is increasing. By 1970, the Center-South contained 61 percent of Brazil's population and received 76 percent of national income; the Northeast, with 30 percent of the country's population, received 11 percent of national income. For the 30 million people in the Northeast, the per capita income of about US$200 in 1970 was less than 38 percent of Brazil's average and less than one-fourth of that in the Center-South. Life expectancy at birth in the Northeast in 1970 was forty-eight years, compared with sixty-six in the South and fifty-six in all of Brazil.

Within the Northeast, Langoni's landmark study found that in 1970 the poorest 40 percent of the population received only 10.7 percent of regional

1. World Bank, *World Development Report, 1979* (New York: Oxford University Press, 1979), pp. 127, 129, 165.

income, which implies that more than 11 million Northeasterners were subsisting on about US$50 each—an annual income too low to ensure adequate nutrition, shelter, health, or education.[2] Indeed, census figures for 1970 showed that fully 75 percent of rural Northeasterners over the age of five could neither read nor write. Illiteracy rates in the Northeast range from 72 percent in Bahia to 78 percent in Piaui, the poorest state in Brazil.

Official concern has not been lacking. Several massive interventions have been attempted throughout this century. Innovative development strategies have been devised, and vast resources—both Brazilian and international—have been spent. Yet there has been little growth or development in the Northeast as a whole. The rural Northeast, in fact, may not have experienced *any* per capita growth: It continues to hold the largest concentration of poverty in the hemisphere. The Northeast problem remains an embarrassment to Brazilians and an immense challenge to economic and social planners.

There are, of course, many dimensions and complexities to the Northeast situation. It is not merely an agricultural problem, nor is it solely a rural problem. It is a problem of defining a role for a region that, having become disparate, can seemingly find no way out of its disparity. Many diagnoses have been made, many solutions attempted, and many other solutions may yet be possible. This study focuses on the agricultural sector, not because it represents the Northeast problem in its entirety but because the origins of this regional problem are rooted in the agricultural system; because the most dramatic effects of the problem are reflected in the lives of the 10 million or more people who continue to scratch out a meager existence in agriculture; and because the dismal conditions within agriculture have had spillover effects on other sectors and other regions, thereby contributing to urban slums, social unrest, an inadequately educated or skilled labor force, and nutritional deficiencies traceable to forgone consumption of basic food-stuffs.

In taking this focus, we do not wish to belittle other approaches nor to discourage other inquiries. Indeed, this study concludes that a comprehensive solution to the Northeast problem cannot lie solely in agriculture—but because agriculture lies at the core of the problem, it demands intense scrutiny. The following section begins to examine the Northeastern agricultural sector with a brief look at its origins, at the subsequent growing realization that a problem exists in agriculture, and at the inadequacies of the numerous indirect attempts to solve the Northeast problem.

2. Carlos Geraldo Langoni, *Distribuicao da renda e desenvolvimento economico do Brasil* (Rio de Janeiro: Editora Expressao e Cultura, 1973).

Development, Decline, and Government Intervention

The narrow, humid coastal strip of land extending no farther than seventy miles inland along the easternmost part of Brazil is called the Zona da Mata (forest zone). Tropical rain forests originally flourished on its dark, rich soils, but in the early sixteenth century cultivation began to transform Brazil's northeast coast into the world's most productive source of sugarcane.[3]

Early Agricultural Development

Portuguese merchants and explorers arrived in the Zona da Mata in the early 1500s, establishing intermittent trading posts along the coast and, not long thereafter, more permanent settlements under captaincies granted by the Portuguese crown. The captaincies, appearing as early as 1530, constituted the first attempt to secure a springboard for colonization, exploration, and commerce in Portuguese America. They provided the base for a thriving brazilwood trade in the sixteenth century and an even more prosperous sugarcane colony in the seventeenth century.[4]

The sugarcane crop has been a potent influence in Brazil's economic, political, and social history.[5] Indeed, Northeastern sugar provided the first growth stimulus for the entire country, drawing large numbers of settlers from Europe and slaves from Africa and yielding export earnings that financed expansion southward and westward.

Another major influence in the development of the Northeast region was the Dutch occupation during the first half of the seventeenth century. Ironically, the period of their occupation coincided with the most prosperous years of the Brazilian sugar economy. Although the Dutch never attempted to reform or contribute to the Northeastern socioeconomic structure, they did make every effort to assimilate, as much as possible, the technological and organizational aspects of the sugar industry. When, after a long struggle, the Dutch were evicted by the Portuguese in 1654, they proceeded to apply this wealth of knowledge to the creation of their own

---

3. Vivianne Lake contributed parts of this section.

4. Fernando de Azevedo, *Brazilian Culture: An Introduction to the Study of Culture in Brazil*, trans. William Rex Crawford (New York: Macmillan Company, 1950), p. 44.

5. For a fascinating discussion, see Gilberto Freyre, *The Masters and the Slaves: A Study in the Development of Brazilian Civilization* (New York: Alfred Knopf, 1946; abridged ed., 1964).

sugar industry in their new Caribbean colonies. This new sugar source was equally as productive as the Northeast, and the resulting glut depressed the world price of sugar for the ensuing century.

From the second half of the seventeenth century, the sugar industry in the Northeast began to decline, and the impetus of Brazil's development moved south with the discovery of gold and other minerals. The excellent harbors and more fertile agricultural land in the South attracted settlement and agricultural development, particularly of coffee, to that region. Even sugar enterprises turned out to be two to three times as productive in the South as in the Northeast.

Thus began a long period of stagnation and relative decline. The vestiges of the sugar-producing system hampered the introduction of the economic and social changes required to avoid agricultural stagnation in the region. The sugar plantations with their *usinas*, or sugar mills, were vast enterprises not unlike city–states, relying on slave and indentured or conscripted Indian labor. Sugar was cultivated to the exclusion of virtually all other crops. Workers were frequently prohibited from planting subsistence crops, in an attempt to preserve all the land for sugar or to bind them further to the usina. Production technology advanced little over centuries, relying on manual labor except in the use of draft power to transport the product.

The socioeconomic and political structures of the Northeast as formulated during the 1600s remained virtually unchanged for centuries as well; nevertheless, each of the factors related to the sugar industry—the plantation, slavery, and free labor—exercised a profound influence on the development of the Northeast life style and its dispersion throughout the interior regions.

The captaincy, for example, spawned the plantation system, which was further subdivided by the landowner into plots rented out to individual farmers. This system, in turn, was emulated in the Northeast interior in the form of estates and sharecropped lands. Thus, from the onset of colonization, the pattern was set for a rural social structure based on economic dependence rather than a legal-political form of social organization.[6]

Slave labor, a factor of great sociocultural significance in the complex network of economic ties, was introduced simultaneously with the sugar plantation as necessary for continued agrarian growth. Its inherent characteristics of "patronage and paternalism" reverberated much beyond abolition in 1889 and influenced the very nature of socioeconomic relations in Brazil as a whole.[7]

6. Shepard Forman, *The Brazilian Peasantry* (New York: Columbia University Press, 1975), p. 23.

7. Ibid., pp. 21–22.

At the other end of the agricultural labor spectrum arose a new class of tenant farmers, the result of the subdivided estates. These tenant farmers represented the first form of free labor in Brazil, and when sugar production fell in the second half of the seventeenth century, many unemployed farmers became the driving force toward settlement of the interior.

Agricultural development progressed inland slowly, to the Agreste and the drought-prone Sertao, but poor access to markets, inadequate or unreliable rainfall, and rough topography have hampered the development of commercial agriculture in the interior even to the present day. Such agriculture as developed in the interior was of three types: slash-and-burn nomadic agriculture; small-scale subsistence farming in scattered areas with adequate water supply, such as river valleys; and large estates and plantations. The latter were similar in institutional structure to the usinas and also relied on dependent labor, but their products were more diverse. Such conditions led neither to the development of family agricultural enterprises nor to adaptable commercial farms.

Though not conducive to farming, the Northeast interior proved suitable for the expanding cattle-breeding population of the coast. The sugar plantations' growing needs for draft power and food led to a disproportionate expansion of the cattle-breeding sector whose nomadic nature, in turn, became increasingly incompatible with the sugar-producing economy. As a result, the Portuguese government finally prohibited cattle breeding in the coastal sugar zone and created, in effect, a new and separate subsistence sector in the interior region.[8]

While the coastal economy was increasingly disturbed by external economic factors and its dependence on imports of labor and capital, cattle breeding continued to extend farther into the Agreste and Sertao unencumbered by external dependencies. Its main asset reproduced itself automatically, entailing few major costs, and the demand for meat and hides continued to increase as a natural consequence of human population growth.[9] Cattle breeding was well suited to the climate and agricultural conditions of the interior and thus provided the first major stimulus to the penetration of a region that, otherwise, would have long remained bleak and neglected.

The second major incentive to inland migration was the discovery in the early 1700s of gold and other mineral deposits in central Northeast Brazil. Following trails already blazed by cattle raisers, the first mining pioneers,

8. Celso Furtado, *The Economic Growth of Brazil: A Survey from Colonial to Modern Times*, trans. Ricardo W. de Aguiar and Eric Charles Drysdale (Berkeley: University of California Press, 1963), p. 62.
9. Ibid., pp. 67–68.

known as the "bandeirantes of Sao Paulo" (mestizo sons of white and Indian parents), initiated a new economic utilization of the interior.[10] The respective quests of miners and cattle breeders soon became intertwined and interrelated: The growing opportunities gained through territorial exploration and expansion resulted from the respective efforts of both groups, to their mutual advantage.[11]

Thus, cattle paths soon developed into well-traveled trails along which towns and villages began to emerge. Cattle and gold not only enhanced the prospects of Northeastern economic growth but also, and perhaps of more significance in the long run, led to increased national unity.[12] The breeding and transporting of cattle and the search for new pasturage and mineral wealth decreased distances between North and South and caused East and West to become more interdependent.

The 1800s witnessed the introduction of cotton to the Sertao as another impulse to internal migration and development of agricultural estates. During a relatively long drought-free period (1845–76), the development of a new strain of drought-resistant cotton attracted masses of rural laborers from the Agreste, thus adding an element of agricultural stability to the otherwise transient nature of the Northeast settler.

The increasing numbers of farmers, cattle breeders, miners, and mere adventurers who migrated inland represented a growing subsistence sector emanating from the coastal population because of the steady decline of the sugar economy. In the words of Celso Furtado, "the expansion of the economy of the Northeast during this long period consisted of a process of retrograde economic evolution: the high-productivity sector was losing its relative importance, whereas productivity in the stockbreeding sector declined in proportion to its own expansion."[13] Thus, while the perimeters of civilization continued to push farther southward and westward, the technological tools either remained unchanged or reverted to more primitive stages to adapt to the more primitive standards of living of the Northeast interior.

Though the nature of settlement in the Northeast, and more especially in the interior, was partially responsible for delaying the process of its own development, a number of other factors—climatic, socioeconomic, and political—have further impeded the development process from the 1800s to the present day.

10. de Azevedo, *Brazilian Culture*, p. 48.
11. Ibid., p. 50.
12. Ibid., p. 51.
13. Furtado, *Economic Growth of Brazil*, p. 70.

Insufficient and irregular rainfall is a major characteristic, if not a handicap, of the Northeast Sertao. Severe droughts occur about once every hundred years, and milder droughts approximately every ten years. Such periods are characterized by the aggravation of poverty, starvation, agrarian unemployment, and migration.[14] Yet, historically, the Northeasterner has been unable to avert the possibility of future disaster, waiting and relying, instead, on government assistance. The government, in turn, faced the same unpredictable climatic situation and thus responded only when the need arose, without any long-term planning or policy objectives.

Yet it was hardly the climate alone that determined governmental reaction to the Northeast problem. From the mid-1700s, when the sugar industry was declining rapidly in the Northeast, mining was becoming a lucrative alternative in the South, the nation's capital was moved from Bahia to Rio (1762), and Brazil's politico-economic centers of activity began thriving in the Center-South. As a result, the Northeast found itself isolated from the major impulses to growth, not only geographically but, of even more significance, politically, economically, and socially. Furthermore, since the creation of the republic in 1889, the Northeast had been divided into many states smaller than those in the South, thus reducing, comparatively, the amount of power the former could wield in the government.[15]

During the past century, the impact of droughts has been increasing in direct proportion to the increasing population of the Northeast. Intermittent attempts have been made to deal with this climatic problem by individuals as well as by federal agencies, but it is only in the past two to three decades that the government has sought to formulate a more systematic and comprehensive development policy.

By the late 1940s, even before Brazil's "economic miracle" had emerged, the plight of the Northeast and its growing disparity from the rest of the country had been recognized as a deep-seated and growing problem, not simply a transitory one overshadowed by the successes of the growth centers of Rio de Janeiro and Sao Paulo.[16] Social disturbances focused attention on the Northeast as conditions worsened. The growing income

14. Anthony L. Hall, *Drought and Irrigation in North-East Brazil* (Cambridge, England: Cambridge University Press, 1978), p. 1.

15. Albert O. Hirschman, *Journeys toward Progress: Studies of Economic Policy-Making in Latin America* (New York: Twentieth Century Fund, 1963), p. 17.

16. Roberto Cavalcanti de Albuquerque and Clovis de Vasconcelos Cavalcanti, "Regional Development Policies in Brazil: Precedents and Prospects," Seminar on Regional Development/Brazil, European Economic Community (Brasilia, October 17, 1972), p. 4.

gap could not be overlooked: By 1955 the state of Sao Paulo had a gross product 2.3 times that of the Northeast, although the latter had twice the population.[17]

Government Intervention

Until relatively recently, the underlying causes of the plight of the Northeast have commonly been viewed as environmental rather than economic or social, and most of the concentrated interventions in this century have been in response to specific droughts. This governmental tendency to take action only in response to impending dire need, together with the presence of Northeasterners in the decisionmaking body, were two key elements influencing the realization and impact of governmental assistance programs.[18]

Government interventions to alleviate the effects of drought date from 1906 (in response to the devastating drought of 1877) and have had two objectives: first, to provide relief through short-term employment in public works; second, to achieve a lasting solution to the drought problem by constructing water storage facilities—the so-called hydraulic solution.[19] Under the auspices of the Department of Works against the Droughts (a newly created federal agency that, having undergone several name changes since then, is known today as DNOCS), the hydraulic program and a serious agricultural research effort were initiated to help the Northeast prepare itself for future droughts. As many as 536,000 workers were employed in temporary relief works in 1958 (when this total amounted to 13 percent of the population affected by drought); such a large-scale mobilization is only one example of the depth of official concern for the region and its poverty. The public and private dams constructed in the Northeast probably number in the thousands. By 1955, public reservoirs had a storage capacity of 7,800 million cubic meters, increasing to 11,400 million cubic meters in 253 dams by 1972.[20]

After the calamitous drought of 1958, in which thousands starved and tens of thousands more were uprooted, attention turned from the shortage

17. Furtado, *Economic Growth of Brazil*, p. 265.

18. Ibid., pp. 4–6; Hall, *Drought and Irrigation*, pp. 5–7; and Stefan H. Robock, *Brazil's Developing Northeast: A Study of Regional Planning and Foreign Aid* (Washington, D.C.: Brookings Institution, 1963), p. 69.

19. Hall, *Drought and Irrigation*.

20. Ibid., p. 7. By comparison, Egypt's share of the net gain in storage from the Aswan High Dam amounts to only 7,500 million cubic meters. See H. A. El-Tobgy, *Contemporary Egyptian Agriculture* (Beirut: Ford Foundation, 1974), p. 28.

of water to its distribution and use. The failure of the hydraulic solution and the irrigation program that followed it have been extensively documented by Hall, Hirschman, and others.[21] The reasons behind the failure are still a matter of debate. Certainly the hydraulic solution suffered from a myopic, if not naive, view of the drought problem, and the irrigation program from poor management, insufficient technical expertise, and corrupt practices in the distribution of aid. It has also become clear that, although water storage may reduce the consequences of drought for people and, especially, animals, the irrigation potential in the Northeast is insufficient to warrant any large-scale program of investment. Hall feels that no level of investment in water resources will overcome the structural bottlenecks in the Northeastern economy, which not only prevent resources from being channeled to the rural poor but also impede economic growth. Earlier, Robock argued that "from the standpoint of formulating development programs for the region, it is crucial to recognize that the most basic problem of the Northeast is not the periodic drought but continuing poverty."[22] Significantly, an economic geographer comes to an almost identical conclusion: "The fact that there is a *coincidental* relationship between the drought area of Northeast Brazil and the area of greatest poverty does not mean that there is a *causal* relationship between them."[23]

The weaknesses inherent in the early intervention attempts came under attack during the administration of Epitacio Pessoa (1919–22), the first and only president from the Northeast. Although his plans for large-scale projects subsidized by foreign capital proved far too ambitious for Brazil's absorptive capacity at the time,[24] his efforts underlined a fundamentally misconstrued perception of government policymakers: In a country where a prosperous and an indigent region exist side by side, governmental intervention and spending are generally directed toward the growing demands of the former until its thriving economy permits surplus funds to be invested in the poor, stagnant region. Such a tendency might imply that the Northeast problem was not so much a climatic consequence as a result of political and administrative incompetence and inefficiency.[25]

In the 1940s, Jose Augusto Trindade, the first director of the DNOCS agricultural research program, further emphasized the need for consistent and effective government intervention, particularly in the form of irrigation

21. Hall, *Drought and Irrigation*, pp. 55–108; Hirschman, *Journeys toward Progress*.
22. Robock, *Brazil's Developing Northeast*, p. 8.
23. Kempton E. Webb, *The Changing Face of Northeast Brazil* (New York: Columbia University Press, 1974), p. 178.
24. Hirschman, *Journeys toward Progress*, pp. 30–31.
25. Ibid., pp. 36–37.

projects. Because Northeasterners had virtually never before been exposed to modern irrigation technology, they were naturally hesitant to integrate it into the region's hitherto primitive agrarian system. The government's responsibility was, therefore, to redirect the inhabitants' socioeconomic behavior by gathering and disseminating information, clarifying their perceptions of the Northeast situation, and reorganizing land distribution.

Not until the aforesaid conditions were met, or at least approximated, would government programs actually yield positive and long-term results. Trindade's perceptions of the Northeast problem have constituted the fundamental guidelines for intervention programs since the 1940s, but it was not until almost twenty years later, during the period Robock has termed "the new era," that serious efforts began.[26]

Before then, however, several other attempts had been made to alleviate the Northeast problem. In hopes of providing new growth impulses to the underdeveloped Sao Francisco River Valley, the federal government created the Sao Francisco Valley Commission (CVSF) in 1946, followed shortly thereafter by the establishment of the Sao Francisco Hydroelectric Company (CHESF). Though the performance of CVSF was rather ineffectual because of ill-defined objectives and geographically dispersed projects relying on annual funding (as opposed to lump sums), CHESF proved more successful in fostering growth incentives in the Sertao by providing an abundant new source of inexpensive energy. Nevertheless, CHESF remained primarily an engineering project and, like CVSF, was unable to transform the Sertao economy.[27]

Similar criticisms were leveled against the DNOCS bureaucracy. By the late 1950s it was channeling most of its funds into dam construction projects, instead of into more needed but controversial irrigation projects, as a result of the growing affiliation between DNOCS directors and engineers and Sertao politico-economic leaders and powerful landowners. Because no efforts were being made to promote self-sufficiency, the Northeast was perceived as a continual sieve for investments that could otherwise prosper in the Center-South.[28] Following a severe drought period in the early 1950s, DNOCS authority began to decline as its continued water storage policy, in a time when irrigation was so drastically needed, became increasingly conspicuous.[29]

26. Robock, *Brazil's Developing Northeast*, p. 88.
27. Martin T. Katzman, *Cities and Frontiers in Brazil: Regional Dimensions of Economic Development* (Cambridge, Mass.: Harvard University Press, 1977), pp. 134–35.
28. Ibid., p. 138.
29. Hirschman, *Journeys toward Progress*, p. 76.

A regional development bank, the Bank of the Northeast (BNB), was created about this time, marking "the first official government acceptance of the economic solution as a federal policy for the Northeast."[30] Unlike most federal development agencies, the BNB was situated in the Northeast to attract individuals dedicated primarily to the advancement of that region and to maintain readily available funds specifically for long-term investment loans that would encourage regional development.[31] The BNB therefore had the twofold purpose of promoting agricultural and industrial growth in the Northeast and simultaneously helping to prevent the continual loss of financial and administrative resources to the Center-South.

Ultimately, however, the BNB's performance was affected by many of the same socioeconomic and political pressures that had constrained Northeastern development in the past. Thus, in response to the calamitous drought of 1958, when disparity in income levels was reaching an all-time high despite the BNB's limited success in stimulating investment, the Working Group for the Development of the Northeast (GTDN), headed by Celso Furtado, produced a report entitled "A Policy for the Economic Development of the Northeast."[32] The Furtado report was an updated and condensed version of various diagnoses and policy prescriptions that Furtado and his colleagues (at BNB and elsewhere) had been producing for several years. It has been heralded as a "highly skillful document" and attacked as "a political document cloaked in the authority of technical economic analysis."[33] Irrespective of the outcome of the debate, few can argue that it has not been the most important document affecting modern Northeastern history. The Furtado report not only plunged national thinking firmly into the "new era" concerning policy prescriptions for the Northeast, it also (perhaps more correctly, Furtado himself) forged the institutional framework (SUDENE) and the programs that had, at least, a strong potential for dealing with the Northeastern problem. Significantly, it emphasized that the Northeast had to be treated as an integral part of the greater nation of Brazil, and its deteriorating economy as part of a national, rather than regional, problem.

Furtado recognized that the Northeastern economy, dependent on sugar and cotton exports to foreign markets as well as food imports from the

30. Robock, *Brazil's Developing Northeast*, p. 88.
31. Hirschman, *Journeys toward Progress*, pp. 62–63.
32. Grupo de Trabalho para o Desenvolvimento do Nordeste, *Uma política de desenvolvimento para o Nordeste* (Rio de Janeiro: Conselho de Desenvolvimento, 1959). This historic document is still a point of reference for development policy in the Northeast. Indeed, SUDENE's participation in the survey employed in the present study was based on the work program outlined in that document.
33. Hirschman, *Journeys toward Progress*, p. 73; Robock, *Brazil's Developing Northeast*, p. 111.

Center-South, had been disadvantaged by overvalued exchange rates and high rates of inflation, a combination that led to a severe deterioration in the interregional terms of trade. This, in turn, led to underinvestment in Northeastern agriculture and a steady capital outflow to the more dynamic regions. His prescription called for a radical transformation of the regional economy, to be achieved through a comprehensive strategy to strengthen the infrastructural, industrial, and agricultural foundations of the Northeast. The key elements consisted of industrial development based on the region's singular comparative advantage, cheap and abundant labor; emigration of the region's surplus population to colonies in Maranhao and to unsettled public land in the more humid areas of central Bahia; and a "more rational" use of land in the sugar zone to produce cheap food for the industrial labor force.

The Furtado prescription entailed further complexities, of course. For political reasons it did not directly address certain issues, and for lack of data it was not couched in convincing empirical terms.[34] Nevertheless, it exhibited the clearest understanding of the root of the Northeast problem: too many people on too little land depending on an agricultural system that needed to be made "more rational."

That the creation of SUDENE resulted directly from the Furtado report and that the majority of subsequent programs in the Northeast owe their origin to that report is now history. These programs have comprised remarkably intensive and innovative regional development strategies, the more important of which are reviewed here.

COLONIZATION. Efforts to colonize western and northern Brazil, including the Amazon region, have been in progress since the rubber boom of the 1940s. Although the GTDN's recommendations concerned the largely virgin Maranhao region, national policy was directed more toward the Amazon region, as was manifested most vividly by the Trans-Amazonic highway. Provisions were made for agricultural settlements along this corridor, and part of their justification was the alleviation of supposed population pressure in the Northeastern interior. A variety of programs and institutions have been created to promote this westward push.

---

34. Admission that the Northeast was overpopulated and, consequently, that emigration was needed was unpopular because it drew attention to the inadequacies of the agricultural system. Furtado resolved this problem by redefining the Northeast to include the frontier state of Maranhao. Land reform in the sugar zone, of course, has been politically explosive in the Northeast, and Furtado has been "noncommittal and reserved" (Hirschman, *Journeys toward Progress*, p. 78) on the topic, calling instead for "more rational land use" and "reorganization."

Though it is too early to evaluate the colonization efforts, there are three indications that such programs will not be sufficient to solve the Northeast problem. First, emigration has proven to be a highly controversial issue among landowners who have traditionally benefited from the comparative advantage of abundant, cheap labor. Sociopolitical leaders have also rejected the colonization proposal because it would reduce their constituencies. Second, where colonization has in fact taken place, agricultural productivity in these areas has been exceedingly disappointing. Even in Maranhao where rainfall is sufficient, yields are poorer than in the drought-prone Sertao, and soil erosion usually confines farming to slash-and-burn techniques followed, after two or three years, by cattle ranching. Third, much of the settlement has been spontaneous; the record of official programs has been poor. By 1972, the Brazilian Institute for Agrarian Reform (IBRA), the agency directly responsible for settlement, had managed to establish only 5,000 families on less than 500,000 hectares.[35] Cavalcanti and Cavalcanti note that even if official settlement goals are reached the various schemes will annually accommodate a number of families equal only to the net annual increase in the rural Northeast.[36] If this judgment is correct, colonization can at best only keep pace with the increase in the rural poor; by no means can it be expected to eliminate poverty.

INDUSTRIAL INCENTIVES. Having ruled out conventional development policy options such as the expansion of exports, the Furtado group emphasized the need for industrialization to develop the Northeast from within by providing employment for the transient Sertao population, establishing a regional entrepreneurial class, and keeping capital in the Northeast.[37] A fourth impulse to internal development would be the creation of an active industrial center that would generate incentives to growth throughout the Northeast through backward linkages.

The recommendation of GTDN that had the greatest impact on the Northeastern economy was the creation of the Northeast Development Superintendency (SUDENE) in 1959. Shortly after it was established, SUDENE began promoting industrial development in the Northeast through a highly in-

35. William H. Nicholls, "The Brazilian Agricultural Economy: Recent Performance and Policy," in *Brazil in the Sixties*, ed. Riordan Roett (Nashville, Tenn.: Vanderbilt University Press, 1972), p. 174. In 1971 IBRA was merged with two other agencies into the National Institute of Colonization and Agrarian Reform (INCRA).

36. Cavalcanti and Cavalcanti, "Regional Development Policies in Brazil," p. 35.

37. Katzman, *Cities and Frontiers in Brazil*, p. 136.

novative system of fiscal incentives named after the law (34/18) by which it was enacted in 1961.

This law enabled Brazilian corporations to reduce their tax liabilities by up to 50 percent by making deposits in a special fund established in the BNB and administered by SUDENE. This fund could then be drawn upon for private investment in the Northeast in projects approved by SUDENE. The 34/18 program resulted in a massive redirection of interregional capital flows, which has brought about an impressive transformation of the region's industrial structure.

Debates continue as to its success in meeting its stated goals,[38] but it seems clear by now that the program has had very little effect on the rural economy. During the scheme's first eight years, only 0.4 percent of the funds were invested in the poorest state, Piaui, generating employment for only 275 persons.[39] Nor has the program had an appreciable impact on the region's underemployment problem: By 1976, no more than 200,000 jobs were to have been created, a number amounting to 5 percent of the urban labor force and only 11 percent of the incremental growth in the labor force since 1960.[40]

If 34/18 has failed to solve the Northeast problem, it is not only because of its inherent emphasis on subsidizing capital in a situation of excess labor but also because the projects supported have been mainly confined to the coastal urban centers and have had very limited backward linkages to primary production.

LAND REFORM. Land reform has been adequately legislated, staffed, and funded but has not enjoyed sustained support. Indeed, there has been substantial official reluctance, along with the traditional opposition of littoral and Sertao landlords, to undertake reform on any appreciable scale despite widespread recognition of the inherent inefficiency of unused

38. See, for example, David Goodman, "Industrial Development in the Brazilian Northeast: An Interim Assessment of the Tax Credit Scheme of Article 34/18," in Roett, *Brazil in the Sixties*; David Goodman and Roberto Cavalcanti, *Incentivos a industrializacao e desenvolvimento do Nordeste* (Rio de Janeiro: IPEA/INPES, 1974); and D. E. Reboucas, "Interregional Effects of Economic Policies: Multisectoral General Equilibrium Estimates for Brazil" (Ph.D. dissertation, Harvard University, 1974). Goodman and Cavalcanti argue that the tax incentive scheme concentrated on capital-intensive sectors and failed to generate the expected employment opportunities. Reboucas, however, reinterpreting the evidence through a two-sector general equilibrium model, concludes that in the years 1959–70 the *net* result of the scheme was to increase industrial employment by about 40 percent over what it would otherwise have been.

39. Goodman, "Industrial Development in the Northeast," p. 260.

40. World Bank, "Rural Development Issues and Options in Northeast Brazil," report no. 665a-BR (Washington, D.C., June 23, 1975; restricted circulation), p. 116.

land's being concentrated on large estates while underemployed labor is abundant.[41]

In evaluating the effects of these three programs, it is important to stress that, despite Furtado's plans, they were introduced piecemeal, rather than being adopted as part of a comprehensive strategy for the development of the region. By 1961 SUDENE was emphasizing the lack of such a strategy:

> The growing populational pressure in the Northeast and the structural incapacity of the region's economy to absorb the surplus population have been the chief cause of some social and political problems of the utmost seriousness. These problems are aggravated by the fact that the Northeastern economy is based substantially on a subsistence agriculture, practiced mostly in zones of poor soils and subjected to periodic droughts. Such problems can be thus summarized: (a) a general climate of dissatisfaction; (b) the upsurge of much resentment toward the country's most developed areas; (c) the rising of rural workers' leagues claiming [that] the solution to the problem [is] immediate access to landownership; (d) increasing unemployment; (e) diminishing prestige of the Public Power in the greatest populational segments.
>
> All these facts, which do constitute a threat to the unity and the internal security of the country, come to a great extent from the inexistence of an overall policy for the economic development of the Northeast, as well as from the failure of only partial solutions that have been tried.
>
> The lack of an integrated conception of the economic problems that assail the Northeast has led the Public Power to a perfunctory action, involving high and growing expenditures of a merely assistential [*sic*] character and investments not always coordinated and complemented, with small positive repercussion on the precarious living conditions of the Northeastern populations.[42]

This assessment was apparently still valid eleven years later, for Cavalcanti and Cavalcanti stated in 1972 that "it is impossible to identify a prevailing policy in the Northeast, either of agricultural development, or industrial development or emigration."[43]

Even SUDENE, which in its first decade represented a politically and economically cohesive force in the Northeast, became guilty of the same

41. Comite Interamericano de Desarrollo (CIDA), *Land Tenure Conditions and Socioeconomic Development of the Agricultural Sector, Brazil* (Washington, D.C.: Pan American Union. 1964).

42. SUDENE, "The Brazilian Northeast and Its Institutions for Economic Development" (English version, Recife, 1961), p. 3.

43. Cavalcanti and Cavalcanti, "Regional Development Policies in Brazil," p. 31.

weaknesses charged against its predecessors. Its early role as an increasingly powerful agency and its determination to transform the traditional socioeconomic infrastructure brought SUDENE under stronger attack by the power elite which upheld that infrastructure.[44] Molded by such pressures, SUDENE programs were thus redirected toward typically noncontroversial transportation, energy, and water storage projects.

A severe drought in 1970 led to the creation of yet another federal program, PROTERRA (Program for Land Redistribution and Stimulation of Agro-Industry in the Northeast), whose financial resources, amounting to about US$1,000 million, by 1976 had grown to US$4,000 million, a figure twice the value of the gross annual production of the Northeast and an investment that attests to the level of official commitment to the Northeast's problems. Though the primary intention was to redistribute land in the Northeastern areas of greatest tension, this program has gradually been forgotten and become a line of credit that has actually made PROTERRA a mechanism of economic concentration.[45] As of the last available tally (1975), 17,000 hectares of land had been redistributed to less than a thousand recipients.[46]

That none of the above approaches had successfully addressed the rural poverty problem of the Northeast was apparent from the creation in 1974 of a major program designed specifically to raise productivity and rural incomes, particularly for small- and medium-scale farmers and sharecroppers. POLONORDESTE (Development Program for Integrated Areas in the Northeast) is a well-financed and staffed set of individual projects, already undertaken and in various stages of planning. The project areas are selected either because they have intense poverty problems or because they hold promise for rapid development with an appropriate infusion of modern inputs and techniques. For the most part, POLONORDESTE operates within the existing agrarian structure and the policies pertaining to it. Unlike previous programs dedicated to the establishment of new public works and social services, POLONORDESTE's main objective was to redirect and fortify existing projects to achieve greater efficiency and productivity.

Despite POLONORDESTE's potential for alleviating pockets of poverty and raising the productivity of its target groups, it does not provide "an overall policy for the economic development of the Northeast." The continuing

44. Hirschman, *Journeys toward Progress*, p. 89.
45. This sentence is translated from a quotation by former minister of agriculture Luis Fernando Cirne Lima, in *Jornal do Brasil*, November 20, 1977; it echoes William Cline's (and others') characterization of the program.
46. World Bank, "Rural Development Issues and Options in Northeast Brazil," p. 31.

plight of the Northeast and the scope of efforts to deal with it are perhaps best illustrated by the scale of recent drought relief works. From January 1976 to January 1977, for example, SUDENE spent about Cr$1,200 million (about US$100 million at that time) out of a fund of Cr$2,500 million to finance temporary work for 279,000 peasants.[47] This expenditure was roughly equal to the annual government contribution to POLONORDESTE. In a bad drought year, the number of workers seeking relief employment can reach 1 million.

Yet the creation of PROTERRA, POLONORDESTE, and EMBRAPA (the Brazilian Agricultural Research Company that has recently exhibited substantial concern for the Northeast) indicates that policymakers in Brazil are giving increased attention to the notion that the Northeast problem is rooted in agriculture and cannot be solved easily through roundabout policies and indirect interventions, no matter how well administered and funded.

The Approach Followed in This Study

The foregoing discussion has hypothesized that the root of the Northeast problem lies in agriculture, but numerous programs and policies have not significantly improved the state of the rural Northeast for decades, perhaps centuries. If the Northeast problem originated in and is perpetuated by the agricultural system, this system demands close scrutiny, unencumbered by political passions and enhanced by quantitative analyses. In short, the solution to the problem demands "fresh" numbers and "fresh" tools. The SUDENE/World Bank survey provides the fresh numbers, and modern econometric and mathematical programming techniques provide the fresh tools.

The approach followed in this study is twofold. First, we shall use data collected by a joint SUDENE/World Bank survey of 8,000 farms to describe the salient features of Northeastern agriculture: the size and distribution of the resources; the products and the inputs employed in the various farming systems; incomes and their distribution; and the performance of the various agents. Second, we shall employ a large-scale mathematical programming model of the agricultural sector, which represents farms of different types in different physiographic zones, to investigate the constraints in North-eastern agriculture. The model will then be used as a simulation tool to explore alternative means of relaxing those constraints and to estimate the

---

47. "O feijao e o sonho," *Veja*, March 2, 1977, pp. 29–30.

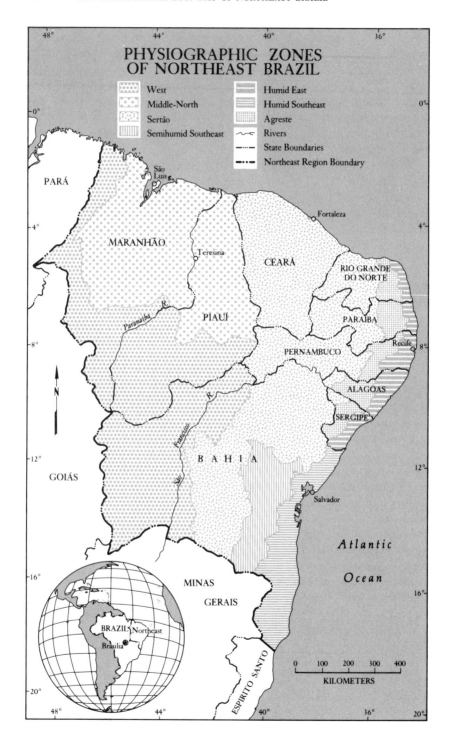

PHYSIOGRAPHIC ZONES OF NORTHEAST BRAZIL

West
Middle-North
Sertão
Semihumid Southeast
Humid East
Humid Southeast
Agreste
Rivers
State Boundaries
Northeast Region Boundary

benefits that might accrue from various policies or programs to assist the agricultural sector. The remainder of this first chapter is a summary of the study.

Summary and Conclusions

Climate and ecology in the Northeast are extremely diverse, and even within the smallest of its nine states as many as three different physiographic zones can be distinguished. This diversity is reflected in farming systems and in production and marketing patterns and may be the single most important reason the formulation of agricultural policy has been so difficult and disappointing. Most of the analysis in this study divides the Northeast into seven physiographic zones delineated in a SUDENE study.[48] These are shown on the accompanying map and described in the appendix to this chapter. They are, briefly:

—The West (zone A), a long strip comprising the westernmost portions of Maranhao, Piaui, and Bahia, of low population density, poor soils, though adequate rainfall, and slash-and-burn subsistence agriculture by often untitled squatters coexisting with extensive cattle ranches.

—The Middle-North (zone B), comprising the northern and coastal portions of Maranhao and Piaui; very similar to the West except for its closer proximity to the markets of Teresina and the port of Sao Luis and the predominance of an inferior variety of rain-fed rice, *arroz seco*.

—The Sertao (zone C), the vast drought-prone interior region where cotton is the most important crop and sharecropping on large *fazendas*, or plantations, is the dominant form of enterprise.

—The Semihumid Southeast (zone D), comprising most of the state of Bahia, with sufficient and timely rainfall and a wide variety of farming operations: subsistence farmers producing mainly manioc; large cattle ranches, which are the dominant agricultural activity; and cacao plantations.

—The Humid East or Zona da Mata (zone E), the traditional sugarcane area along the coastal portions of Bahia through Rio Grande do Norte.

—The Humid Southeast (zone F), a fertile pocket in the state of Bahia where cacao plantations dominate economic activity.

48. M. Lacerda de Melo, "Espacos geograficos e politica espacial: O caso do Nordeste," *Boletim economico*, vol. 5, no. 2 (July 1967/December 1971), pp. 7–139.

—The Agreste (zone G), a transitional zone between the drought-prone Sertao and the Humid East, characterized by mixed farming on small to medium-size enterprises and only rarely subject to drought.

Most observers have concluded that the heart of the Northeast problem lies in the paucity of its resource base. Chapter 2 describes the labor force, land, and capital in the region. Of the 18 million rural Northeasterners, between 5 and 8 million are members of the labor force, depending upon the definition used. The demographic census of 1970 found 5.2 million persons "economically active in agriculture." The agricultural census of the same year found 7.8 million persons "occupied in agriculture," of whom 2.2 million were "producers," in the sense of being a landowner, renter, sharecropper, or "occupier."

The SUDENE/World Bank survey undertaken for the present study distinguished different groups in the agricultural labor force according to the tenurial arrangements that affect their access to land: proprietors or landowners; renters, who are relatively rare in the Northeast and pay a fixed fee in money or product for the use of land; sharecroppers, who pay the landlord a share of their product, usually under an annual verbal contract; squatters, who work public or private land without compensating the owner and often without the owner's knowledge; permanent workers, who are either *moradores*, resident workers who receive, as part of their compensation, a dwelling and a small parcel of land for family production of subsistence crops, or nonmoradores, who are contracted annually but receive no housing or land; and temporary workers, who are employed when labor demand is at its peak and are paid daily or weekly at rates slightly more than US$1 a day.[49] The survey reported a total of 5.7 million agents in agriculture, and we take the figure of 6 million as a compromise estimate of the agricultural labor force.

Of the 6 million, less than 800,000 own land. Another 900,000 are working members of landowners' families; 26,000 are renters; and 1.14 million are either sharecroppers or permanent workers. Nearly 3 million agricultural workers have no formal or legal access to land and subsist on temporary employment or scratch out a living on landholdings so poor or so

---

49. Unless otherwise stated, the U.S. dollar figures in this study were converted from cruzeiros at the CR$6.4:US$1 rate prevailing in spring 1974 (the harvesttime in the Northeast, during which the largest number of monetary transactions occur). Because many observers believe the cruzeiro to have been overvalued by 20–25 percent during that time, the 1974 dollar figures quoted in this study may be unrealistically high.

remote that they were not registered by any of the censuses, the cadastral survey, or the SUDENE/World Bank survey.[50]

About 50 percent of the available labor appears to be underemployed. Seasonal fluctuations clearly account for part of this, but the lack of continuous access to productive land seems to be the single greatest cause of unemployment and poverty in the rural Northeast. Most landowners (even if they own only two or three hectares of poor land), sharecroppers, and permanent workers obtain twice or three times as much employment in a given year as do temporary workers. Temporary workers and their dependents make up the hard core of poverty in the Northeast. On the average, these workers are employed for only 50–60 days a year, at wage rates that give them family incomes of only about US$200 a year (1974 dollars). It is not possible to determine the number of workers in a typical landless family or what incomes they may obtain outside of agriculture, but it is obvious that many such families have incomes far below the absolute poverty line and that there may be up to 5 million people in this group.

Half of the 80 million hectares of agricultural land in the Northeast is concentrated in properties larger than 500 hectares. These farms number only about 33,000 and account for 4 percent of all landowners and a negligible percentage of all workers. One third of the farms in the Northeast have an average size of five hectares, on 1.4 percent of the region's agricultural land. Farms larger than 200 hectares, a size large enough to provide an adequate family income, make up nearly 70 percent of the agricultural land; their owners number 83,000—10 percent of the landowners and little more than 1 percent of all agricultural workers. In essence, 99 percent of the labor force does not have entrepreneurial access to nearly 70 percent of the agricultural land.

The survey data make it possible to value the capital embodied in on-farm structures, livestock, and equipment.[51] On this basis, the total agricultural capital of the Northeast amounts to about US$5,000 million, which gives a capital/output ratio of about 2. It is, however, concentrated in

50. This estimate of the number of temporary workers should be treated cautiously, as some may have been double-counted and some small farmers or their family workers may be included if, at the time of enumeration, they were working on farms other than their own. (Permanent workers and sharecroppers are not generally allowed to work part-time on other farms.)

51. Though the value of structures per farm appears to be correlated with farm productivity, rigorous analysis of the influence of structures is difficult because it is not possible to distinguish items such as housing from directly productive assets.

structures (which include housing) and livestock; factors such as equipment that contribute directly to modern production practices account for only 3 percent of the value of agricultural capital. Farm equipment inventories are extremely small and are particularly limited on small farms. In much of the Northeast, farms of less than 10 hectares have equipment inventories averaging about US$18—only three times the cost of a single hoe. The estimation of capital/output ratios suggests that substantial returns are possible from investment in Northeastern agriculture. Average capital/ output ratios vary little among different zones and size classes of farms, however, despite the fact that land/labor ratios vary dramatically. There appear to be severe distortions in the region's markets for capital items usually considered prerequisites for modern agricultural development.

Chapter 3 discusses agricultural production and incomes. Crops account for the bulk of agricultural production in the Northeast,[52] and virtually half of crop production is made up of subsistence crops, particularly rice, corn, beans, and manioc (cassava). Cotton and perennial or tree crops such as sugar, cacao, *babacu*, and *carnauba* (varieties of palm) are exportable and contribute about 38 percent of the value of crop output; the remainder is composed of fruits and vegetables that are perishable and have high income elasticities and limited markets within the Northeast. Almost all farms have animals of some type, whether cattle, pigs, goats, or chickens, though few can be said to specialize in livestock, and organized dairy production for the market is virtually nonexistent. Beef, mostly poor in quality and produced by fazendas, is by far the most important animal product in the Northeast.

That the bulk of Northeastern production is inferior and consumed locally suggests that the product mix itself contributes to the region's stagnation. No product has emerged to take the place of sugar in providing an export base to fuel growth in the rural sector. Indeed, most Northeastern products, including those currently exported, are of a type or quality for which there is a low income elasticity of demand, so that the region has not been able to respond to the growth of markets either in other parts of Brazil or abroad.

The gross value of agricultural production in 1973, a year not affected by drought, amounted to US$2,100 million. This implies that the gross output per hectare of agricultural land was less than US$30 and that the output per

---

52. Crops accounted for between 66 percent and 75 percent of gross agricultural output in 1973, depending on the source of the estimates: The first percentage is based on survey estimates for both crops and livestock production; the second is based on a combination of Instituto Brasileiro de Geografia e Estatistica (IBGE) estimates for crops with survey estimates for livestock.

member of the labor force was US$400. If the Northeast is not a net importer (there is no evidence that it is) and if one ignores stocks and savings, agricultural consumption valued at farm-gate prices in that year in the region was at most only US$66 a person, since some crops are exported.

A breakdown of production costs sheds some light on the reason for such low productivity. Expenditures on purchased inputs of all types (other than hired labor) average less than US$2 a hectare, but even this figure understates the primitive nature of Northeastern agriculture. In most zones, inputs for livestock account for at least half the average expenditures. The bulk of the expenditures in the Northeast are for fertilizer on sugar and cacao plantations and for insecticides and pesticides, which in some areas are prerequisites for cropping. The "green revolution" has not touched the Northeast: Less than 10 percent of all farms use selected seeds of any variety, and many of these are "selected" because they are available only from specialized sources such as cotton gins.

Income from agriculture in the Northeast amounted to about US$2,200 million, or US$120 per rural resident, in 1973. Its distribution was highly skewed. Farmers, owners, and their families accrued 75 percent of this total, although they made up only about 28 percent of the agricultural families. The remaining 2 million agricultural families earned total incomes from agriculture (both in money and in kind) of US$530 million, or US$265 per family. Because the average family consists of five persons, per capita incomes from agriculture do not exceed US$50 by much for these 10 million people. Permanent workers and their families probably have incomes slightly above absolute poverty levels, but the employment and wage rates of temporary workers suggest that they are much worse off. Monetary incomes, however, may have limited meaning in the rural Northeast. The National Study of Family Expenditures (ENDEF) undertaken by the Instituto Brasileiro Geografia e Estatistica (IBGE) in 1974–75 found that nearly half the welfare of rural residents accrued from goods and services produced and consumed outside the marketplace.

Farm incomes are highly skewed, depending partly on farm size and partly on location. In most size classes and zones, average farm incomes exceed US$250 a year by at least a factor of 2. For the class of farms of less than ten hectares in the interior regions, however, even the average income does not exceed US$207. About a fourth of the farm income accrues to the 4 percent of farms of more than 500 hectares; it is noteworthy that though farm income generally rises with farm size it does so rather erratically.

Because poverty in the rural Northeast is closely linked to lack of entrepreneurial access to sufficient cultivable land, or lack of full-time employment on such land, the performance of farms of different sizes and types is examined. The analysis in Chapter 4 of factor use and productivity on farms of different sizes and types strongly suggests that the large farm sector is not using resources with maximum efficiency to produce profits. Survey data reveal that the intensity with which land and labor are used declines sharply and consistently as farm size increases, from the smallest of six size groups (under ten hectares) to the largest (over 500 hectares). The smallest farms employ about half their land in crops; the largest, only one-tenth. About 85 percent of all land on farms larger than 500 hectares is not used for production of crops or of fodder. Farms in this size class control 48 percent of the land area and contribute 31 percent of crop production and 34 percent of livestock production. The smallest farms control 1.4 percent of the land, contribute 8 percent and 7 percent, respectively, of crop and livestock production, and produce up to 100 times as much output per hectare as the largest. The reason for the difference in land use lies almost entirely in the use of labor: Small farms throughout the entire Northeast apply twenty-five to forty-five times as much labor per hectare as the largest.

Different size farms perform very differently even though they have similar capital/output ratios, land quality, and crop yields and receive and pay similar prices. Farmers have substantial freedom to choose what they produce and to substitute among most factors of production, and production possibilities do not seem to differ according to farm size. Nonetheless, large farms tend to employ less labor than they would require to maximize profits, even though there is no shortage of labor available. On these farms the marginal productivity of labor is, in general, twice as great as the going wage rates. Small farms tend to employ more labor than profit maximization would warrant, probably in part because family members have difficulty obtaining employment elsewhere.

Labor is potentially the only factor in the region for which markets, delivery systems, and mobility are sufficient to balance demand and supply. There are strong suggestions of distortions in the markets for land and capital that, even more noticeably than labor, do not appear to be allocated according to rules for profit maximization. The marginal productivity of land on large farms is far below reasonable opportunity costs, whereas for permanent land improvements (structures) and livestock the marginal rates of return are erratic and generally below those from comparable assets outside the Northeast. For modern inputs and credit, the rates of return are consistently extremely high. Utility maximization, and farmers' expectations about prices and yields, may account for the divergences from optimal behavior. An alternative explanation may be that in the use of inputs other than labor the majority of the Northeastern farmers have very little freedom of choice because credit is unavailable and delivery systems are inadequate.

Although size is the single most important determinant of farm performance, farm characteristics vary substantially within the six size classes, and the need to aggregate these classes to a smaller, more manageable number for the programming model requires a more formal farm typology (derived in Appendix C, Chapter 5). Discriminant analysis based on the degree of commercialization (percentage of output marketed) and the percentage of labor supplied by the farm family, as well as farm size, yields three relatively homogeneous types of farms: family farms, medium-size or transitional farms, and estates. Family farms have an average size of ten to thirty hectares. They typically rely on family members for at least three-fourths of their labor needs, market only about 35–40 percent of their output, and are all highly land constrained. Medium-size farms, averaging fifty to a hundred hectares, are large enough to require hired labor and market a much higher percentage of output, and they have mixed patterns of constraints. Those referred to as estates, with an average size of more than 500 hectares, are generally plantations, ranches, or mixed fazendas.[53] Much of their land is not intensively used, and they generally exhibit the poorest performance in terms of output and employment.

The second part of this study uses a linear programming model, which is described in Chapter 5. The model was designed to provide a consistent, quantitative framework within which to identify the factors constraining development in the sector and which could then be used to simulate the effects of policy interventions. The model differs from other agricultural sector models in two important ways. First, it is based on survey information collected specifically for it; in particular, the technology data set, based on nearly 40,000 observations of individual activities, should provide a more satisfactory base than the secondary or informal data sets that have generally been available in the past. Second, because it was realized that the constraints on agricultural production in the Northeast differ among sizes and types of farm, the full sectoral model was built up of individual representations of farm types. In each zone, three or four farm types are distinguished so that any solution to the model yields not only aggregate indexes of production, employment, income, and so forth but also a detailed account of the operations and performance of each farm type included. Because the model contains an accounting framework for employment and income by type of agent (farmers of different types, share-

53. The generic term "estates" is used for these large farms for the sake of convenience, but many of them are not richly endowed; nor are their owners necessarily wealthy.

croppers, permanent workers, and temporary workers), the distributional characteristics of alternative solutions can be made explicit.

Solutions against the data base year, 1973, reported in Chapter 6, were undertaken primarily to test how accurately the model captures the important facets of Northeastern agriculture. The simulated aggregate levels of production and labor use revealed a relatively small but consistent bias toward more production and employment than was recorded by the survey. This is typical of optimization models because they *do* optimize, whereas the real world obviously includes some elements of nonoptimal behavior, and any mathematical representation cannot include all constraining elements. The source of the bias, however, lies mostly in the simulated performance of the estates. The model results fully support the hypothesis raised in the cross-sectional analysis that the estates do not behave optimally in their choice of production patterns and their use of resources. These farms, controlling half of the Northeast's agricultural land, would employ nearly twice as many workers as they do at present if they wished to maximize profits in the neoclassical sense. In sharp contrast, the model reveals that the family farms, all of which have a severe land constraint, are using family labor and working their land far more intensively than is optimal from the same profit-maximizing criterion. These results suggest two conclusions: First, strong elements of noneconomic behavior exist in the use of both land and labor on estates; and second, if developmental goals include employment generation, output increases, more intensive use of the resource base, and provision of adequate consumption, family farms are the most viable units for achieving those goals.

The model is employed to simulate and evaluate a range of interventions undertaken within the existing agrarian structure. The effects are mixed and in general not very significant. Technological progress, for example, is the goal of several massive programs in Brazil supported by international institutions. If it succeeds in raising crop yields in the Northeast by 25 percent, this will benefit consumers and small farmers but could cause a net reduction in employment and is likely to result in even *less* intensive land use on the larger farms. The subsidization of employment, simulated up to a rate of 20 percent of permanent laborers' wages, would promote employment and raise production somewhat but would have no appreciable influence either on overall employment rates or on the hiring practices and land use patterns of larger farms. Furthermore, intervention that affects the contractual basis of sharecroppers is likely to lead to their eviction, because landowners are close to being indifferent between sharecropping arrangements and other, less labor-intensive modes of operation.

The influence of demand is investigated through simulations of a guaranteed price support program (which does exist in the Northeast but is ineffective because of institutional weaknesses, the remoteness of most producers, and a lack of storage and transport infrastructure) and of raising the general level of demand by 25 percent through roundabout means. Effective price guarantees would substantially increase the incomes of smaller farms (by 17 percent) but would have negligible effects on gross output and employment. This disappointing result reflects a lack of response from estates: Even though the model assumes that they optimize, the simulated price supports do not raise gross margins enough to affect the employment and land use practices on these farms. The promotion of demand by 25 percent, through marketing and urban incomes policies, would appreciably raise output (by about 8 percent) and the incomes of nontenured labor (by about 16 percent). This result suggests that market-oriented schemes might be profitably adopted in the Northeast, but the outcome would largely depend on whether the estates adopt economically optimal behavior.

When development strategies based on combinations of the above interventions were simulated, the best that any of them could accomplish was a 20 percent increase in output, with gains to consumers through a 13 percent decline in the output price index or, alternatively, a 10 percent rise in output with a 14 percent increase in the general level of employment. None of these strategies is Pareto-optimal, and none provides a panacea for the Northeast. Even if all the instruments were applied simultaneously, with output rising by 20 percent and consumer prices falling by 13 percent, total employment would increase by less than 2 percent. None of the strategies would have a substantial effect on poverty or on employment for the landless.

The results force us to consider the fully legislated, adequately funded, but officially unsupported issue of land reform. Chapter 8 describes a simulation in which the land in the estate subsector is redistributed into module farms, a unit proposed in the Brazilian Land Statute of 1964 and defined in detail by the National Institute of Colonization and Agrarian Reform (INCRA). As simulated by the model, the modules are very attractive farming units. They are large enough to provide acceptable family incomes, to employ family labor fully, to satisfy family consumption needs, and also to take advantage of improving markets and advances in production technology.

The 37,000 existing estates, averaging 740 hectares each, could be converted into 790,000 modules.[54] With such a reform there would be moderate

---

54. Those referred to as estates include all 33,000 farms larger than 500 hectares and an additional 4,000 medium-size farms that are similar to the large ones in their use of resources and degree of commercialization.

gains in production: Output of all commodities, including exportables, would increase by nearly as much as under any of the nonstructural policy interventions. More important, such a redistribution would ensure employment and adequate consumption for more than twice the number of families the agricultural sector is currently accommodating. Of the policy and project interventions described and analyzed by this study, land reform appears to be the only intervention with any hope of alleviating the poverty of the landless rural workers and their families.

A land reform may be a prerequisite for solving the problem of the Northeast. Such a course of action, however, would pose an immense political and administrative challenge without giving any guarantee that its results would be sufficient. The resource base is simply not large enough to provide adequate incomes for the 18 million rural Northeasterners. Measures to help increase farm productivity (agricultural research, extension services, and more efficient and flexible marketing channels) need to be supplemented by interventions in other sectors. In particular, programs are needed to develop human resources and promote the emigration of adequately educated and trained Northeasterners, and the industrial subsidization scheme needs to be restructured to meet the employment goals it originally embraced.

This "fresh" view using fresh numbers and fresh tools is not an optimistic one. The Northeast problem demands political action, recommendations for which lie outside the scope and expertise of the authors. Without such action, the analysis reveals little hope for solving the problem in a region where up to 10 million people remain near absolute poverty while agricultural land the size of France lies idle or greatly underused.

Appendix: Zonal Delineation of the Northeast

Although the Northeast region comprises nine states (plus a part of a tenth, Minas Gerais, which was not included in this study), there are such large physiographic, climatic, and agroeconomic variations even within states that state boundaries cannot be used as delimiters. Paraiba, for example, one of the smallest states in the Northeast, includes no less than three distinctly different ecological zones: the humid coastal Mata, the relatively fertile Agreste, and the semiarid, drought-prone Sertao. This ecological diversity causes differences in all aspects of agricultural activity.

IBGE, the Brazilian statistical bureau, has defined homogeneous microregions in all states for use in presenting the results of the agricultural census. These microregions comprise clusters of *municipios* (counties) that have similar ecological characteristics. The 114 such microregions defined for the entire Northeast, however, are too numerous for this kind of presentation.

We have adopted a zonal delineation proposed in a 1971 SUDENE study that combined demographic, climatic, and agronomic factors to divide the Northeast into seven physiographic zones.[55] With few exceptions, these zones are aggregates of the IBGE microregions and thus allow some comparisons to be made with census results.

The map on p. 20 shows the seven zones superimposed on the nine states. Some of the principal characteristics of each zone are shown in Table 1-1.

Zone A: The West

Zone A, comprising the western portions of the states of Maranhao, Piaui, and Bahia, stretches from the coast in the north to the border of Minas Gerais in central Brazil; its western border is a frontier area near the Amazon region. Population density averages less than three inhabitants a square kilometer; this is the most sparsely populated zone in the Northeast.

Annual precipitation varies between 600 and 2,000 millimeters, evenly distributed over six to eight months. Drought is seldom a problem, but the zone's poor soils and lack of access to markets prohibit intensive agricultural activities. The zone has no paved roads and no market centers, although the ports of Belem and Sao Luis and the Federal District of Brasilia all lie about 200 kilometers from its borders.

Three types of agricultural activity predominate. The swidden or slash-and-burn practices of nonpropertied farmers can be found scattered throughout the zone. After clearing the land, subsistence crops of rice, corn, beans, and manioc are planted for two or three years or until the nutrient value of the soil is depleted and the farmers move to another plot. The cleared land left behind is often taken over by cattlemen, usually nomadic, who use land-intensive methods. Purchased inputs for livestock in this zone average only about US$1.50 per animal a year. The third type of activity is extractive, involving wild carnauba and babacu palms.

Zone B: The Middle-North

The Middle-North zone—the northern parts of Maranhao and Piaui—shares many of the physical characteristics of the West, but because it contains two major cities, the port of Sao Luis and Teresina on the Parnaiba

---

55. Lacerda de Melo, "Espacos geograficos."

Table 1-1. *Principal Characteristics of the Physiographic Zones*

Characteristics	A West	B Middle-North	C Sertao	D Semi-humid Southeast	E Humid East	F Humid Southeast	G Agreste
Component states (parts)	Maranhao Piaui Bahia	Maranhao Piaui	Ceara Rio Grande do Norte Paraiba Pernambuco Alagoas Sergipe Bahia	Bahia	Rio Grande do Norte Paraiba Pernambuco Alagoas Sergipe Bahia	Bahia	Rio Grande do Norte Paraiba Pernambuco Alagoas Sergipe Bahia
Major city or port	None	Sao Luis Teresina	Fortaleza	None	Recife Salvador	Salvador	None
Rainfall (millimeters a year)	600–2,000	600–2,000	400–600	800–1,600	1,000–2,000	1,200–2,000	600–1,000
Susceptibility to drought	Negligible	Moderate	Severe	Negligible	Negligible	Negligible	Moderate
Principal crops	Rice Beans Manioc Corn	Rice Babacu Beans Manioc Corn	Cotton Beans Manioc Corn	Coconut Beans Manioc Corn	Bananas Sugar Coconut Beans Manioc Corn	Cacao	Cotton Beans Manioc Corn
Percentage of Northeast's total							
Agricultural land	18.0	21.3	36.5	7.5	3.2	5.5	8.0
Crop output	3.5	6.3	28.1	5.5	4.2	39.8	12.5
Livestock output	9.9	7.5	41.1	10.7	4.5	0.3	25.9
Agricultural employment	11.5	7.2	41.8	8.0	3.8	7.5	20.3

River, there are better opportunities for marketing agricultural products. As in zone A, slash-and-burn, extensive ranching, and the extraction of babacu and carnauba are important. The Parnaiba River, which stretches throughout the zone, allows the cultivation of irrigated rice, either on small plots adjacent to the river or with water carried to nearby plots surrounded by bunds. Modern irrigation techniques are little used in the Northeast except in the other major river valley, that of the Sao Francisco. Where modern irrigation has been attempted, salinity has usually rendered the soil useless after a few years.

The eastern parts of the zone, bordering on Ceara, are more akin to the Sertao. Here scattered patches of cotton are often interplanted with various subsistence crops. These areas of zone B are quite susceptible to drought, unlike areas near the river and the coast.

Zone C: The Semiarid Sertao

With the possible exception of the coastal sugar zone, the Sertao is the most famous and interesting part of the Northeast from historical, sociological, and folkloric as well as economic points of view. This vast zone begins about 100 kilometers inland from the east coast and stretches almost to the pre-Amazonic frontier. North to south, its boundaries are the sea and the Center-South state of Minas Gerais.

The overriding characteristic of the Sertao is its susceptibility to drought. Over the past century, major droughts have occurred every eight to ten years, causing almost total crop failure, decimation of cattle, and the starvation of thousands. Annual rainfall is usually between 400 and 600 millimeters but is irregularly and unpredictably distributed over four to six months. Under such circumstances, the water hole and adequate stocks of food or money are vital to sustain life. Massive emigration to both the coastal centers and the Center-South takes place. More often than not, the opportunities for migrants there are so limited and the urban slum conditions so squalid that the news of "rain in the Sertao" sends them scurrying back.

The people, the crop varieties, and the farming practices have evolved to cope with the harsh conditions. The Sertao farmer or sharecropper who is able to maintain a family has been called "a hero and a genius."[56] With little more than a hoe and leftover seeds from the previous year, he produces subsistence crops (corn, beans, and manioc) for his family and a cotton crop to purchase minimum necessities. Over perhaps centuries, he has de-

---

56. From conversations with a Brazilian agricultural economist (unnamed).

veloped interplantings of crops that unquestionably increase his chance of survival.[57]

Zone D: The Semihumid Southeast

The Semihumid Southeast, wholly within the state of Bahia, lies between the Bahian Sertao and the fertile cacao-producing coastal areas. Its soils and climate are similar to those of the Agreste (described below). Annual rainfall varies between 800 and 1,600 millimeters, and its regularity permits the cultivation of cash crops such as cacao, coffee, and tobacco as well as corn, beans, and manioc. Livestock ranching is the dominant activity.

Zone E: The Humid East

The Humid East, a narrow strip of eastern coast running from Bahia in the south to the northeasternmost part of Rio Grande do Norte in the north, is part of what is commonly called the Zona da Mata (forest zone), although the forest was cut four centuries ago to allow intensive cultivation of sugar. Rainfall is almost always greater than 1,200 millimeters a year, and droughts do not affect the zone. With the major ports of Recife and Salvador, as well as four other state capitals, the access to urban and export markets is excellent.

The history of this zone is the history of sugar. The intensive cultivation of sugar over the centuries, usually to the exclusion of all other crops, has depleted the once excellent soils. As a result, sugar as well as many other crops require fertilization. The yields of crops other than sugar are quite good in this zone and better than in most other areas of the Northeast. In addition to the usual Northeastern food crops, coconut is planted along the coast.

Zone F: The Humid Southeast

The Humid Southeast is the smallest zone in the Northeast and is the southern extension of the Humid East, which it resembles in its rainfall and soils. Its slightly cooler climate allows cacao production, by far the most important activity in the zone. This zone is quite small and has relatively few farms; land and incomes are more evenly distributed than in the other

---

57. A background study employed mathematical programming models to simulate farmers' behavior in the Sertao. It found that no better risk-reducing farm plans could be devised for their circumstances than those the farmers were already using.

zones; the productivity of the land is the highest in the Northeast; and our survey accordingly covered only one municipio in the zone.

Zone G: The Agreste

The Agreste is a wide belt bounded on the west by the Sertao, on the east by the Zona da Mata, and on the south by the Humid Southeast. Rainfall between 600 and 1,000 millimeters a year, fairly good soils, and low likelihood of drought permit a wide range of agricultural activities, and mixed farming predominates.

Although the zone has no major cities, much of it lies within 200 kilometers of the coast, and thus access to markets is good. This locational advantage and the relatively high productivity of several varieties of planted pasture make livestock a productive enterprise, highly competitive with the wide range of crops that can be grown in this zone.

Apart from the humid zones, many observers view the Agreste as having the highest development potential: It suffers neither the locational disadvantages of the interior and western zones nor the drought susceptibility of the Sertao, and there is evidence that improved crop varieties would thrive, given the right combination of modern inputs.

The seven-zone delineation is used for the cross-sectional analysis in Chapters 2 through 4, but it is sometimes necessary to omit specific reference to zone F because of the limited size of the sample for that zone. The seven zones are aggregated to five in the second part of the study, where a programming model is used for the analysis, so as to keep the model to a manageable size. Because the West and Middle-North have similar production patterns and technology, these are combined into the "West," and the cacao-producing zone F is combined with the larger Semihumid zone D.

2

Labor, Land, and Capital Resources

Most observers have concluded that the heart of the Northeast problem lies in the paucity of its resource base; consequently, many of the policy interventions have been designed at least in part to augment that base. Before proceeding to any analysis of the region's problems, one must examine the nature, magnitudes, distributions, and uses of the primary factors of production in the rural Northeast—labor, land, and agricultural capital.

The Agricultural Labor Force

The 1970 demographic census found a total Northeast population of 28.1 million, of whom 16.4 million, or 58 percent, were rural. The state-by-state totals are given in Table 2-1. By 1973, when the survey for the present study was undertaken, the Northeast population had passed 30 million, and its rural population, despite continued emigration, had risen to nearly 18 million.

Various definitions of the agricultural labor force are available. The demographic census, which uses the term "economically active" in agriculture (including a presumably small proportion engaged in mining, hunting, and fishing), found 5.2 million persons, or about one-third of rural Northeasterners, so engaged in 1970. The agricultural census of the same year, which used more disaggregated definitions, found 7.8 million people "occupied" in agriculture, as reported in Table 2-2.[1] The agricultural census

---

1. The problems of reconciling different Brazilian data sources have plagued other researchers. Cavalcanti and Goodman, for example, found "vast discrepancies" between demographic and sectoral censuses and opted for the former's "economically active population" as the most reliable labor force data. See David Goodman and Roberto Cavalcanti, *Incentivos a industrializacao e desenvolvimento do Nordeste* (Rio de Janeiro: IPEA/INPES, 1974).

Table 2-1. *Total and Rural Population and Number Economically Active in Agriculture, by State, 1970*

State	Total population	Rural population	Percentage of population in rural areas	Economically active in agriculture[a]
Rio Grande do Norte	1,550,244	812,976	52.4	240,955
Paraiba	2,382,617	1,380,461	57.9	437,937
Pernambuco	5,160,640	2,349,797	45.5	764,719
Ceara	4,361,603	2,581,510	59.2	749,090
Piaui	1,680,573	1,143,961	68.1	346,875
Maranhao	2,992,686	2,240,659	74.9	762,900
Alagoas	1,588,109	956,370	60.2	323,155
Sergipe	900,744	485,392	53.9	161,815
Bahia	7,493,470	4,407,987	58.8	1,437,364
Northeast total (average)	28,110,686	16,359,613	(58.2)	5,224,810

a. Includes mining, hunting, and fishing.
Source: Instituto Brasileiro de Geografia e Estatistica, *Censo demografico* [by state] *VIII: Recenseamento geral, 1970*, vol. 1, nos. 5–10 (Rio de Janeiro, 1972).

Table 2-2. *Agricultural Labor Force, by State, 1970*

State	Producers					Occupied persons
	Propri-etors	Renters	Share-croppers	Occu-pants	Total pro-ducers	
Rio Grande do Norte	62,927	17,479	2,400	21,571	104,377	315,377
Paraiba	108,801	33,063	5,569	22,563	169,996	613,176
Pernambuco	202,683	59,138	10,108	59,757	331,686	1,157,039
Ceara	159,135	21,238	27,672	37,910	245,955	1,081,501
Piaui	73,744	50,402	43,853	49,993	217,912	519,931
Maranhao	48,397	147,629	10,493	190,405	396,924	1,196,611
Alagoas	74,270	18,192	1,883	11,051	105,396	440,342
Sergipe	71,700	11,975	406	11,842	95,923	275,751
Bahia	455,017	18,750	7,903	62,384	544,054	2,214,914
Northeast total	1,256,674	377,866	110,287	467,476	2,212,303	7,814,648

Source: Instituto Brasileiro de Geografia e Estatistica, *Dados preliminares gerais do censo agropecuario VIII: Recenseamento geral, 1970* (Rio de Janeiro, 1972).

divides "producers" into the categories of proprietors, renters, sharecroppers, and occupants, a better term for whom is "squatters." Together the producers recorded by this census numbered 2.2 million, or 28 percent of the occupied persons.

The present study sought new definitions of agents in the agricultural labor force for several reasons. First, the number of proprietors recorded by the agricultural census does not coincide with the number of properties given by a 1972 cadastral survey undertaken by the National Institute of Colonization and Agrarian Reform (INCRA). This cadastral survey was the basis for the SUDENE/World Bank survey undertaken for the present study.[2] It found only about 850,000 properties, or 400,000 fewer than the number of proprietors recorded by the census. The SUDENE/World Bank survey had as its basis the farm, defined as a property or collection of properties under the same *administration*, and found only 800,000 such entrepreneurial units, as some individuals farmed more than one property.

Similarly, the SUDENE/World Bank survey found far fewer renters than did the agricultural census, 26,000 versus 378,000, and about 240,000 sharecroppers, compared with 110,000 found by the agricultural census. These discrepancies probably again reflect differences in the classifications used. Most sharecroppers (*parceiros*) in the Northeast tended to describe themselves as renters (*arrendatarios*) even though the rent they pay is a portion of the harvest, whereas the SUDENE/World Bank survey distinguished such agents on the basis of the form of rental contract.

The number of occupants or squatters given by the agricultural census is difficult to verify from the SUDENE/World Bank survey. Because the survey was based on agricultural properties as recorded by INCRA, it took account of squatters only when the owner of the property was aware that they were occupying it. A supplementary subsample was taken of squatters on public land in Maranhao, but it is certain that the information obtained was by no means complete. The authors' observations indicate that a very large population of migratory slash-and-burn agriculturalists in the Northeast is not adequately captured by any census or survey, including the SUDENE/World Bank survey. The implication from the agricultural census is that one-fifth of the producers neither hold a title nor have any contract, written or unwritten, to the land they are working.

A more functional breakdown of the agricultural labor force, employed by the SUDENE/World Bank survey and this analysis, is as follows:

2. Preliminary data from the INCRA cadastral survey were made available to SUDENE in raw form in 1973 to provide the sampling base for the SUDENE/World Bank survey.

—*Owner-operator:* the entrepreneur who owns part or all of the farm and resides thereon.

—*Administrator:* a nonowner who performs the entrepreneurial function.

—*Permanent worker:* a permanently contracted worker who may or may not perform entrepreneurial or managerial tasks. A morador is a permanent worker who receives, as part of his compensation, a dwelling on the farm and a plot for family cultivation of subsistence crops; a nonmorador is contracted annually but receives no housing or land.

—*Sharecropper:* an agent who pays a previously agreed-upon share of the produce in exchange for the use of a plot of land; he may or may not receive compensation for work performed off the sharecropped plot.

—*Family worker:* a member of the entrepreneur's or sharecropper's immediate family who is economically active on the farm.

—*Temporary worker:* a worker contracted and paid on a short-term (daily, weekly, or monthly) basis, usually to assist in planting and harvesting crops.

—*Renter:* an agent who pays a fixed fee in money or produce for the use of a plot of land.

—*Squatter:* an occupant of private or public land who makes no compensation to the owner, often using the land without the owner's knowledge.

The number of these agents estimated by the SUDENE/World Bank survey are reported in Table 2-3 for the different physiographic zones of the Northeast. The Northeast total of 5.7 million in 1973 is nearer to the demographic census total of 5.2 million economically active persons than it is to the 7.8 million occupied persons found in the agricultural census. For the rest of the analysis we shall take 6 million as the approximate size of the agricultural labor force.

The average farm household in the Northeast has five persons (adults and children), of whom 2.2 man-equivalents are members of the labor force. (Casual observation suggests that members of the extended family, including parents, brothers, and more distant relatives, often depend on a single farm even if it is very small.) Table 2-3 shows that of the 6 million in the labor force less than 800,000, or 13 percent, own the land they operate; this percentage rises to 30 when their family workers are included. Nearly half the labor force, or 2.9 million workers, rely on temporary employment with no continuous access to land.[3]

3. See Chapter 1, note 50.

Table 2-3. Agricultural Labor Force, by Zone, 1973

Zone	Owner-operators[a]	Hired administrators	Renters	Family workers	Share-croppers	Permanent workers[b]	Temporary workers	Zone total
West	88,213	1,271	621	85,905	7,159	36,668	375,833	595,670
Middle-North	72,533	3,204	4,215	57,560	56,045	84,825	387,773	666,155
Sertao	321,420	3,312	3,179	438,388	172,108	159,119	1,149,551	2,247,077
Semihumid Southeast	55,991	0	131	55,991	1,680	38,634	169,653	322,080
Humid East	29,771	1,130	1,510	23,176	927	46,970	109,390	212,874
Humid Southeast	57,381	0	0	29,838	0	384,453	215,179	686,851
Agreste	139,639	3,654	16,276	237,866	2,860	144,726	465,702	1,010,729
Northeast total	764,948	12,571	25,932	928,724	240,785	895,395	2,873,081	5,741,436

a. Includes squatters on public lands.
b. Includes both moradores and nonmoradores.
Source: SUDENE/World Bank survey (extrapolated results).

Table 2-4 reports the actual use of labor from the various categories of workers by zone. The Northeast total of 1.77 million man-years of labor use implies un- and underemployment of up to 70 percent. Because the sudene/World Bank farm survey did not capture employment in nonagricultural sectors (nor does any other data source permit estimates of such employment for rural residents), nothing conclusive can be said of un- and underemployment rates. Casual observation suggests that nonfarm employment opportunities are quite limited, a view supported by expenditure survey data in the appendix to Chapter 3 that indicate 93 percent of rural households depend mainly on agriculture. That there is substantial underemployment in agriculture is beyond question. It is partly due to the seasonal nature of cropping in the Northeast and is strongly associated with the degree of access to land. Farmers and their family workers, as well as permanently employed workers and sharecroppers, work two to three times as many days a year as do the temporary workers. Temporary workers average only sixty days of agricultural employment annually; thus, if not productively employed in other sectors, they are clearly the most impoverished group.

Nonetheless, all types of agents in all zones appear to be underemployed. Although Table 2-4 includes only labor directly related to cropping, stock raising, and farm maintenance, there may be up to 4 million man-years of labor available for productive employment in the rural Northeast. This reservoir represents an untapped resource of potentially immense dimensions.

Land: Its Distribution and Quality

At the risk of stating the obvious, it must be emphasized that landownership alone does not guarantee an adequate income. Many factors determine whether a property is, or can be, economically viable: its size, soil quality, and access to markets; the attitudes, skills, and motivation of the proprietor; and the climate (in particular, sufficient and timely rainfall).

Tables 2-5 through 2-7, summarized in Table 2-8, reveal that farm sizes vary dramatically throughout the Northeast but that in all zones land is concentrated in large farms. About 33,000 farms (4 percent) contain 49 percent of the agricultural land and are larger than 500 hectares; 32 percent of all farms have an average size of five hectares, on 1.4 percent of all agricultural land. Gini coefficients of concentration, reported in Table 2-8, range from 0.75 to 0.89 for the various zones and average 0.83 for the entire

Table 2-4. Intensity of Agricultural Employment, by Zone

| Zone | Average days worked a year | | | | | Man-years worked per average farm | Total man-years worked per zone |
	Family workers	Permanent workers	Share-croppers	Temporary workers	Total per farm		
West	152	183	113	46	494	1.94	173,599
Middle-North	138	118	69	43	368	2.15	162,835
Sertao	153	171	119	53	496	2.31	754,751
Semihumid Southeast	162	222	100	64	548	2.25	125,979
Humid East	130	180	100	68	468	2.51	77,562
Humid Southeast	109	234	—	162	505	7.81	96,591
Agreste	126	211	150	59	546	2.63	376,861
Northeast total							1,768,178

— Not applicable.
Note: The typical working month in the Northeast is twenty-five days; the typical working year, 300 days.
Source: SUDENE/World Bank survey.

Table 2-5. *Estimated Size Distribution of Farms, by Zone*
(number of farms)

Zone	Farm size (hectares)						Zone total
	0–9.9	10–49.9	50–99.9	100–199.9	200–499.9	500 +	
West	20,218	30,708	12,290	10,534	8,460	7,274	89,484
Middle-North	10,791	19,666	11,584	16,217	10,198	7,281	75,737
Sertao	94,174	122,521	48,081	30,412	20,594	10,950	326,732
Semihumid Southeast	9,286	27,034	9,621	4,565	2,895	2,590	55,991
Humid East	15,166	10,714	2,321	1,048	956	696	30,901
Humid Southeast	14,637	22,610	7,056	7,870	3,460	1,748	57,381
Agreste	84,665	39,334	8,188	5,394	3,358	2,354	143,293
Size class total	248,937	272,587	99,141	76,040	49,921	32,893	779,519

Source: SUDENE/World Bank survey.

Table 2-6. *Average Size of Sampled Farms,*
by Farm Size and Zone
(hectares)

	Farm size (hectares)					
Zone	0–9.9	10–49.9	50–99.9	100–199.9	200–499.9	500 +
West	3.70	25.45	71.94	138.90	313.22	1,178.03
Middle-North	3.69	26.57	68.80	138.93	317.20	1,395.89
Sertao	4.88	27.51	72.37	143.27	288.11	1,059.15
Semihumid Southeast	4.75	24.20	71.84	138.42	282.47	1,210.60
Humid East	3.71	26.11	72.82	143.62	283.51	2,303.59
Humid Southeast	5.60	27.09	70.63	142.29	294.60	620.00
Agreste	4.01	26.52	73.36	143.40	299.12	1,135.33

Source: SUDENE/World Bank survey, based on INCRA cadastral survey.

Northeast.[4] Concentration is highest in the Zona da Mata where, historically, the usinas dominated all economic activity and were sufficiently
wealthy to absorb small farms. The cacao zone appears to have the most
even land distribution, but another study argues that here the land distribution is much more concentrated than it appears because of the prevalence of
multiple-property holdings.[5]

Property size, of course, is only one dimension of the potential value of a
farm as a productive asset. If small farms had a higher percentage of good
soils, better access to water, or more capital invested in their land (for
example, through clearing and leveling, prior fertilization to build up soil
quality, irrigation and drainage, or stocks of tree crops), the distribution of
productive potential would be less skewed. By the same token, if the land
concentrated in large holdings were composed of poorer soils and located in
areas far removed from market opportunities, the skewness in the distribu-

4. An anonymous reviewer has pointed out the likelihood that the INCRA cadastral survey of
properties was biased toward a more *equal* land distribution because large landowners may
have attempted to disguise the size of their holdings by subdividing their properties among
family members and friends. This observation is consistent with popular accounts of one
family's owning the western half of Pernambuco and two families' controlling the Paraiba
sugar zone. See Joseph A. Page, *The Revolution that Never Was: Northeast Brazil, 1955–1964*
(New York: Grossman Publishers, 1972), pp. 3–4, 224.

5. Gervasio Castro de Rezende, "Plantation Systems, Land Tenure, and Labor Supply: An
Historical Analysis of the Brazilian Case with a Contemporary Study of the Cacao Regions of
Bahia, Brazil" (Ph.D. dissertation, University of Wisconsin, Madison, 1976), pp. 248–51.

Table 2-7. *Total Area in Farms, by Farm Size and Zone*
(thousands of hectares)

Zone	Farm size (hectares)						Zone total
	0–9.9	10–49.9	50–99.9	100–199.9	200–499.9	500 +	
West	74.8	781.5	884.1	1,463.2	2,649.8	8,569.0	14,422.4
Middle-North	39.8	522.5	797.0	2,253.0	3,234.8	10,163.5	17,010.6
Sertao	460.5	3,371.8	3,475.8	4,354.4	5,933.3	11,597.7	29,193.5
Semihumid Southeast	44.1	654.2	691.2	631.9	817.8	3,135.5	5,975.0
Humid East	56.3	279.7	169.0	150.5	271.0	1,603.3	2,529.8
Humid Southeast	82.0	612.5	498.4	1,119.8	1,019.3	1,083.8	4,415.8
Agreste	339.5	1,043.1	600.7	773.5	1,004.4	2,672.6	6,433.8
Total	1,097.0	7,265.6	7,116.2	10,746.3	14,930.4	38,825.4	79,980.9

Source: SUDENE/World Bank survey, based on INCRA cadastral survey.

Table 2-8. Distribution of Farms and Farm Area, by Size and Zone
(percent)

Farm size (hectares)	West		Middle-North		Sertao		Semihumid Southeast		Humid East		Humid Southeast		Agreste		Northeast	
	Farms	Area	Farms	Area	Farms	Area	Farms	Area	Farms	Area	Farms	Area	Farms	Area	Farms	Area
0–9.9	22.6	0.6	14.2	0.2	29.0	1.6	16.6	0.7	49.1	2.2	25.5	1.9	59.1	5.3	32.0	1.4
10–49.9	34.3	5.4	26.0	3.1	37.7	11.6	48.3	10.9	34.7	11.1	39.4	13.9	27.4	16.2	35.1	9.1
50–99.9	13.7	6.1	15.3	4.7	14.2	11.4	17.2	11.6	7.5	6.7	12.4	11.3	5.7	9.4	12.5	8.7
100–199.9	11.8	10.1	21.4	13.2	9.4	15.0	8.1	10.6	3.4	5.9	13.7	25.3	3.8	12.0	9.8	13.5
200–499.9	9.5	18.4	13.5	19.0	6.3	20.4	5.2	13.7	3.1	10.7	6.0	23.1	2.4	15.6	6.4	18.7
500 +	8.1	59.4	9.6	59.8	3.4	40.0	4.6	52.5	2.2	63.4	3.0	24.5	1.6	41.5	4.2	48.6
Gini coefficient	0.82		0.84		0.80		0.81		0.89		0.75		0.85		0.83	

Source: SUDENE/World Bank survey, based on 1972 INCRA cadastral survey.

tion of land would only compensate for these factors.[6] Furthermore, questions of performance differentials, taken up in Chapter 4, would have no meaning. Therefore, we take up the issues of land value, location, and quality at this juncture. We employ several different approaches because several dimensions of productive potential are involved, and some of the data are subjective and possibly prone to bias.

If such data were completely reliable, land values would provide the most meaningful comparators because they would reflect differences in locational advantage, soil qualities, and capital embodied in the land. In the rural Northeast, however, land sales and rental markets are probably the least perfect of all markets, and because land taxes—notwithstanding the insignificance of their rates—depend on land value, the available land value data must be cautiously analyzed. Three sources (Getulio Vargas Foundation, INCRA, and the SUDENE/World Bank survey) of land value data are available, but only two will be used here. (The most up-to-date INCRA land valuations were not available; however, this source is probably the most bias-prone because tax rates and land reform plans depend on them.)

In a related World Bank study of land distribution by state (as opposed to distribution by zone, as in this study), Gini and Pareto coefficients of landownership concentration were calculated for both physical area alone and physical area adjusted by a land value index based on reported sales prices and rental values.[7] For seven of the nine states, the distribution adjusted for land value was even more skewed than the distribution of physical area. For Sergipe, one of the smallest states, the skewness was the same before and after adjustment for land value. Only for Piaui, the poorest and least productive state, did the adjustment improve the distribution of land.

The SUDENE/World Bank survey asked farmers to give a subjective estimate of the value of their land, not including the replacement value of the structures, as a proxy for its productive potential. Table 2-9 reports the average land values per hectare, by farm size class and zone, based on the valuations by farmers. These averages vary wildly throughout the Northeast, ranging from a low of Cr$77 (US$12) per hectare for the largest farms

6. Schuh, for example, suggests that "large farms may be large of necessity because the soil productivity is low" and says that "many of the large land holdings are relatively isolated from the mainstream of economic life, and are being held for purely speculative purposes." G. Edward Schuh, *The Agricultural Development of Brazil* (New York: Praeger, 1970), pp. 415–16.
7. World Bank, "Rural Development Issues and Options in Northeast Brazil," report no. 665a-BR (Washington, D.C., June 1975; restricted circulation), pp. 8–9. The index employed was constructed by the Getulio Vargas Foundation and was based on reported sales prices and rental rates.

Table 2-9. *Average Land Values, by Farm Size and Zone*
(cruzeiros per hectare)

Zone	Farm size (hectares)						Zone average[a]
	0–9.9	10–49.9	50–99.9	100–199.9	200–499.9	500 +	
West	1,348	192	218	196	227	93	142
Middle-North	821	189	142	113	113	77	97
Sertao	785	359	330	723	205	216	329
Semihumid Southeast	900	1,532	955	928	786	950	989
Humid East	2,273	1,282	784	886	1,037	2,317	1,878
Humid Southeast	2,993	6,168	9,428	8,057	8,098	10,824	8,544
Agreste	1,453	1,016	1,039	947	972	653	875
Size class average[a]	1,266	1,054	1,064	1,318	785	625	838
Analysis of variance from comparisons of class means	degrees of freedom: $df_1 = 5$, $df_2 = 36$, $F = 0.05$ $F_{0.05}(5, 36) = 2.5$						

a. Weighted by total area of farms in each size class.
Source: SUDENE/World Bank survey.

in the Middle-North to a high of Cr$10,824 (US$1,600) per hectare for the cacao estates in the Humid Southeast. Such variation may be partly due to the unreliability of subjective (and possibly bias-prone) valuations, but it undoubtedly reflects the diversity of the ecological base within the rural Northeast.

In the three westernmost zones and the Agreste, there appears to be a significant downward trend in land value with respect to farm size. For the Northeast as a whole, such a trend does not appear until farm size exceeds 200 hectares. This fact raises the suspicion that owners of the largest farms may indeed have attempted to conceal the value of their farms (a suspicion supported by the location and land quality tests that follow). Land values, however, are quite stable throughout the size groups in the Semihumid Southeast, show a strong tendency to increase with farm size in the Humid Southeast, and exhibit a U-shaped pattern in the Humid East. A possible explanation for this pattern is that in the West and Middle-North larger farms may have lower-valued land because many of them have absorbed the smaller slash-and-burn farms for grazing purposes after the soils have been depleted. Similarly, the larger farms in the Sertao, and to a lesser extent the Agreste, are predominantly pasture, possibly because their soils are less fertile. The U-shaped pattern in the Humid East may partly reflect the proximity of the largest and smallest farms to urban centers. The largest farms, which are invariably sugar plantations, have relatively high levels of investment, and many small farms have very fertile land used to produce vegetables for the coastal urban markets. In the Humid Southeast, the higher land values of large farms may reflect the denser cacao plantings on these farms, whose more ready access to credit makes it easier for them than for small farms to meet the investment costs of cacao planting.

Although such interfarm variations in average land value are important in some parts of the Northeast, they are not significant for the Northeast as a whole. The *F*-test on size-group mean values reveals that there are no statistically significant differences in these means (at the 95 percent confidence level). This result is due partially to the wide variation within size groups (Table 2-9) but mostly to the overwhelming weight of the variation across zones. The analysis-of-variance test implies that the interzone variation is about twenty times as great as the intrazone variation.[8]

The average values for the zones decline markedly as the distance from the coast increases, reflecting not only the locational advantages of the

8. In layman's terms, if the value per hectare were to be estimated for a farm picked at random in the Northeast, knowledge of the zone in which the farm was located would be far more useful than knowledge of the farm's size.

Humid East and Humid Southeast over the West and Middle-North but also the investment in perennial crops in the former zones. In the Humid Southeast, with its large plantings of cacao trees, land values are markedly higher in all farm size classes. Climate and the probability of drought also appear to influence land values heavily. Large parts of the Sertao are no less favorably situated than the Semihumid Southeast or the Agreste, but land values there are roughly one-third of those in the latter two zones, which are less prone to drought. Regardless of these latter factors, it is clear that the SUDENE/World Bank survey did capture the locational differences in land value, and these differences are far more marked between zones than among farm size groups within a given zone.

The location hypothesis can be addressed at the more micro level because the SUDENE/World Bank survey tabulated the distance of the sampled farms from the nearest municipio seat. In the rural Northeast, the municipio seat is usually the largest nearby town and constitutes the market for the farms as well as the transportation hub for goods not consumed locally.

Table 2-10 reports the average distances in kilometers from the sampled farms to the municipio seats, by zone and farm size group. As was the case with land value, no clear pattern emerges. Farms in all size groups and all zones are quite widely dispersed. In most zones, the medium-size farms are, on the average, farthest from the municipio seat, rather than the largest farms, as might have been expected. Also, the smallest farms appear to have a locational advantage in zones E and D, but this advantage is very small. When the smallest size class (0–10 hectares) was compared with the largest class (more than 500 hectares), it was found that a difference-of-means test was significant at the 95 percent confidence level only in zones A, B, and D. For the Northeast as a whole, there is no difference in the mean distances for the two extreme size groups, again at the 95 percent confidence level. The analysis-of-variance test reported in Table 2-10 also reveals no statistically significant locational differences across all size groups within given zones.

Variations in land quality were investigated through a study of the fertility and topography of a special subsample of about 2,200 farms scattered in the seven zones. These two dimensions of land quality are particularly important in Northeast Brazil because the chemical composition of the soil varies greatly and because many farms are narrow strips of land stretching from a river valley to the top of an altiplano. Farmers were asked to classify their land as high, medium, or low yield. Their classifications were cross-checked by the interviewer (generally an agronomist) with

Table 2-10. *Average Distance from Sampled Farms to Municipio Seat*
(kilometers; standard deviations in parentheses)

Zone	Farm size (hectares)					
	0–10	*10–50*	*50–100*	*100–200*	*200–500*	*500 +*
West	49.1	44.5	62.6	54.1	56.6	60.9
	(51.9)	(53.3)	(100.5)	(53.4)	(78.3)	(55.0)
Middle-North	24.1	22.3	40.2	34.8	38.6	29.6
	(30.8)	(23.1)	(54.6)	(55.1)	(53.6)	(18.1)
Sertao	22.5	21.5	22.8	22.8	24.2	22.8
	(54.3)	(19.0)	(22.8)	(17.3)	(33.6)	(16.5)
Semihumid Southeast	31.0	37.1	42.1	36.1	34.4	34.9
	(29.3)	(23.4)	(21.2)	(22.7)	(21.5)	(23.8)
Humid East	10.0	18.8	31.0	17.2	18.2	11.0
	(10.4)	(14.2)	(122.4)	(11.8)	(18.5)	(8.1)
Humid Southeast	5.5	9.0	13.1	13.1	15.5	13.0
	(5.0)	(7.0)	(10.4)	(5.9)	(8.2)	(0.)
Agreste	16.1	24.2	21.1	21.1	13.4	14.4
	(65.8)	(83.1)	(57.3)	(36.3)	(11.7)	(14.1)
Analysis of variance from comparisons of group means	degrees of freedom: $df_1 = 5$, $df_2 = 36$, $F = 0.04$ $F_{0.05}(5, 36) = 2.5$					

Source: SUDENE/World Bank survey.

further inquiries on the yields of the three types of land crop by crop.[9] Farmers then classified the topography of their land into three groups—lowland, hillside, and highland.

Table 2-11 reports the results of statistical tests on the land quality subsample. The first test involves a log-linear regression of the quantity of the most productive land qualities against total farm size.[10] Apart from the Humid Southeast (cacao region), none of the elasticities is significantly different from one at the 95 percent confidence level. In other words, the proportion of a farm's land that is composed of either high- or medium-

9. Some additional control is provided by the data on yields. In fact, yields varied less within groups of homogeneous soil quality than they did between groups of different soil qualities.

10. The remaining land qualities were omitted from the tests because they are generally unsuitable for crop cultivation.

Table 2-11. *Tests for Independence between Land Quality and Farm Size, by Zone*

Zone	Log-linear relation between quantity of land by quality and farm size[a]		Chi-square (χ^2) test for independence between proportion of land by quality and farm size[b]
	Elasticity	R^2	
West			
High-yield land	1.027	0.991	9.73
Medium-yield land	0.975	0.998	1.53
Middle-North			
High-yield land	0.954	0.998	4.86
Medium-yield land	1.217	0.587	0.69
Sertao			
High-yield land	0.928	0.998	6.32
Medium-yield land	1.051	0.999	2.32
Semihumid Southeast			
High-yield land	1.002	0.996	4.23
Medium-yield land	1.036	0.994	4.44
Humid East			
High-yield land	1.074	0.998	7.84
Medium-yield land	0.957	0.994	6.68
Humid Southeast			
High-yield land	0.817	0.892	41.47
Medium-yield land	1.467	0.939	16.86
Agreste			
High-yield land	0.973	0.998	1.70
Medium-yield land	1.031	0.997	3.09

a. An elasticity greater (less) than one implies the proportion of land of a given quality expands faster (slower) than the size of farms in a given zone. None of the elasticities in the table are significantly different from one, at the 95 percent confidence level, except for those pertaining to the Humid Southeast.

b. The χ^2 is computed from unweighted, grouped data to test the hypothesis that the percentage of land of different quality is not significantly related to farm size. The 5 percent critical value of the χ^2 for five degrees of freedom is 11.07.

Source: SUDENE/World Bank survey.

yielding soils is invariant with the size of the farm. In the Humid Southeast, larger farms appear to have lower proportions of high-yielding land but much larger proportions of medium-yielding land. This does not, however, adversely affect the value of these farms; as shown in Table 2-9, the average land value per hectare has a marked tendency to increase as farm size increases in this zone.

The chi-square test reported in the far-right column of Table 2-11 supports the regression tests. Again, only in the Humid Southeast are the

Table 2-12. *Agricultural Capital, by Zone*
(thousands of cruzeiros)

Zone	Structures	Animals	Equipment	Total capital Cruzeiros	Total capital Percent
West	995	1,649	79	2,723	8
Middle-North	930	1,212	133	2,275	7
Sertao	5,472	4,996	479	10,947	32
Semihumid Southeast	2,019	2,470	77	4,566	13
Humid East	966	497	76	1,559	5
Humid Southeast	5,596	194	85	5,875	17
Agreste	2,983	2,995	192	6,170	18
Northeast total	18,961	14,013	1,143	34,117	100

Note: By type of capital, percentages are: structures, 56 percent; animals, 41 percent; equipment, 3 percent.
Source: SUDENE/World Bank survey.

proportions of high- and medium-yielding land not independent of farm size.

From these investigations into the value and quality of agricultural land and the distance from the sampled farms to the nearest markets, several conclusions can be made that will have important implications for later analysis. First, the skewness in the distribution of land throughout the entire Northeast is not mitigated by the consideration of land value. Although there is a clear trend for average land value per hectare to decline as farm size increases in the Agreste and the interior zones, this is not true for the rest of the Northeast comprising the humid and semihumid zones of highest productive potential and best locational advantage. Second, for the Northeast as a whole, the zone in which a farm is located has far greater importance in determining its land value than does the size of the farm. Third, within sampled municipios, the smallest farms do not have a statistically significant locational advantage over the larger farms. And, fourth, there is no evidence that larger farms outside the Semihumid Southeast have smaller percentages of high- and medium-yielding soils than do small and medium-size farms.

Agricultural Capital

Other forms of capital such as structures, livestock, and equipment are much easier to value than those embodied in land. Table 2-12 reports the

Table 2-13. *Average Agricultural Capital per Farm, by Zone*
(cruzeiros)

Zone	Structures	Animals	Equipment	Total
West	11,123	18,432	886	30,441
Middle-North	12,292	15,999	1,759	30,050
Sertao	16,748	15,290	1,474	33,512
Semihumid Southeast	36,067	44,120	1,367	81,554
Humid East	24,765	12,730	2,469	39,964
Humid Southeast	97,519	3,376	1,480	102,375
Agreste	20,818	20,904	1,340	43,062
Northeast average[a]	24,324	17,976	1,466	43,766

a. Weighted by estimated farm distribution.
Source: SUDENE/World Bank survey.

total values of these items by zone, and Table 2-13 reports the average value per farm of the same items.

Structures account for over half the value of capital items recorded by the survey. They include the houses of the proprietor and those of any permanent resident workers, storage buildings, livestock pens, and water storage and distribution facilities. Though the value of structures per farm appears to be correlated with productivity (being lowest in the poorest zones, the West and Middle-North, and highest in the more humid eastern zones), rigorous analysis of the influence of structures is difficult because it is not possible to distinguish items such as housing from directly productive assets.

Animals account for about 40 percent of the value of the three capital items discussed here. Virtually all farms have cows, pigs, sheep, goats, chickens, and turkeys. Animals are treated as a capital item in the sense that farms invest in them to obtain either a flow of services (for example, draft power) or a flow of production (meat, dairy products, eggs, hides). The use of animals for draft power is relatively rare in the Northeast, but cattle are highly significant in generating income. Other animals are kept largely for home consumption. There is also widespread evidence that many animals are maintained as a store of value, particularly in the interior where financial markets are primitive, but also perhaps as a hedge against runaway inflation. The authors' observations suggest that farmers rely heavily on the occasional marketing of a goat or a flock of hens for cash between harvests.

Only 3 percent of the agricultural capital considered here is in equipment. This category covers virtually any nonfixed item directly or indirectly related to production or marketing, ranging from simple hoes[11] to tractors and implements, water pumps, scales, carts, jeeps, and trucks. The values of the equipment inventories reported in Tables 2-12 and 2-13 are extremely low. They range from Cr$886 per farm (US$138 in 1973 dollars) in the West to Cr$2,469 (US$386) in the sugar zone; in the other zones they are closely clustered about the Northeast mean figure of Cr$1,466.

The distribution of equipment among farm size groups is shown in Table 2-14. Comparison of this table with the size distribution of farms in Table 2-8 gives another indication of the paucity of resources with which small farms have to work. In the Sertao, for example, 29 percent of the farms possess only 2 percent of the equipment; in the Agreste, 59 percent of the farms possess 6 percent of the equipment. If those in the relatively wealthy zones, the Humid Southeast and the Humid East, are omitted, farms under 10 hectares have an average equipment inventory of Cr$115 (US$18 in 1973 dollars). Inasmuch as a single hoe costs about one-third of this amount, the level of technology on these 249,000 farms is obviously very low.

Casual observation suggests that, apart from the land distribution, the key factors constraining agricultural progress in the Northeast are the paucity of equipment and of structures directly related to production (particularly storage facilities and water storage and distribution facilities). This hypothesis may be crudely tested by estimating incremental capital/output ratios (ICOR). Table 2-15 reports log-linear regressions of capital (defined as housing, other structures, and equipment) on gross output.

The high elasticities observed in all zones but the Semihumid Southeast imply that substantial returns are possible from investment in Northeastern agriculture: The elasticity of annual gross output with respect to housing, other structures, and equipment is always greater than 0.4, and these types of capital have very long lives. Its importance to Northeast production is further substantiated in Table 2-16, which reports average capital/output ratios (ACOR). These are remarkably stable across zones and farm size groups, though land/labor ratios vary widely. (As shown in Chapter 4, these ratios vary by as much as a factor of 45 over size groups.) Clearly, farms in different size groups and in different zones freely substitute along the land/labor isoquant, but the relative constancy of the ACOR and their closeness to the ICOR imply rigidities in the markets for housing, other structures, and equipment.

---

11. The typical hoe in the Northeast is a combination hoe-ax-pick; it is heavy, durable, and employed for a variety of uses. For more than a few Northeastern agriculturalists, it is the only equipment available.

Table 2-14. *Distribution of Equipment, by Farm Size and Zone*
(cruzeiros; percentages in parentheses)

Zone	Farm size (hectares)						Total
	0–9.9	10–49.9	50–99.9	100–199.9	200–499.9	500 +	
West	3,494	10,685	17,118	4,949	21,521	21,543	79,310
	(4)	(13)	(22)	(6)	(27)	(27)	(100)
Middle-North	1,231	17,461	26,318	19,168	25,896	43,175	133,249
	(1)	(13)	(20)	(14)	(19)	(32)	(100)
Sertao	9,047	83,600	73,909	74,431	71,294	166,489	478,770
	(2)	(17)	(15)	(16)	(15)	(35)	(100)
Semihumid Southeast	540	24,628	12,920	7,837	6,085	24,528	76,538
	(1)	(32)	(17)	(10)	(8)	(32)	(100)
Humid East	20,767	12,263	6,907	7,117	20,462	8,782	76,298
	(27)	(16)	(9)	(9)	(27)	(16)	(100)
Humid Southeast	n.a.	5,810	9,551	25,612	42,336	1,588	84,897
	n.a.	(7)	(11)	(30)	(50)	(2)	(100)
Agreste	10,777	31,160	15,900	49,369	53,477	31,310	191,993
	(6)	(16)	(8)	(26)	(28)	(16)	(100)

n.a. Not available.

Table 2-15. *Regression Results: Incremental Capital/Output Ratios (ICOR)*

Zone	Constant	Elasticity of output with respect to value of capital	ICOR	R^2
West	67.93	0.513	1.95	0.796
Middle-North	− 314.27	0.902	1.11	0.928
Sertao	268.29	0.525	1.90	0.997
Semihumid Southeast	471.37	0.274	3.65	0.962
Humid East	1,244.30	0.474	2.11	0.920
Agreste	126.50	0.403	2.48	0.997

Note: Table is based on grouped data. Dependent variable: annual gross output. Independent variable: capital = value of housing, other structures, and equipment.

Table 2-16. *Capital/Output Ratios: Value of Housing, Other Structures, and Equipment*

Farm size (hectares)	Average capital/output ratios (ACOR)						
	West	Middle-North	Sertao	Semi-humid South-east	Humid East	Humid South-east	Agreste
0–9.9	1.81	1.72	1.85	1.81	1.96	0.44	1.26
10–49.9	1.95	1.40	1.62	2.62	1.84	0.85	1.64
50–99.9	1.67	1.80	1.63	1.47	1.52	1.14	1.41
100–199.9	1.87	1.87	1.73	3.37	1.62	0.74	2.28
200–499.9	2.61	1.68	1.66	3.50	1.32	0.81	2.23
500 +	1.52	1.11	1.95	3.51	2.21	0.54	2.30
ACOR, all farms	1.89	1.46	1.73	2.80	1.80	0.77	1.81
ICOR, all farms	1.95	1.11	1.90	3.65	2.11	0.59	2.48

3

Outputs, Inputs, and Incomes

Before we analyze the way the principal factors—labor, land, and capital—
are employed on different types of farms, it is necessary to discuss the ends
of agricultural production: outputs and incomes. Because markets are
primitive in much of the Northeast and many farmers and sharecroppers
produce largely for subsistence, output and income are closely intercon-
nected.

Agricultural Products

The size of the Northeast region and the diversity of its farming systems
mean that no fewer than sixteen crops must be considered to obtain a
representative picture of the region's crop output. The crops currently
produced are described briefly below.

Short-Cycle Crops

Five principal short-cycle (annual) crops are cultivated in the Northeast:
herbaceo cotton, rice, corn, manioc, and two varieties of beans, *de arranca* and
de corda. Cotton is the principal cash crop in the Sertao and Agreste regions;
the other four crops are grown throughout the Northeast and make up a
large proportion of the typical diet. Rice is grown on both irrigated and
rain-fed land, though the scarcity of irrigation works largely confines
irrigated rice production to the river valleys in the western regions. About
80 percent of the corn produced is a common maize variety; several hybrid
varieties make up the remainder. Virtually all farms, save the sugar and
cacao plantations, produce at least two annual food crops, both for their
own consumption and for the market. Manioc is grown very commonly,
partly because storage facilities on most farms are limited and manioc roots
can be left in the ground for up to two years.

Long-Cycle Crops

Agricultural resources in the Zona da Mata have been almost entirely devoted to sugar production since the sixteenth century. Sugar remains the largest source of foreign exchange for the rural Northeast, followed by cacao, which is produced mainly in the central region of Bahia (the Humid Southeast zone in this study). Whereas most of the agricultural technology in the Northeast is primitive, sugar and cacao production techniques rely to some extent on mechanized equipment and chemical fertilizers. Of the farms sampled by the SUDENE/World Bank survey, at least 30 percent of those in the Humid East and Humid Southeast used chemical fertilizers, whereas only 1 percent of those in the interior (West, Middle-North, and Sertao) did so.

Cotton is the dominant long-cycle crop in the interior zones. The most common variety is the long-fiber *moco*, which is highly drought-resistant and has a life cycle of five to eight years. A hybrid between moco and the annual herbaceo is *verdao*, which has a life cycle of about three years. Although it is inferior to moco, verdao shares some of moco's drought-resistant qualities and, because it is more bushlike, leaves the land easier to clear.

Tropical fruits, particularly bananas, oranges, and coconut, are also widely cultivated in the Northeast.

Two types of long-cycle fibers, sisal and *tucum*, were once relatively important in the Northeast, but their production has declined rapidly in the face of competition from synthetic substitutes and instability in international markets.

Extractive Activities

Apart from forestry, which is not considered in this study, extractive activities from babacu and carnauba, two types of indigenous palm, are prevalent in the West and Middle-North. The babacu produces nuts, which are gathered in the slack agricultural season for a variety of uses and for their oil. The carnauba is of economic importance to the frontier areas and to the Sertao because of the high-quality wax derived from its leaves.

Livestock

Stock raising of some type is observed in all zones and on almost all farms, though few, except in the western zones, can be said to specialize in livestock. This study will not consider the small animals kept on most farms; it is difficult to attribute particular inputs to their production, and they account for a negligible proportion of marketed output. Roughly 18 million head of cattle are maintained in the Northeast. Dairy products are best considered as by-products, except in a few farms near major market centers. In the interior, because of poor transport and a dearth of refrigeration facilities, organized dairy production for the market is almost nonexistent.[1]

By far the most important output from stock raising, therefore, is beef. The singular advantage of beef cattle appears to be that they can transport themselves (often 200 miles or more) to market and, unlike crops, their sales can be timed to yield a steadier flow of income. The quality of beef produced, however, is extremely poor. Little or no effort is made to preserve breeds, and the resulting mixture of bloodlines, combined with primitive technology, yields very low carcass weights.

Agricultural Output

Official Brazilian figures estimate the gross output from crops in the Northeast in 1973 at Cr$11,281 million, or US$1,763 million.[2] The crop yields reported by the SUDENE/World Bank survey suggest that this figure may be biased upward, even when allowance is made for the possibility that it takes less than full account of production consumed on the farm by either people or animals or of payments in kind to workers. Nevertheless, it is the best available starting point to analyze agricultural productivity in the Northeast. Data on the consumable output from livestock are not available from official sources,[3] but the survey suggests that meat and dairy production for 1973 amounted to Cr$2,316 million or US$362 million, giving a total of Cr$13,597 million or US$2,125 million for all agricultural production.

For the rural population of 18 million in 1973, gross output from agriculture thus amounted to US$125 per capita. Aside from the fact that farm

1. In every interior market that we have observed, all perishable products (meat and dairy) are sold on the same day they are brought to market.
2. Instituto Brasileiro de Geografia e Estatistica (IBGE), *Anuario estatistico do Brasil* (Rio de Janeiro, 1975).
3. IBGE reports animal population but not production. Production estimates from other sources, principally the Ministry of Agriculture, have been termed "highly suspect . . . unreliable and often inconsistent." William H. Nicholls, "The Brazilian Agricultural Economy: Recent Performance and Policy," in *Brazil in the Sixties*, ed. Riordan Roett (Nashville, Tenn.: Vanderbilt University Press, 1972), pp. 162–63.

profits and labor remuneration make up the bulk of value added in agriculture, the virtual absence of industry and the visibly meager tertiary activities in the rural Northeast suggest that rural per capita incomes may not be much higher than this figure. If the balance of trade between the Northeast and the rest of Brazil and the world is zero,[4] the gross output figures imply that per capita annual consumption of agricultural products in the Northeast is at most US$66, if stocks and savings are ignored. The data that were given in Tables 2-3 and 2-4 imply that the output per capita of persons in the agricultural labor force is US$400. The output for each man-year of full-time employment is US$1,202.

For all agricultural land—that is, land contained in properties registered by the INCRA cadastral survey—gross output is US$29 per hectare (1973 dollars). For land actually cultivated and harvested, gross output is US$183 per hectare.[5] As noted above, it is possible that the estimate of aggregate crop output may be too high, and hence that these yield figures may be overstated.[6] Although the survey results are generally quite close to census figures for comparable aggregate items and for prices and cropped areas, there are some substantial differences for crop yields. Table 3-1 reports IBGE's estimates of yields with those from the survey for both good- and medium-quality cropland, for the principal crops that were reported in comparable units.[7]

The survey and the census are remarkably close for crops (cotton and sugar) that require processing and for which formal control over production statistics is thus possible. They differ dramatically for crops, particularly beans and manioc, that are primarily subsistence crops with the bulk of production never reaching a formal market or processing center. This

---

4. The Northeast exports sugar, cocoa, cotton, babacu, sisal, and carnauba, but information on its food imports is not available.

5. This may be broadly compared with a world average grain yield of about US$350 per hectare.

6. Gross crop output may have been overestimated if the procedures used in the census (on which the estimate is based) double- or triple-count the output of crops from land that is interplanted. A hectare interplanted with manioc and beans, for example, may have been recorded as one full hectare of manioc and one full hectare of beans and the size of the harvest then deduced on this basis. IBGE does not report the procedures it uses in such cases, but the yield data shortly to be discussed suggest that some overcounting does occur. Survey estimates (based on the INCRA land registration) indicate that 13.8 million hectares were harvested in 1973, nearly 2 million more than the 11.6 million reported by the Bank of the Northeast from IBGE sources.

7. Whereas IBGE reports yield data in kilograms per hectare, the survey employed the most common units of measurement used by the farmer. Most fruits and some vegetables were reported in hundreds of fruits, which cannot be strictly compared with the weight measures.

Table 3-1. *Average Yields of Principal Crops, 1973:*
Alternative Estimates
(kilograms per hectare)

| Crop | IBGE[a] | SUDENE/World Bank survey[b] | |
		Good land	Medium land
Cotton	276	265	236
Rice	1,300	1,052	900
Sugar	45,788	48,000	45,000
Beans	516	262	166
Manioc	11,324	6,891	4,584
Corn	687	515	392

Note: Survey estimates are based on 1,000 or more observations of each crop.

a. IBGE, *Anuario estatistica.*

b. Averages over all varieties and techniques for the zone in which the crop predominates. Coefficients of variation of these estimates generally average 0.10 to 0.15.

suggests that the IBGE sampling technique may be biased toward market-oriented production, which probably takes place on more productive farms and yields higher-quality products.

The composition of the crop production provides a first insight into the stagnation of Northeastern agriculture. In value terms, only 38 percent of output is from export crops—cotton, sugar, cacao, and sisal. All the export crops suffer marketing problems: cotton and sisal because they compete with synthetics,[8] sugar because of international marketing restrictions and severe competition from more efficient southern Brazil producers, and cacao because of inelastic world demand. Fully 47 percent of crop output is from subsistence types of crop—rice, corn, beans, manioc, bananas, potatoes, tobacco, and coconuts. These crops are inferior goods, produced largely for on-farm consumption or for the local market because their quality is too poor for exportation. Income elasticities for the main food crops have been estimated to be: rice, 0.34; manioc, 0.27; corn, 0.25; beans, 0.50; bananas, 0.34.[9] Most of the crops composing the remaining 15 percent of crop output are either highly perishable (melons, tomatoes) or commod-

8. The 1973 oil crisis did not improve the Northeast's scope for exporting cotton, either abroad or to the rest of Brazil, because most of the cotton production was diverted to internal uses to substitute for imported petroleum-based products.

9. Unpublished estimates by the United Nations Food and Agriculture Organization and the Superintendency for Planning, Ministry of Agriculture.

ities that are predominantly consumed by high-income groups and hence have rather limited Northeastern markets (grapes, citrus, pineapples).

Industrialization, urbanization, and rising incomes are unlikely to cause a substantial rise in the demand for the traditional foodstuffs.[10] This is not to say that the production of these foodstuffs should not be promoted, for they compose the vast bulk of the typical Northeastern diet, which, in view of the per capita output estimated above, is presumably grossly inadequate for the majority of the population. Rather, a search must continue for products that not only are amenable to Northeastern growing conditions but also have alternative, less constrained outlets.

The dominance of crop and livestock production in the generation of gross agricultural income can be seen from the top part of Table 3-2. The other two items captured by the survey—income from rental of land and equipment—account for only 1 percent of the composition of gross receipts. Rental transactions do not of course affect production directly, but their small size attests that these markets are not operating as efficiently as one might expect.

Inputs and Costs

If there are difficulties in measuring output in cross-sectional studies (because of interfarm transfers, measurement errors, and possible biases), the measurement of production costs is even more perplexing. First, many costs are of the nonmarket variety: Not only is it difficult to measure the opportunity costs of family farm labor and land, but many of the inputs employed in Northeastern agriculture are produced on the farm (seeds) or are by-products of other activities (manure). Hired laborers are often remunerated partly in kind, not only in foodstuffs, which can be approximately valued, but in services such as housing and the extension of credit for consumption purposes. Second, it is often difficult to decide whether

10. The role an inferior product mix may play in a stagnant region has long been recognized. Hollis B. Chenery, "Development Policies for Southern Italy," *Quarterly Journal of Economics*, vol. 76 (November 1962), pp. 515–47, found "demand limitations" and "concentration of production in sectors (mainly agriculture) that do not offer the possibility of rapid growth" to be "one of the most basic Southern problems" (p. 539). His analysis also has implications for strategies discussed later in this study: for example, "price support for Southern agriculture [is] of a palliative nature and conflict[s] with the national policy of freer trade and economic integration" (p. 540); and "the 'overhead approach' [to investment] either ignores the other structural changes that are needed in the rest of the economy or assumes that they will take place automatically" (p. 546).

Table 3-2. *Percentage Composition of Agricultural Receipts and Costs, by Zone*

Receipts and costs	West	Middle-North	Sertao	Semi-humid South-east	Humid East	Humid South-east	Agreste	North-east total
Receipts								
Crops	50.6	69.5	66.9	58.6	70.2	99.9	60.4	66.0
Livestock	48.0	28.4	32.5	39.9	25.4	0.1	38.7	33.0
Rental of land	0.4	1.2	0.3	1.2	4.3	0.0	0.7	0.7
Rental of equipment	1.0	0.9	0.3	0.3	0.1	0.0	0.2	0.3
Total	100.0	100.0	100.0	100.0	100.0	100.0	100.0	100.0
Costs								
Wage labor	53.7	47.5	41.1	36.8	45.3	60.5	42.8	44.8
Purchased inputs for livestock	2.6	7.4	8.2	10.1	10.1	0.1	8.8	7.2
Other purchased inputs	3.3	9.2	7.1	4.3	14.4	8.0	16.7	8.8
Rental of equipment	0.3	0.5	0.7	0.7	1.7	0.9	0.7	0.7
Maintenance	19.7	16.5	15.6	18.5	9.1	9.2	14.8	14.2
Depreciation of structures and equipment	20.4	18.8	25.4	29.6	19.3	21.3	16.2	24.3
Total	100.0	100.0	100.0	100.0	100.0	100.0	100.0	100.0

Source: SUDENE/World Bank survey.
Note: Receipts and costs include subsistence production and wage payments in kind.

facilities should be characterized as productive, and their costs measured, if they are also used by the family for other purposes. Examples are the costs of maintaining a water supply for the family's needs as well as for crops and livestock, or the costs of maintaining a burro that is used for family transportation as well as to haul agricultural inputs and outputs. Third, it is often difficult to distinguish current costs of production from investment costs. This is of particular importance for farms concentrating on long-cycle crops; unless they all have trees with a uniform age distribution, input expenditures in any one year may vary enormously among farms.

The bottom part of Table 3-2 reports the percentage composition of the main costs—hired labor, purchased inputs for livestock and for crops, equipment rentals, maintenance, and depreciation. As could be expected, wage payments compose the bulk (45 percent) of expenditures. The wage percentage is lowest in the Semihumid Southeast, where production is dominated by livestock, and highest in the Humid Southeast. Rental of equipment is again negligible in all zones. Maintenance and depreciation costs account for nearly 40 percent of expenditures. The percentage of expenditures used for maintenance appears to be progressively higher, the more remote the zone: lowest in the coastal Humid East and highest in the West. Depreciation takes a higher percentage of total costs in zones where livestock is important; in the Sertao and the Semihumid Southeast it accounts for over a quarter of total costs.

Purchased inputs for livestock and crops, which together account for only 16 percent of total agricultural costs, deserve closer scrutiny. The levels of expenditure on purchased inputs for each head of cattle indicate that items such as vaccines, veterinary services, and supplemental rations, commonly accepted in many other parts of the world as essential for livestock production, are so infrequently used in the Northeast as to have a negligible effect. In the West, admittedly the most remote zone, less than US$1 an animal was spent in the survey year. Even in the Semihumid Southeast, which is less remote and where ranching is the dominant activity, livestock inputs averaged only US$2 an animal. The averages are somewhat higher in the Sertao and the Agreste, but they reflect the more common use of cottonseed cakes to supplement rations in these cotton-producing areas rather than the use of more advanced technology. Because of the long distances, and the difficulties and costs of transport, markets for livestock inputs in the interior have remained at a rudimentary stage of development, as is evident from the observed prices: In 1972, for example, animal salt sold for Cr$0.16 a kilogram in Rio Grande do Norte, a coastal state, and for Cr$0.29 in Maranhao, the westernmost state covered by the survey.[11]

The data on inputs partly explain why stock raising in the Northeast is a highly land-extensive activity. In few areas can one hectare of pasture support one head of cattle; usually at least three are necessary. As will be explored in the next chapter, the presence of livestock goes far toward explaining the underutilization of large tracts of Northeastern land. Table 3-3 shows the average expenditures on livestock per farm.

Table 3-4 reports average expenditures per farm and per hectare on other purchased inputs. These include all items not directly related to either stock raising or maintenance of structures and equipment, and most of them are used for crop production—seeds, fertilizers, insecticides, and pesticides being the major items. The expenditures are extremely low in relation to farm size as well as income. On the smallest farms in the West, expenditures on inputs for crops averaged only about US$1 per farm and about US$0.30 per hectare. This group of farms is, of course, an extreme

---

11. Fundacao Getulio Vargas, *Precos pagos pelos agricultures* (Rio de Janeiro, 1972), p. 25.

Table 3-3. *Average Expenditure per Farm on Inputs for Livestock,*
by Farm Size and Zone
(cruzeiros)

Zone	Farm size (hectares)					
	0–9.9	*10–49.9*	*50–99.9*	*100–199.9*	*200–499.9*	*500 +*
West	5	64	39	155	222	416
Middle-North	26	448	111	297	516	1,121
Sertao	59	259	344	555	1,516	2,813
Semihumid Southeast	7	651	170	484	2,419	7,459
Humid East	1,831	38	285	233	668	751
Agreste	33	983	725	1,736	2,638	21,117

Note: Humid Southeast is omitted from the table because there were too few observations of cattle.
Source: SUDENE/World Bank survey.

Table 3-4. *Average Expenditure per Farm and per Hectare*
on Other Purchased Inputs, by Farm Size and Zone
(cruzeiros)

Zone	Farm size (hectares)					
	0–9.9	*10–49.9*	*50–99.9*	*100–199.9*	*200–499.9*	*500 +*
	Expenditure per farm					
West	7	109	268	111	256	214
Middle-North	34	54	64	103	195	4,063
Sertao	238	157	539	339	674	1,620
Semihumid Southeast	15	149	749	429	812	1,816
Humid East	710	455	2,906	2,505	11,669	8,420
Humid Southeast	214	635	1,356	5,666	5,186	n.a.
Agreste	323	802	1,396	3,231	8,820	18,652
	Expenditure per hectare					
West	1.86	4.29	3.72	0.80	0.82	0.18
Middle-North	9.18	2.02	0.93	0.74	0.61	2.91
Sertao	48.78	5.70	7.44	2.37	2.34	1.53
Semihumid Southeast	3.12	6.20	10.43	3.10	2.87	1.50
Humid East	183.46	17.44	39.90	17.44	41.15	3.65
Humid Southeast	38.29	23.44	19.21	39.81	17.60	n.a.
Agreste	80.55	30.23	19.03	22.53	29.49	16.43

n.a. Not available.
Source: SUDENE/World Bank survey.

case, but the tables reveal that the majority of Northeastern farms have no green revolution.

Agricultural Incomes

The distribution of income in Brazil has received almost as much attention in the literature as the impressive growth record of the economy. Although the debate continues, it seems clear that the distribution of income is highly skewed in Brazil; that the majority (at least two-thirds) of those in poverty are rural; and that about half of Brazil's poor are in the Northeast.

The SUDENE/World Bank survey did not attempt to measure incomes in the rural Northeast directly, and a size distribution of incomes cannot be derived from it. Other inquiries, including censuses and household surveys, have produced size distributions, although with conflicting and sometimes debatable results.[12] The most recent and comprehensive attempt to measure expenditures—and hence welfare—in Northeast Brazil is described in the appendix to this chapter. The purpose here is to employ the income data from the SUDENE/World Bank survey to arrive at a functional distribution of incomes from agriculture and to identify those poorest who depend on agriculture for their livelihood.

The SUDENE/World Bank survey provides income estimates for certain classes of agricultural agents: farmers, sharecroppers, permanent workers, and, to a less precise extent, temporary workers.[13] The definitions of these incomes are as follows: For farmers, income is measured as the gross value of crop and livestock production (including that consumed on the farm), plus receipts from land and equipment rentals and net income from share-

12. See, for example, Carlos Geraldo Langoni, *Distribuicao da renda e desenvolvimento do Brasil* (Rio de Janeiro: Editora Expressao e Cultura, 1973); Albert Fishlow, "Brazilian Size Distribution of Income," *American Economic Review*, vol. 62, no. 2 (May 1972), pp. 391–402; Gary Fields, "Who Benefits from Economic Development? A Re-examination of Brazilian Growth in the 1960s," *American Economic Review*, vol. 67 (September 1977), pp. 570–82; Guy Pfeffermann and Richard C. Webb, *The Distribution of Income in Brazil*, World Bank Staff Working Paper no. 356 (Washington, D.C., September 1979); and Montek S. Ahluwalia, John H. Duloy, Graham Pyatt, and T. N. Srinivasan, "Who Benefits from Economic Growth? An Examination of Fields' Reexamination for Brazil," *American Economic Review*, vol. 70, no. 1 (March 1980), pp. 242–45.

13. Because the sample frame was the farm defined as an entrepreneurial unit, rented parcels were excluded from the survey unless the entire farm was under rental contract. Therefore, the survey does not permit a complete accounting of incomes from the agents operating the 26,000 rental parcels (at most 3 percent of farms).

Table 3-5. *Agricultural Incomes, by Type of Agricultural Agent*

Type of agent	Total income (thousands of U.S. dollars)	Number of households (thousands)	Household average (U.S. dollars)	Percentage of households	Percentage of income
Farmers	1,648	779	2,116	27.7	75.1
Sharecroppers	80[a]	241	332[a]	8.6	3.6[a]
Permanent workers	248[a]	895	277[a]	31.8	11.3[a]
Temporary workers	218[b]	897	243[b]	31.9	9.9[b]
Total	2,194[c]	2,812		100.0	100.0

Note: It is assumed that *all* temporary labor income accrues to the households headed by a temporary worker.

a. Lower bound.

b. Upper bound.

c. This total is slightly larger than the estimate of gross value of production, based primarily on census sources, reported earlier. Although one would expect value added to be nearly as large as gross production when purchased input usage is minimal, it certainly cannot be *greater*. The most likely explanation for this discrepancy lies with the previously mentioned inadequate sample of the cacao zone (zone F) in which only one municipio was sampled, and that municipio turned out to be one of the most productive and wealthiest in the zone. Thus, farmers' income in the table is undoubtedly overstated.

Source: SUDENE/World Bank survey.

cropped plots, less expenditures for purchased inputs, equipment rental, hired labor, and maintenance of structures and equipment. For sharecroppers, income is the value of the retained share of the product, plus the value of any foodstuffs produced on the plot and consumed by the sharecroppers' family, less the cost of inputs purchased by the sharecropper. For hired workers, income is the sum of wages paid in money and in kind.

A first approximation to the functional distribution of these incomes among the broad classes of agricultural agents is given in Table 3-5. This distribution is a first approximation because it is based on the extreme assumption that none of the temporary labor income accrues to members of households of the first three types and that it accrues entirely to households in the residual category, those headed by and composed of temporary workers. Many small farmers, sharecroppers, and members of their families do work off their plots occasionally, although the survey did not record the extent. It is doubtful that many permanent workers are allowed to work temporarily on other farms; the months of peak labor demand for nearby farms would presumably be the same for the farm on which the permanent worker is employed. This restriction would not apply to permanent workers' families who most likely do find occasional temporary employment.

Table 3-6. *Average Permanent Workers' Wages, by Zone*

Zone	Number of permanent workers	Average annual wage	
		Cruzeiros	U.S. dollars
A, B (West)	122,000	1,492	233
C (Sertao)	159,000	1,532	240
D, F (Southeast)	420,000	1,825	285
E (East)	47,000	2,097	328
G (Agreste)	145,000	2,054	321
Northeast average	895,000	1,760	277

Note: Wages include payments in kind.
Source: SUDENE/World Bank survey.

The gap in the earnings accrual information, combined with the probable overstatement of farm incomes in the cacao zone, precludes a precise derivation of an agricultural income distribution. Nevertheless, some observations are possible. First, and not surprisingly, landownership appears to be the single most important factor in assuring an adequate income. Farm-owning households, making up about 28 percent of agriculture-dependent households, accrued about 75 percent of agricultural incomes.

The information further reveals that income per household is closely tied to the degree of access to land. For the purposes of this study, access to land is defined as entrepreneurial access. In general, this definition is met only under ownership criteria. Sharecroppers in the Northeast do not appear to have entrepreneurial control of the plots they cultivate, although they probably do contribute to the decisionmaking process on use of inputs, particularly labor.[14] This marginal degree of control corresponds to somewhat higher income levels for sharecroppers than for their permanently employed counterparts. As Table 3-6 reports, permanent workers' average wages are below the sharecroppers' average of US$332 in all zones,

14. In a separate but related study, the authors found that the farm plans *desired* by sharecroppers and landowners for a typical sharecropped plot in the Sertao (where sharecropping is concentrated in the Northeast) could differ widely, the former preferring more intensive foodstuff production and the latter more intensive cash crop (cotton) production. That cotton does dominate sharecropped production indicates that the landowners' preferences prevail. See Gary Kutcher and Pasquale L. Scandizzo, "A Partial Analysis of Share-tenancy Relationships in Northeast Brazil," *Journal of Development Economics*, vol. 3 (December 1976), pp. 343–54.

Table 3-7. *A Low-cost Northeastern Diet*

	Foodstuff			
Item	*Rice*	*Manioc (flour)*	*Beans*	*Total*
Grams a day	150.00	400.00	200.00	750.00
Calories per gram	3.13	2.99	3.21	—
Protein per gram	0.075	0	0.214	—
Calories a day	470.00	1,200.00	640.00	2,310.00
Grams of protein a day	11.00	0	43.00	54.00
1973 U.S. dollars a year	6.57	8.76	22.63	37.96

— Not applicable.

although they are quite close in the more productive East and Agreste zones.

Clearly, and not surprisingly, households depending on temporary employment are the least well off. These households—an estimated total of 897,000 (see the appendix to this chapter)—earn, at most and including income in kind (principally foodstuffs), US$243 a family from agriculture. These households, not owning land or having a sharecropping or permanent employment arrangement, are thus in the most precarious income position and constitute the hard core of Northeastern rural poverty. Given that the average temporary worker receives about sixty days' employment a year (from Table 2-4) at wage rates between Cr$6 and Cr$10 per day and that the typical household has 2.2 workers,[15] family incomes for this group could range between US$124 and US$206 a year. Given family sizes in the range of three to four for the poorest income group, per capita incomes for families depending on temporary agricultural employment are about US$50 and possibly lower—a level that begs the question of survivability. People *do* starve in the rural Northeast but usually only in drought periods.[16] Presumably, a good deal of unrecorded farming activity takes place on unregistered plots not covered by the SUDENE/World Bank survey, and these activities supplement the incomes from casual labor on more formal farming enterprises. The very low level of farm-gate prices for foodstuffs, however, and the relatively high protein and energy content of the typical rural diet indicate that it is possible to survive on as little as US$40 per capita a year, even if the purchased commodities are not supplemented by self-produced foodstuffs. Table 3-7 describes a low-cost

15. SUDENE/World Bank survey estimate for small farmers and sharecroppers.
16. For a lucid account, see Josue de Castro, *Death in the Northeast* (New York: Random House, 1966).

diet composed of typical Northeastern subsistence commodities that approximates Food and Agriculture Organization (FAO) estimates for protein and calorie consumption for all of Brazil and can be purchased at farm-gate prices for under US$40.[17]

That families dependent on casual agricultural employment are the poorest is not surprising; but it *is* surprising that sharecropping families and permanently employed workers' families are very near reasonable absolute poverty lines—arbitrarily defined as US$300 per household.[18] Seventy-eight percent of permanent workers (from Table 3-6) average less than this poverty line, and even the sharecroppers average only 8 percent more. Even though some of the temporary employment accrues to households headed by sharecroppers and permanent workers, it is significant that 40 percent of agricultural households hover around or not substantially above absolute poverty levels, while another 32 percent are probably below this level.

Although farmers' incomes on the average are seven or more times the average of other agricultural agents, it does not follow that all landowning households have acceptable incomes. Table 3-8 reports average farm incomes by zone and size class, and Table 3-9 reports farm income per hectare.

The smallest size class (less than ten hectares) in the four westernmost zones comprises about 56,000 farmers who have average incomes well below the US$300 poverty level we have adopted, and unless they are receiving substantial off-farm employment and income, many of them apparently fare worse than permanent workers and sharecroppers in other zones. These farms, averaging three to four hectares each and not located in areas of adequate soils and rainfall, do not appear large enough to be viable income-producing units.[19]

Several other comments concerning farm incomes are warranted. First, even within size classes of farms, there are vast differences in average income among the zones, largely as a reflection of differences in climate, soil quality, and access to markets. Even apart from the atypical cacao zone, in many cases average incomes in the East and Agreste are four times those in the West and Middle-North. Second, although incomes generally rise with farm size, they do so rather erratically. In the Middle-North, for example,

17. United Nations, Food and Agriculture Organization, *Agricultural Commodity Projections, 1970–1980*, vol. 2 (Rome, 1971), p. 111.

18. Fishlow's poverty line in 1970 was US$230—roughly comparable, when inflated to 1974, to this $300 line.

19. Andrade has argued that only under exceptional circumstances can a farm smaller than five hectares support a Northeastern family, regardless of location within the Northeast. Manuel Correia de Andrade, *A terra e o homen no Nordeste* (Sao Paulo: Editora Brasiliense, 1963), p. 202.

Table 3-8. *Average Net Income per Farm, by Farm Size and Zone*
(U.S. dollars)

	Farm size (hectares)											
	0–9.9		10–49.9		50–99.9		100–199.9		200–499.9		500 +	
Zone	Income per farm	Percentage of zone's farms	Income per farm	Percentage of zone's farms	Income per farm	Percentage of zone's farms	Income per farm	Percentage of zone's farms	Income per farm	Percentage of zone's farms	Income per farm	Percentage of zone's farms
West	207	23	425	34	552	14	670	12	696	10	1,261	8
Middle-North	163	14	541	26	618	15	669	21	1,047	14	3,571	10
Sertao	179	29	711	38	1,401	14	1,762	9	2,855	6	7,647	3
Semihumid Southeast	247	17	885	48	841	17	965	8	1,631	5	3,969	5
Humid East	675	49	1,007	35	1,698	8	2,167	3	4,504	3	9,716	2
Humid Southeast	682	25	5,402	40	15,785	12	37,127	14	59,200	6	119,357	3
Agreste	551	59	771	27	2,353	6	2,333	4	3,031	2	5,976	2

Note: Average net income per farm includes the gross value of crop and livestock production, plus receipts from land and equipment rentals, less expenditures for purchased inputs, equipment rental, hired labor, and maintenance of structures and equipment.
Source: SUDENE/World Bank survey.

Table 3-9. *Average Net Income per Hectare, by Farm Size and Zone*
(U.S. dollars)

Zone	Farm size (hectares)					
	0–9.9	10–49.9	50–99.9	100–199.9	200–499.9	500 +
West	56	17	8	5	2	1
Middle-North	44	20	9	5	3	3
Sertao	37	26	19	12	10	7
Semihumid Southeast	52	37	12	7	6	3
Humid East	182	39	23	15	16	4
Humid Southeast	122	199	223	261	197	193
Agreste	138	29	32	16	10	5

Note: Average net income per hectare includes the gross value of crop and livestock production, plus receipts from land and equipment rentals, less expenditures for purchased inputs, equipment rental, hired labor, and maintenance of structures and equipment.
Source: SUDENE/World Bank survey.

income only doubles from stratum 3 to stratum 5, although the average farm size increases by a factor of ten. The same is true in the Agreste, where there is no appreciable increase in average incomes from stratum 3 to stratum 5, although average farm size quadruples over this range.

Appendix: The National Study of Family Expenditures

Farm surveys, such as the SUDENE/World Bank survey, typically do not include comprehensive coverage of income or expenditure and hence cannot provide an adequate measure of the welfare of those depending primarily—though not necessarily entirely—on agriculture. By the same token, expenditure surveys do not typically address questions of income origin and thus are of limited value for policy analysis. The two types of surveys, if used conjunctively, can provide a more complete picture.

The most recent and potentially most reliable expenditure information for Brazil is provided by the 1974–75 ENDEF survey of household expenditure and nutrition.[20] Preliminary and partial results became available in 1978. ENDEF surveyed 55,000 households in all of Brazil, of which 15,675 were in the Northeast and 5,946 were rural. The fieldwork procedures

20. Unless noted otherwise, all references to ENDEF are from Estudo Nacional da Despesa Familiar, *Despesas das familias, dados preliminares*, Regiao V (Rio de Janeiro: FIBGE, 1978).

involved daily visits for a single week to measure the consumption of those commodities, such as food, that are prone to problems of recall. Other items were measured on a monthly or annual basis. Extensive efforts were made to distinguish monetary expenditures from "global" (monetary plus nonmonetary) expenditures. This distinction is particularly important in the rural Northeast where much consumption probably arises from payments in kind of self-production on unorganized plots not covered by the SUDENE/World Bank farm survey. Neither source would be captured by a tabulation of monetary expenditures alone. ENDEF is also of interest because the survey unit was the household, which does not always correspond to the farm, sharecropped plot, or agricultural worker.

In this appendix, we shall briefly report the number and types of households reported by ENDEF, the two concepts of expenditures, and some limitations of the ENDEF tabulations. Some issues are suggested for further survey work and more precise definitions and delineations of income, expenditure, and their origins.

Agricultural Households

ENDEF reports 3.274 million rural households in the Northeast. Of these, 2.838 million are classified as agricultural,[21] broken down as follows:

	Number of households	Family size	Number of heads and dependents
Employers	487,000	6	2,922,000
Self-employed	1,239,000	6	7,434,000
Employees	1,112,000	5	5,560,000
Total	2,838,000		15,916,000

The total number of agricultural households, as well as the total population depending on agriculture, appear consistent with other estimates and were used in this study to determine the number of temporary worker-headed families as a residual.

The functional breakdown, however, leaves much to be desired. As discussed in Chapter 2, the variety of contracts found in Northeastern agriculture and the varying degrees of decisionmaking control found in

21. ENDEF, table 6, p. 55. Households were classified as agricultural if the principal activity of the head was in farming, livestock raising, or agricultural extractive pursuits. ENDEF's table 6, summarized here, covers the entire Northeast, and 12.8 percent of the total number of households are missing. The documentation (ENDEF, p. 16) states that the missing either are in religious or military professions or are "inactive."

Table 3-10. *Mapping of Agricultural Households between the SUDENE/World Bank and ENDEF Surveys*

SUDENE/World Bank		ENDEF	
Category	Number	Number	Category
Large farms	498,000 ———————➤ 487,000		Employers
Small farms	282,000		
Sharecroppers	241,000 ———————➤ 1,239,000		Self-employed
Renters	26,000		
Permanent workers	895,000		
Temporary workers	897,000 ———————➤ 1,112,000		Employees
Total	2,838,000	2,838,000	

those agents who have some access to land require a much more specific taxonomy.

The employers category presumably covers those farms or agribusinesses large enough to employ nonfamily workers. The total of 487,000 employers is approximately consistent with the SUDENE/World Bank estimate of 498,000 farms that did hire outside labor. The ENDEF tabulation system, however (as well as the ENDEF questionnaire), obscures landownership information because it groups squatters, partners, contractors, and leaseholders together on the sole criterion of whether the households had employees.

The employees category includes both permanent and temporary workers, but again some confusion is possible. A morador, for example, who resides on a small plot on the owner's farm and produces some subsistence crops, could be classified as an employee or as self-employed with equal ease.

The self-employed category suffers from further ambiguities. These households presumably include small farmers, sharecroppers, and workers who perform tasks without contracts.[22]

Although the functional breakdown of agricultural households by ENDEF is inappropriate for the analysis of agricultural development questions (as could be expected, since ENDEF did not address such questions), mapping and reconciliation of the household classifications are desirable. Such a mapping is attempted in Table 3-10.

22. The Portuguese term used by ENDEF for this category is *conta-propria*, literally, "without contract."

Table 3-11. Selected ENDEF Expenditure Data: Current Monetary Expenditure

Expenditure class (U.S. dollars)	Household average (U.S. dollars)	Family size	Per capita (U.S. dollars)	Number of families (thousands)	Percentage of households	Percentage of expenditures
0–308	181	4	45	1,109	33.9	10.8
309–456	378	5	76	657	20.1	13.4
457–603	525	6	87	485	14.8	13.7
604–751	673	6	112	348	10.6	12.6
752–912	826	7	118	217	6.6	9.7
913–1,060	983	7	140	131	4.0	6.9
1,061–1,207	1,126	7	161	77	2.6	4.7
1,208–3,033	1,716	7	245	222	6.8	20.5
3,034+	5,115	7	731	28	0.9	7.7
All rural	567	5	113	3,274	56.5	28.5
All nonrural	1,849	5	370	2,527	43.5	71.5
All Northeast	1,124	5	225	5,791	100.0	100.0
Gini coefficient = 0.45						

Source: ENDEF, table 9.

76

From this mapping, it appears that ENDEF may have classified as many as two-thirds of our so-called permanent workers as self-employed. Because the SUDENE/World Bank survey found at least half the permanent workers to be moradores, such a conclusion is reasonable. But many or most of the temporary worker households could be squatters, and thus self-employed. Because the SUDENE/World Bank survey covered squatters only if they resided on a registered farm and the owner was aware of their presence, or if they were discovered in one of the squatter areas in Maranhao specifically included in the survey, their true status remains open to question.

Two conclusions emerge from this discussion, however. First, only 17 percent of agricultural households employ nonfamily labor; the others rely solely on family labor, either because they farm plots too small to require additional labor or because they are totally dependent on off-farm employment. Second, as many as 897,000 or 32 percent of agricultural households could depend entirely on casual employment.

Monetary Expenditures

The preliminary ENDEF results provide a distribution of monetary expenditure by rural households.[23] This distribution is reproduced in Table 3-11, in U.S. dollars comparable to figures given elsewhere in this study. Although the vast majority (94 percent, according to ENDEF) of rural households depend primarily on agriculture, and although items such as savings and decrements to assets, which would cause a divergence between monetary income and monetary expenditure, can safely be ignored in an impoverished and inflation-ridden region, this distribution is not equivalent to an income distribution because it ignores income arising from nonmonetary transactions and nonagricultural sources and includes expenditures financed from nonagricultural activities.

Nevertheless, Table 3-11 verifies the existence of extreme poverty and disparity in the rural Northeast. Interpolating the income classes and extrapolating family size to population totals, we find that at least 50 percent of the rural population, or 9 million persons, had monetary expenditures below US$100 per capita; nearly 25 percent had expenditures below US$50 per capita. The per capita rural expenditure was only about half that

23. The ENDEF method of tabulating the data obscures important information. The ENDEF tables distribute households to expenditure classes on the basis of household, not per capita, expenditure. Thus, within a given class, a wide range of per capita expenditure is possible. In addition, the tables include expenditures by nonfamily members such as guests and employees, but these persons are excluded from the family size averages (ENDEF, p. 14). Thus little, if anything, can be said about per capita expenditure levels.

Table 3-12. *Selected* ENDEF *Expenditure Data: Global Expenditure*

Expenditure class (U.S. dollars)	Household average (U.S. dollars)	Family size	Per capita (U.S. dollars)	Number of families (thousands)	Percentage of households	Percentage of expenditures
0–308	220	3	73	282	8.6	1.9
309–456	389	4	97	377	11.5	4.4
457–603	529	4	132	482	14.7	7.7
604–751	675	5	135	460	14.1	9.4
752–912	828	5	166	410	12.5	10.3
913–1,060	984	6	164	315	9.6	9.4
1,061–1,207	1,136	6	189	208	6.4	7.1
1,208–3,033	1,715	7	245	656	20.0	34.0
3,034+	6,123	7	875	85	2.6	15.8
All rural	1,012	5	202	3,274	56.5	32.2
All nonrural	2,769	5	554	2,527	43.5	67.8
All Northeast	1,776	5	355	5,791	100.0	100.0
Gini coefficient = 0.40						
Agricultural households						
Employers	2,132	6	355	487	17.2	33.7
Self-employed	979	6	163	1,239	43.7	39.5
Employees	739	5	148	1,112	39.1	26.7
All agricultural	1,083		193	2,838	100.0	100.0

Source: ENDEF, table 7.

of all Northeasterners and less than one-third that of nonrural Northeasterners.

Even though the Gini coefficient of the distribution of these monetary expenditures is quite high (0.45), these data do not reveal many very well-to-do households. Indeed the top 1 percent of wealthiest households average only US$5,115 or US$731 per capita, which does not seem to square with the distribution of landholdings described in Chapter 2 and the average income for the largest farms reported in Chapter 3. This observation supports commonly held views of such intense household surveys: that the most well-off refuse to cooperate and are thus underreported; and that the poorest, who may be itinerant workers with no fixed abode, would not be captured by a survey based on a delineation of domiciles.

Global Expenditures

Recognizing that monetary expenditures do not account for all sources of welfare in a developing rural area, ENDEF tabulated all household expenditures in physical terms and imputed values to those components that were not obtained through monetary transactions. The distribution of these "global" expenditures for rural households is reproduced in Table 3-12. Although the available ENDEF documentation does not report monetary expenditures for agricultural households as broken down above, it does so for global expenditures, and these data are reported at the bottom of the table.

As could be expected, the global expenditures are far higher for all expenditure groups than the monetary expenditures, a result indicating that a good proportion of welfare is derived from nonmarket transactions. For all rural households, nonmonetary expenditures account for nearly half of total expenditures; but even for nonrural Northeastern households, the proportion is one-third.

Differences of such magnitude deserve further inquiry, particularly as the origins of the expenditures are not available from the reported data. Food reported as a nonmonetary expenditure, for example, could either have been produced by the households or have been a payment in kind for work performed outside the household.[24] For all rural households, food

---

24. The ENDEF volume that reports consumption differentiates the origin of foodstuffs only between purchased and not purchased. For the major categories of foodstuffs, the percentages not purchased for all rural households are: cereals and derivatives, 63.8 percent; roots and tubers, 57.6 percent; sugar and derivatives, 15.5 percent; legumes, 68.9 percent; vegetables, 82.8 percent; fats and oils, 22.7 percent; beverages, 13.1 percent. Estudo Nacional da Despesa

accounted for 57 percent of total global expenditures, followed by housing at 14 percent and clothing at 8 percent.[25]

A large part of the differences in the expenditure concepts probably arises from the manner in which food is evaluated. Although the imputed values of particular commodities are not reported, it appears that these values are far higher than farm-gate prices. The implicit price for cereals and derivatives is about Cr$10 a kilogram, yet the average farm-gate price for rice, the most important cereal, was less than Cr$1. Although costs of milling, transportation, storage, and marketing would account for part of this difference, such costs are largely irrelevant because 64 percent of this commodity group was not purchased.

An additional clue is given by the method ENDEF used to evaluate clothing and similar items produced in the household. Here the documentation states that the global expenditures "included the difference between the market value of goods made at home and the costs of raw material and services necessary to make them."[26] This procedure requires the strong assumptions that goods produced within the households are marketable and that they are of similar quality to those available in the market.

Despite these shortcomings, which probably overstate expenditures in comparison with more traditional measures of income, ENDEF highlights the importance of welfare arising from nonmarket transactions within the rural Northeast. Clearly, monetary income is not an appropriate measure of the welfare of the poorest when nearly half the expenditures may derive from income in kind, self-produced goods, or barter. When such sources are taken into consideration, the poorest are not so badly off in relation to other income classes.

Expenditure surveys such as ENDEF could be far more useful to policy-makers if they provided a breakdown of income by source and outlays by category,[27] such as:

Income by source
Monetary
    a. from agriculture
    b. from other sectors

Familiar (ENDEF), *Consumo alimentar antropometria, dados preliminares*, Regiao V (Rio de Janeiro: FIBGE, 1977), p. 50.

25. ENDEF, table 7, p. 62.
26. Ibid., p. 16.
27. This classification was suggested by John H. Duloy.

Nonmonetary
  a. wage income in kind
  b. imputed income
Expenditures by category
Monetary
  a. monetary expenditures
  b. savings
Nonmonetary
  a. wage income in kind
  b. imputed expenditures

4

Farm Sizes, Types, and Performance

Several characteristics of the rural Northeast emerge from the survey data. The great majority of its residents depend directly on agriculture, and many are in absolute poverty or not substantially above it. The poor natural resources of the region—its poor soils and uncertain or untimely rainfall—are compounded by the illiteracy and lack of training of its workers, the use of primitive cultural practices, and a virtual absence of modern inputs. As Chapter 3 has suggested, however, the causes of the low levels of agricultural productivity must also be sought in the nature of the markets.

Product markets in the Northeast are not well developed; the production of many Northeastern farmers is geared to their own subsistence needs, and much of the crop output of the region is of goods for which demand is highly inelastic. Questions of demand are considered in the second half of this study. With regard to factor markets, movements of capital appear to be extremely limited, while only 3 percent of the agricultural land is operated under rental contract.

In this chapter econometric analysis is used to examine obstacles to the expansion of farm production and employment. In particular, we analyze differences among groups of farms in the availability and use of resources and their levels of production and seek reasons for these differences in economies of scale, imperfections in the labor market, the use of modern inputs, and the diverse objectives of farmers.

Land and Labor Use

If all farms used the same technology and land and labor markets were functioning efficiently, the marginal productivity of all factors should be the same across farms. Comparison of the marginal productivity of different farms can give an idea of the gaps in the efficiency of resource use and suggest the potential gains for the agricultural sector from a reallocation of

Table 4-1. *Gross Output per Hectare, by Farm Size and Zone*
(cruzeiros)

| | Farm size (hectares) | | | | | |
Zone	0–9.9	10–49.9	50–99.9	100–199.9	200–499.9	500 +
West	543	197	101	56	31	14
Middle-North	464	211	94	51	38	28
Sertao	369	222	174	116	99	67
Semihumid Southeast	135	320	298	89	91	62
Humid East	2,025	397	298	234	285	48
Humid Southeast	1,109	1,574	1,720	2,012	1,622	1,456
Agreste	1,098	370	344	204	198	155

resources from low-productivity to high-productivity farms. The use of machinery, modern inputs, and credit in the Northeast is extremely limited. Substitution possibilities are measurably high, however, and isoquants show unit elasticities for all combinations of inputs.[1] Thus, one must address the use of the two primary factors: land and labor.

Most of the empirical evidence from developing countries points to an inverse relation between farm size and output per hectare, and between farm size and labor use per hectare.[2] Using average productivity as a proxy for marginal productivity, Table 4-1 shows that in the Northeast, also, gross output per hectare declines as farm size rises, and does so dramatically.

Table 4-2 reports on the use of a multiple regression model to examine, in more detail, the effects of size on productivity, distinguishing the possible influences of the proportion of farmland used for crops, as well as of land value, both of which may be higher on small farms. It shows, first, that farm size, the proportion of land under crops, and land value together explain only a relatively small part of the variation in land productivity across farms. Second, the relation between output per hectare and farm size is generally inelastic, so that increases in farm size tend to decrease land

1. These are analyzed in P. L. Scandizzo and T. Barbosa, "Substituicao e produtividade de fatores na agricultura Nordestina," *Pesquisa e planejamento economico*, vol. 7, no. 2 (August 1977), pp. 367–404.
2. See, for example, R. Albert Berry and William R. Cline, *Agrarian Structure and Factor Productivity in Agriculture* (Baltimore, Md.: Johns Hopkins University Press, 1979); World Bank, *Land Reform*, Sector Policy Paper (Washington, D.C., 1974); and D. K. Britton and Berkeley Hill, *Size and Efficiency in Farming* (Lexington, Mass.: Saxon House Studies/Lexington Books, 1976).

Table 4-2. *Relations between Gross Output per Hectare, Farm Size, Percentage of Farmland under Crops, and Land Quality*
(log-linear relations; standard errors are in parentheses)

| Zone | Con-stant | Elasticities | | | R^2 | Degrees of freedom |
		Farm size	Crop-land	Land value (per hectare)		
West	4.779	−0.890	0.538	0.120	0.600	515
	(0.189)	(0.035)	(0.039)	(0.029)		
Middle-North	3.796	−0.600	0.302	0.168	0.398	640
	(0.197)	(0.034)	(0.029)	(0.040)		
Sertao	3.895	−0.635	0.563	0.079	0.386	1,884
	(0.094)	(0.021)	(0.021)	(0.014)		
Semihumid Southeast	2.241	−0.397	0.408	0.343	0.389	276
	(0.290)	(0.052)	(0.059)	(0.040)		
Humid East	4.496	−0.971	0.909	0.090	0.462	305
	(0.255)	(0.064)	(0.046)	(0.039)		
Humid Southeast	5.348	−1.165	1.181	0.066	0.138	42
	(0.542)	(0.547)	(0.539)	(0.056)		
Agreste	4.226	−0.643	0.567	0.107	0.388	700
	(0.149)	(0.033)	(0.036)	(0.024)		

Note: Except for Humid Southeast, all the coefficients are significant at the 1 percent level.

productivity less than proportionally. Third, for five of the seven regions, the value of output per hectare is much more strongly associated with the proportion of farmland under crops than with the size of the farm. Fourth, the value of land appears to have only a minor effect on output. Although it is not possible to reach definite conclusions without a more complete model, these results suggest that the main reason output per hectare declines as farm size increases is that large farms use land less intensively than do small farms.

The differences in the intensity of land use may be associated with the amounts of labor and capital applied. Although it is reasonable to expect large farms to use less labor per hectare than small farms, it is less likely that they would also use less capital. As Table 4-3 shows, however, both labor and capital per hectare decline dramatically as farm size increases. Except in the Humid Southeast, in which there appears to be no systematic relation between the variables considered, the smallest farms apply, on the average, about twenty-five times as much labor per hectare as do the largest. Capital intensity also decreases noticeably as farm size rises; this, together with the fact that capital/output ratios vary little with farm size (see

Table 4-3. *Man-years of Labor and Capital per Hectare, by Farm Size and Zone*

	Farm size (hectares)						Zone average
Zone	0–9.9	10–49.9	50–99.9	100–199.9	200–499.9	500 +	
	Man-years of labor						
West	0.45	0.80	0.03	0.02	0.01	0.01	0.14
Middle-North	0.23	0.08	0.03	0.01	0.01	0.01	0.06
Sertao	0.23	0.08	0.04	0.02	0.02	0.01	0.11
Semihumid Southeast	0.23	0.08	0.04	0.02	0.01	0.01	0.09
Humid East	0.44	0.09	0.05	0.03	0.04	0.01	0.25
Humid Southeast	0.25	0.16	0.09	0.10	0.07	0.10	0.16
Agreste	0.51	0.10	0.05	0.04	0.03	0.02	0.33
	Capital (cruzeiros)[a]						
West	985	384	168	105	81	21	75
Middle-North	799	295	170	96	63	31	63
Sertao	681	359	283	201	164	134	203
Semihumid Southeast	2,406	840	438	300	318	219	351
Humid East	3,975	733	453	363	375	106	332
Humid Southeast	489	1,335	1,953	1,481	1,312	787	1,286
Agreste	1,380	605	485	465	443	355	489

a. Value of housing, other structures, and equipment.

85

Table 4-4. *Trends in Capital and Labor Use as Farm Size Increases, by Zone*
(percentage increase in value of capital and use of labor in response to a 1 percent increase in farmland area)

Zone[a]	Value of land	Value of structures	Value of equipment	Value of livestock	Permanent workers	Temporary workers
West	0.82	0.33	0.52	0.34	0.29	0.55
Middle-North	0.61	0.41	0.63	0.50	0.58	0.37
Sertao	0.78	0.67	0.90	0.73	0.78	0.67
Semihumid Southeast	0.96	0.56	0.82	1.00	0.78	0.66
Humid East	0.99	0.47	0.46	0.58	0.56	0.35
Agreste	0.88	0.76	0.92	0.99	0.25	0.69

Note: Capital refers to the value of housing, other structures, and equipment; labor is measured in man-days.
a. The Humid Southeast is excluded because the test revealed no statistically significant relation between farm size and the variables considered.
Source: SUDENE/World Bank survey, regression estimates on grouped data.

Chapter 2), suggests that large-scale farmers face severely limited capital markets or that they are not interested in using their land with maximum efficiency.

Table 4-4 gives additional details of trends in capital and labor use as farm size increases. Though the aggregate value of land rises roughly in proportion to area, the value of all other capital items, including livestock—an important part of the capital stock on larger farms—shows a rather mixed pattern of response and usually rises less than proportionally with area.

That the various indicators of farm performance decline as farm size increases is to be expected; that they decline so dramatically and so consistently, over both zones and variables, requires explanation. Before delving more deeply into the typology of farms in the Northeast and into questions of profit-maximizing behavior, we will briefly consider several possible hypotheses.

The first and most obvious may be termed the ecological/locational hypothesis. In this view, the larger farms are operated less intensely, simply because they have poorer soil and are located in more remote areas with tenuous links to markets. This hypothesis is undoubtedly true for some individual farms, but the evidence presented thus far strongly indicates that it is not true in the aggregate. In Chapter 2 the various statistical tests showed no systematic deterioration in locational advantage or land quality over farm sizes in all zones. The variation in land value per hectare appears to be too erratic to draw any firm conclusions except to say that the interzone variation is far greater than the intrazone. Nonetheless, the relations in Table 4-2 show that these variations have a negligible effect on productivity. Furthermore, the variation in the elasticities over zones in Table 4-2 lend little support to the locational component of this hypothesis. Apart from the cacao zone, the fastest rate of decline in productivity with respect to farm size occurs in the East (elasticity of -0.971), which is closest to both the Northeast's urban markets and export channels. If anything, the data show that the farther inland a zone is located, the *slower* is the decline in productivity with respect to farm size (Agreste, -0.643; Sertao, -0.635; Middle-North, -0.600) until the trend reverses in the most remote zone (West, -0.890), as might be expected.

A second explanation for lower productivity of large farms concerns implicit taxation of agriculture through distorted or chronically overvalued exchange rates. At least one student traces the origin of the Northeast problem to the mid-nineteenth-century system of exchange rates, which favored export earnings of coffee, produced mostly in southern Brazil, while virtually pricing out of the market the Northeast's export crops, sugar and cotton.[3] Most observers feel that the exchange rate has been overvalued throughout the postwar period and that this has been a conscious government policy designed to assist import substitution in the industrial sectors. The effect has clearly been to tax agriculture to the extent that the overvaluation has resulted in lower prices paid to farmers for exported crops. This explanation has some validity, but it is questionable whether all the performance differentials can be attributed to it. First, the "tax" affects all agricultural producers except the smallest, subsistence-oriented farms. Why, then, do farms in the range of 100 to 200 hectares produce on the average twice as much per hectare as do farms larger than 500 hectares when they face the same "tax" rate? Second, less than 25 percent of Brazilian agricultural production is exported. Why has the estate sector not adapted to the large and growing domestic market to effectively avoid the "tax"?

A second explanation related to macroeconomic policies is inflation, which has often exceeded 50 percent a year in the postwar period. Inflation adversely affects agricultural productivity in at least two ways.[4] First, the ex post results of production decisions are often quite different from the ex ante expectations because inflation rates are difficult to predict and different products are affected to different extents. This serves to diminish incentives to utilize resources at their full capacity and to invest in new agricultural capital. Second, inflation increases the value of land as a speculative asset relative to its value as a factor of production. When inflation leads to disorganized capital markets, land is one of the few assets available as a hedge against losses in purchasing power. As was the case with the exchange rate "tax," inflation is likely to affect small, subsistence-oriented producers to a far lesser extent than larger, potentially commercial operations.

Finally, the social unrest and periodic calls for land reform throughout much of this century have also contributed to uncertainty and to lower levels of productivity than would have occurred in a more stable political environment. The possibility of a land reform undoubtedly lessens the incentive of large landowners to engage in labor contracts with sharecroppers and permanent residents (moradores) because these agents would presumably be the beneficiaries of a reform. Such disincentives, therefore, make less labor-intensive activities such as stock raising more attractive and lead to a heavier reliance on temporary labor.

3. Nathaniel H. Leff, "Economic Development and Regional Inequality: Origins of the Brazilian Case," *Quarterly Journal of Economics*, vol. 86, no. 2 (May 1972), pp. 243–62.
4. G. Edward Schuh, *The Agricultural Development of Brazil* (New York: Praeger, 1970), p. 346.

Apart from the ecological/locational explanation, all the above-mentioned factors probably do have an adverse impact on the operations and productivity of the large-farm sector. It is questionable, however, whether they can explain, even if taken together, the sheer size of the performance differentials. When labor-to-land ratios vary by a factor of twenty or more, and output per hectare by a factor of 100 or more, the full answer must be sought in the functioning of the factor markets and in the behavioral responses of farms of different sizes and types to productive opportunities.

Market Dependency: Family and Nonfamily Farms

Extensive experimentation convinced us that there were no significant differences in the production functions of farms of different size classes.[5] To further investigate the reasons for the differences in patterns of factor use on farms of different sizes, it is necessary to look at the organization of production. Theoretical studies, supported by most of the empirical literature on Brazilian agriculture,[6] suggest a sharp dualism between a subsistence sector and a market-oriented sector, each of which has stylized characteristics:

Subsistence sector
—Labor is mainly supplied by the family.
—Output is mainly consumed on the farm so that the marketable surplus is relatively small and not increasing.
—There is little or no technical change.
—The returns to capital and labor are low so that there is little incentive to save, to invest, or to employ labor beyond the activities strictly required for subsistence.

Market-oriented sector
—Labor is mainly supplied by hired workers.
—There is a high reliance on the market both to dispose of the marketable surplus and to procure inputs.

5. These tests are reported in SUDENE, *A economia agricola do Nordeste: Diagnostico parcial e perspectivas* (Recife, 1976).
6. See the discussion on technological dualism in Brazilian agriculture in Ruy Miller Paiva, "Modernizacao e dualismo tecnologico na agricultura," *Pesquisa e planejamento economico*, vol. 1, no. 2 (December 1971), pp. 171–234; W. H. Nicholls, "Paiva e o dualismo tecnologico na agricultura: Um comentario," in *Pesquisa e planejamento economico*, vol. 3, no. 1 (March 1973), pp. 15–50; G. E. Schuh, "Modernizacao e dualismo tecnologico na agricultura: Alguns comentarios," *Pesquisa e planejamento economico*, vol. 3, no. 1 (March 1973), pp. 17–94.

Figure 4-1. A Farm Classification Scheme Based on Market Dependency

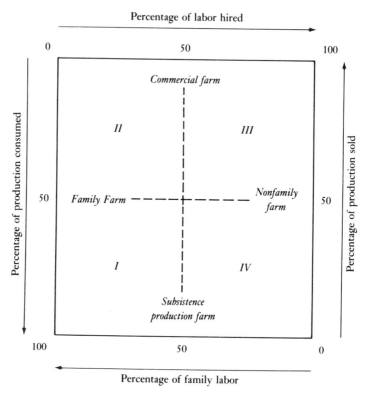

Percentage of labor hired

Percentage of family labor

Percentage of production consumed

Percentage of production sold

Source: C. Nakajima, "Subsistence and Commercial Farms: Some Theoretical Models of Subjective Equilibrium," in *Subsistence Agriculture and Economic Development*, ed. C. R. Wharton, Jr. (Chicago: Aldine, 1970).

—Technical change, as reflected in the adoption of new techniques, is rapid.

—The returns to capital and labor are substantial, and the supply of these factors is responsive to movements in their relative prices.

Nakajima has suggested that all farms can be classified according to two continuous variables relating to the proportion of family labor in total labor use, and the proportion of production consumed on the farm.[7] Figure 4-1

7. Chihiro Nakajima, "Subsistence and Commercial Farms: Some Theoretical Models of Subjective Equilibrium," in *Subsistence Agriculture and Economic Development*, ed. C. R. Wharton, Jr. (Chicago: Aldine, 1970).

Figure 4-2. Preliminary Classification of Sampled Northeastern Farms

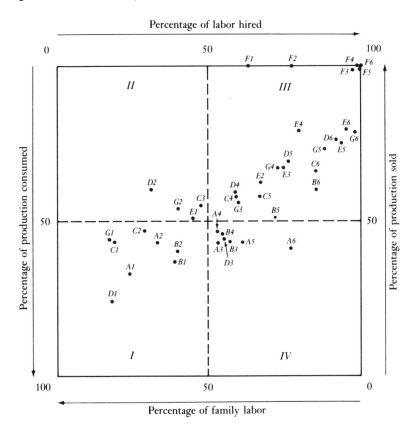

Note: Farms are denoted by zone (*A*, West, through *G*, Agreste) and by size class (*1* = 0–9.9 hectares; *6* = 500+ hectares).

represents this two-dimensional continuum. Two of the four quadrants in the figure (I and III) indicate, respectively, family subsistence farms and commercial enterprises that hire labor. Farms in the other two quadrants, II and IV, are more difficult to characterize, and their classification requires additional criteria.

Figure 4-2 shows the mean values of the two Nakajima variables for the different farm size classes and zones of the Northeast. It shows, first, that the two elements of market dependency (proportion of produce sold and proportion of labor hired) are highly correlated. Exceptions include a few farms of small and medium size in the Zona da Mata, Semihumid Southeast, and Agreste, which rely on family labor but market at least half their produce, and all the farms over fifty hectares in the West, which rely on hired labor but market less than half their output. Second, the more commercial farms tend to be large, whereas the subsistence farms tend to be small. Third, agriculture is noticeably more market-oriented closer to the coast. All farms in the Zona da Mata and the cacao zone are commercial: Except for those under ten hectares in the sugar zone, at least two-thirds of their labor is hired, and they market at least two-thirds of their output. As the distance from the coast increases, it is only progressively larger farms that are commercial. Fourth, except in the sugar and cacao zones, farms of medium size (50–200 hectares) are neither distinctly commercial nor distinctly oriented to subsistence. More variables will be necessary if we are to characterize their activities.

More systematic tests of the efficiency of family subsistence and non-family commercial farms are needed to establish whether the differences in the performance of farms of different sizes are associated with differences in the production functions of family and nonfamily farms; whether different factor intensities are caused by imperfections in the factor markets; and whether there is evidence of non–profit-maximizing behavior. For these tests, farms are classified into two subsamples according to the proportion of labor that is hired. The first subsample comprises all the farms that employ more family labor than wage labor (designated family farms), and the second comprises all the others (nonfamily farms).

To test for differences in production functions, for each subsample and each zone we fitted a simple Cobb–Douglas production function using ordinary least squares,[8] according to the following model:

$$\log Q_i = a_0 + \Sigma_{j=1}^{8} a_j \log X_{ij} + u_i,$$

where
Q_i = total output for the ith farm (cruzeiros)
X_{i1} = total value of farm land (cruzeiros)
X_{i2} = labor in man-years
X_{i3} = quantity of insecticide used (kilograms)
X_{i4} = quantity of fertilizer used (kilograms)
X_{i5} = value of credit received in the last two years (cruzeiros)
X_{i6} = value of structures and permanent land improvements (cruzeiros)
X_{i7} = value of equipment (cruzeiros)

---

8. The use of this type of function is justified in Scandizzo and Barbosa, "Substituicao e produtividade."

X_{i8} = value of livestock (cruzeiros)

u_i = error term.[9]

Table 4-5 reports the regression results. With few exceptions the estimated equations are similar for family and nonfamily farms. A simultaneous test for differences among the regression parameters (the Chow test) also yielded negative results for all zones except the Agreste.[10] Furthermore, there are no significant differences in marginal rates of return to land and capital between the two types of farms.

There do appear to be significant differences in the labor markets facing the two types of farms, as is shown by the comparison of marginal productivities and wage rates reported in Table 4-6.[11] If their objectives were simply to maximize profits, the family farms, where workers' marginal products are much smaller than their wages, would employ fewer workers than they actually do, and the nonfamily farms would employ more. If one interprets the marginal products of family laborers as their reservation wages, there appears to be a considerable incentive for them to seek employment on large farms, where wages are much higher.

There are obviously many possible reasons the excess labor on small farms is not absorbed by the large farms through downward movements in the wage rate. People may prefer to work on their own farms, and there may be institutional barriers, such as legislated minimum wages or restrictions to labor movement. But the widespread unemployment and the large seasonal variations in agricultural labor requirements suggest that another possible reason lies in the family workers' limited opportunities for finding outside employment. Table 4-7 shows the results of a test of this hypothesis. It compares the ratio of marginal products of labor on family farms to the wage rates on nonfamily farms with estimates of the probability of family workers' finding temporary employment off their own farms.[12] In all

9. Variables X_{i1} and X_{i5} through X_{i8} are measured as stocks and hence are representative of the productive capacity of the farm rather than of its input levels. For all these variables, however, a flow measure was either impossible by definition (as for structures or permanent land improvements) or impractical (as for livestock or equipment).

10. See G. S. Chow, "Tests of Equality between Sets of Coefficients in Two Linear Regressions," *Econometrica*, vol. 28, no. 3 (July 1960), pp. 591–605. In all cases, except for the Sertao, the results of this test do not permit us to reject the hypothesis that the two sets of coefficients are equal at the 5 percent significance level.

11. For the theoretical basis of this type of comparison, see, for example, E. O. Heady and J. L. Dillon, *Agricultural Production Functions* (Ames: Iowa State University Press, 1960).

12. See J. R. Harris and M. P. Todaro, "Migration, Unemployment, and Development: A Two-Sector Analysis," *American Economic Review*, vol. 60, no. 1 (March 1960), pp. 126–42.

Table 4-5. *Cobb-Douglas Production Functions,*
by Type of Farm and Zone
(standard errors in parentheses)

Variable	West		Middle-North		Sertao	
	Non-family	Family	Non-family	Family	Non-family	Family
Constant	4.873[a]	4.626[a]	4.620[a]	3.973[a]	4.039[a]	3.610[a]
	(0.364)	(0.292)	(0.300)	(0.363)	(0.219)	(0.166)
Land value	0.096[a]	−0.0018	0.167[a]	0.166[a]	0.111[a]	0.065[a]
	(0.042)	(0.041)	(0.037)	(0.043)	(0.012)	(0.033)
Labor	0.770[a]	0.566[a]	0.451[a]	0.409[a]	0.433[a]	0.507[a]
	(0.081)	(0.093)	(0.066)	(0.079)	(0.039)	(0.041)
Pesticides	0.061	0.075	—[d]	—[d]	0.082[a]	0.080[a]
	(0.063)	(0.155)	—[d]	—[d]	(0.028)	(0.033)
Fertilizer	—[d]	—[d]	—[d]	—[d]	—[d]	—[d]
	—[d]	—[d]	—[d]	—[d]	—[d]	—[d]
Credit	0.0035	0.031	0.014	0.037	0.028[a]	0.048[a]
	(0.020)	(0.03)	(0.020)	(0.030)	(0.011)	(0.013)
Structures	−0.0059	0.061	0.084[b]	−0.0007	0.152[a]	0.127[a]
	(0.0036)	(0.038)	(0.034)	(0.037)	(0.029)	(0.025)
Equipment	0.071[a]	0.148[a]	0.034	0.077[a]	0.073[a]	0.125[a]
	(0.024)	(0.036)	(0.022)	(0.035)	(0.015)	(0.014)
Livestock	0.064[a]	0.095[a]	0.040	0.130[a]	0.077[a]	0.129[a]
	(0.27)	(0.033)	(0.026)	(0.030)	(0.016)	(0.016)
Coefficient of scale ($\Sigma \beta_i$)	1.060	0.974	0.692	0.560	0.956	1.080
R^2	0.609	0.428	0.369	0.355	0.553	0.535
Degrees of freedom	237	266	378	250	888	984

Note: Family farms are defined as having 50 percent or more of total farm employment supplied by family labor. The Humid Southeast is excluded because there were too few family farms in the sample.

a. Significant at the less than 0.1 percent level.

cases the two measures are indeed very close and, when sample variability is considered, not significantly different from each other at any reasonable degree of confidence.

Farm Sizes and Types: A Multiple Classification

Though the distinction between family and nonfamily farms may be adequate to illustrate the mechanisms at work in the allocation of labor, other dimensions of economic behavior that vary with farm size may be

Semihumid Southeast		Humid East		Agreste		Northeast	
Non-family	Family	Non-family	Family	Non-family	Family	Non-family	Family
3.505[a]	1.758[a]	6.239[c]	4.039[a]	5.716[a]	4.420[a]	4.795[a]	4.073[a]
(0.888)	(0.651)	(0.421)	(0.541)	(0.322)	(0.258)	(0.125)	(0.115)
0.441[a]	0.367[a]	0.011	0.055	0.083[a]	0.061[b]	0.105[a]	0.087[a]
(0.111)	(0.064)	(0.035)	(0.057)	(0.027)	(0.027)	(0.013)	(0.013)
0.426[a]	0.492[a]	0.708[a]	0.437[a]	0.784[a]	0.497[a]	0.582[a]	0.510[a]
(0.124)	(0.173)	(0.068)	(0.141)	(0.075)	(0.078)	(0.026)	(0.031)
0.130[b]	0.144[c]	—[d]	—[d]	0.078[b]	0.182[a]	0.060[a]	0.043[a]
(0.042)	(0.077)	—[d]	—[d]	(0.033)	(0.047)	(0.016)	(0.024)
—[d]	—[d]	0.047[c]	0.091[c]	—[d]	—[d]	0.043[a]	0.062[a]
—[d]	—[d]	(0.023)	(0.055)	—[d]	—[d]	(0.012)	(0.019)
0.025	−0.110[c]	0.020	0.062	0.025[b]	0.089[a]	0.015[a]	0.047[a]
(0.022)	(0.118)	(0.025)	(0.062)	(0.016)	(0.021)	(0.007)	(0.010)
−0.071	0.055	−0.0012	0.0009	−0.005	0.034	0.090[a]	0.056[a]
(0.139)	(0.081)	(0.049)	(0.0055)	(0.04)	(0.034)	(0.016)	(0.015)
0.047	0.032	0.050[c]	0.063	0.043[c]	0.021	0.057[a]	0.095[a]
(0.032)	(0.055)	(0.028)	(0.062)	(0.024)	(0.028)	(0.0028)	(0.011)
−0.042	0.060	0.059[c]	0.124[b]	0.0012	0.088[a]	0.039[a]	0.107[a]
(0.047)	(0.048)	(0.029)	(0.043)	(0.026)	(0.023)	(0.010)	(0.011)
0.957	1.050	0.894	0.833	1.009	0.972	0.991	1.007
0.509	0.446	0.646	0.364	0.489	0.436	0.528	0.435
132	132	184	109	327	361	2,225	2,146

b. Significant at the 0.1–1 percent level.
c. Significant at the 1–10 percent level.
d. Too few observations to estimate the coefficient.
Source: SUDENE/World Bank survey.

overlooked. To try to capture these, multiple comparison methods are used to estimate Cobb–Douglas production functions, with dummy variables representing: (1) five size classes, or strata, of farms (the first five used in the tabulations by farm size, excluding farms of 500 hectares and over); (2) the family or commercial nature of the enterprise (defined according to the proportion of hired labor in its total labor use, as specified in the previous section); (3) the presence of sharecropping; (4) the use of irrigation and of mechanical or animal traction equipment; and (5) the seven physiographic zones. These variables are used to test the hypothesis that farms of different sizes and modes of organization and in different zones may operate on

Table 4-6. *Comparison of Marginal Products of Labor with Wage Rates, by Type of Farm and Zone*
(geometric averages)

Zone	Nonfamily farms			Family farms		
	M/W	t-statistic	Degrees of freedom	M/W	t-statistic	Degrees of freedom
West	1.11	−2.33	345	0.55	−6.75	175
Middle-North	1.04	0.74	481	0.52	−8.89	183
Sertao	1.18	4.76	978	0.75	−6.72	633
Semihumid Southeast	0.97	−0.39	160	0.48	−4.66	86
Humid East	1.45	5.30	216	0.50	−4.87	71
Humid Southeast	1.08	1.73	41	1.18	2.09	41
Agreste	1.46	6.98	378	0.54	−7.92	218

Note: The hypothesis tested is that the marginal product of labor (M) is significantly different from the wage rate (W), or that M/W is significantly different from one. The M/W variable is assumed to be (asymptotically) lognormally distributed.

more—or less—technologically advanced production functions. The nature of the test is such that only intercept levels, which indicate the level of technological efficiency abstracting from differences in the amounts of resources used, can be compared. As noted earlier, however, no significant differences in the production function coefficients could be detected by comparing the performance of farms of different size groups.

The results of one series of tests are reported in Table 4-8, analogous to Table 4-5, which shows the effects of the scalar and dummy variables on output.[13] As can be seen from the second part of Table 4-8, farm size generally has a large and significant effect on efficiency at a high confidence level, and, except in the Humid East, this relation is apt to be stronger as farm size increases. This implies that for a given quantity of resources used, smaller farms appear to obtain less output than larger farms (and family farms obtain less than nonfamily farms). For four zones out of seven, however, classification by size yields coefficients that imply substantial diseconomies of scale. This is a somewhat surprising result, given that the test (Table 4-5) of the effects of farm size alone—that is, with no account taken of other effects that may be associated with size—showed that the

13. Because the dummy variable is equal to one when the farm belongs to the corresponding stratum and is zero otherwise, and because the dummies correspond to the first five strata, a positive effect of farm size will show up as a negative coefficient. When a farm belongs to the sixth (highest) stratum, all size dummies are zero, and farm production will just equal the positive intercept.

Table 4-7. *Comparison of Marginal Products of Labor on Family Farms with the Probability of Finding Alternative Employment*

Zone	Labor marginal products on family farms/Wage rate on nonfamily farms	Probability of alternative employment[a]	t-statistic
West	0.52	0.51	0.01
Middle-North	0.55	0.46	0.31
Sertao	0.57	0.51	0.15
Semihumid Southeast	0.30	0.54	0.81
Humid East	0.39	0.43	0.11
Humid Southeast	0.34	0.42	1.10
Agreste	0.51	0.48	0.08

a. The probability of finding temporary off-farm employment is estimated as the ratio of average yearly employment per family worker outside his own farm, in man-days, to the standard availability for employment of 300 man-days a year.

returns to scale were constant. Our interpretation is that economies of scale as generally measured in agriculture tend to capture the combined effects of several variables associated with the size of the operation. These may include technical efficiency, the proportion of labor supplied by the family, or the degree of decentralization of farm management, all of which are variables whose effect is at least partly captured by the dummy shifters of the equations in Table 4-8. Once these variables are taken into account, the coefficient of scale expresses the economies (or diseconomies) associated with residual factors such as managerial ability and the organization and supervision of farm operations.

Some Conclusions

The production function analysis leads to some conclusions about returns to scale, efficiency in factor allocation, and profit-maximizing behavior on Northeastern farms.

Returns to Scale

There is some mixed evidence of constant or decreasing returns to scale. Although small farms are much less efficient than large farms at the same level of input use, when allowance is made for differences in input use there appear to be substantial diseconomies of scale. Once appropriate allowance is made for input use and other aspects of farm structure, however, small

Table 4-8. Scalar and Dummy Variable Analysis of Effects on Gross Output of Farm Size, Sharecropping, and Three Types of Equipment
(standard errors in parentheses; dependent variable = gross output)

Variable	West	Middle-North	Sertao	Semihumid Southeast	Humid East	Humid Southeast	Agreste	Northeast
Scalar variable								
Land value	0.045	0.073[b]	0.067[a]	0.354[a]	0.009[a]	0.026	0.060[b]	0.096[a]
	(0.032)	(0.030)	(0.015)	(0.062)	(0.034)	(0.062)	(0.020)	(0.009)
Labor	0.679[a]	0.518[a]	0.477[a]	0.511[a]	0.623[a]	0.505[c]	0.674[a]	0.603[a]
	(0.062)	(0.050)	(0.028)	(0.102)	(0.075)	(0.207)	(0.056)	(0.020)
Insecticides	0.087	-0.164	0.060[b]	0.138[a]	—[d]	—[d]	0.112[a]	0.047[a]
	(0.060)	(0.158)	(0.021)	(0.039)			(0.027)	(0.013)
Fertilizer	—[d]	—[d]	—[d]	—[d]	0.050[b]	—[d]	—[d]	0.063[a]
					(0.022)			(0.010)
Credit[e]	0.017	0.019	0.036[a]	-0.014	0.038	—[d]	0.061[a]	0.021[a]
	(0.017)	(0.015)	(0.008)	(0.021)	(0.024)		(0.013)	(0.005)
Structures	0.028	0.031	0.088[a]	0.062	0.026	0.174	0.011	0.063[a]
	(0.027)	(0.024)	(0.019)	(0.046)	(0.038)	(0.173)	(0.028)	(0.011)
Equipment	0.106	0.078[a]	0.055[a]	0.043	0.052[a]	0.024	0.036	0.052[a]
	(0.031)	(0.025)	(0.015)	(0.046)	(0.040)	(0.044)	(0.027)	(0.010)
Livestock	0.072	0.070[a]	0.085[a]	0.026	0.069[b]	-0.080	0.045[a]	0.071[a]
	(0.021)	(0.019)	(0.011)	(0.033)	(0.025)	(0.098)	(0.019)	(0.007)
Coefficient of scale ($\Sigma\beta_i$)	1.034	0.625	0.868	1.120	0.866	0.699	0.999	1.016
t test ($t|\Sigma\beta_i - 1|$)	(0.012)	(-6.015)	(-2.134)	(0.812)	(-2.174)	(-1.715)	(0.001)	(0.131)
Constant	4.917[a]	5.616[a]	4.766[a]	2.500[a]	5.454[a]	8.106[a]	5.511[a]	4.984[a]
	(0.282)	(0.293)	(0.210)	(0.801)	(0.576)	(1.608)	(0.374)	(0.116)

Dummy variable								
Stratum 1 (0–9.9 hectares)	−0.316 (0.212)	−1.122ᵃ (0.235)	−0.896ᵃ (0.148)	−0.807ᵃ (0.490)	−0.309 (0.414)	−3.061ᶜ (1.276)	−0.792ᵇ (0.286)	−0.834ᵃ (0.085)
Stratum 2 (10–49.9 hectares)	−0.232 (0.153)	−0.962ᵃ (0.163)	−0.551ᵃ (0.119)	−0.025 (0.343)	0.688 (0.366)	−2.104ᶜ (1.079)	−0.499ᵇ (0.286)	−0.521ᵃ (0.085)
Stratum 3 (50–99.9 hectares)	−0.241 (0.160)	−0.796ᵃ (0.157)	−0.422ᵃ (0.114)	−0.023 (0.309)	0.310 (0.373)	−1.581 (1.105)	−0.519ᶜ (0.242)	−0.435ᵃ (0.067)
Stratum 4 (100–199.9 hectares)	−0.090 (0.154)	−0.688ᵃ (0.138)	−0.350ᵃ (0.108)	−0.493ᶜ (0.028)	0.560 (0.357)	−1.251 (1.049)	−0.205 (0.230)	−0.330ᵃ (0.063)
Stratum 5 (200–499.9 hectares)	−0.102 (0.130)	−0.546ᵃ (0.119)	−0.167ᵃ (0.107)	−0.104 (0.258)	0.545 (0.366)	−1.286 (1.123)	−0.067 (0.238)	−0.228ᵃ (0.061)
Proportion of farm labor supplied by family[f]	−0.353ᵃ (0.095)	−0.430ᵃ (0.093)	−0.340ᵃ (0.049)	−0.703ᵃ (0.166)	−0.810ᵃ (0.148)	−0.0001 (0.379)	−0.612ᵃ (0.097)	−0.487ᵃ (0.035)
Sharecroppers	0.114 (0.213)	1.011ᵃ (0.123)	0.666ᵃ (0.061)	0.791ᶜ (0.347)	0.848 (0.590)	—	0.835ᵃ (0.198)	0.761ᵃ (0.052)
Equipment								
Irrigation	−0.722 (0.306)	−0.247 (0.634)	0.136 (0.196)	−0.820 (1.138)	0.080 (1.186)	—	0.233 (0.348)	−0.048 (0.164)
Mechanical	−0.056 (0.184)	−0.152 (0.172)	0.073 (0.081)	0.358 (0.261)	0.051 (0.233)	0.263 (0.214)	−0.028 (0.135)	0.084 (0.058)
Animal traction	0.031 (0.130)	−0.164 (0.159)	0.233 (0.063)	−0.460 (0.212)	0.167 (0.220)	0.111 (0.561)	−0.093 (0.113)	−0.041 (0.046)
R^2	0.560	0.514	0.623	0.640	0.645	0.869	0.614	0.589
Degrees of freedom	502	627	1,871	263	292	32	687	4,366

— Not applicable.
a. Significant at the less than 0.1 percent level.
b. Significant at the 0.1–1 percent level.
c. Significant at the 1–10 percent level.
d. Too few observations to estimate the coefficient.
e. The credit variable has to be interpreted as a shifter that absorbs the effect of several "residual" or unspecified variables related to managerial ability and the ability to obtain financial resources. It is very difficult, however, to separate credit from other forms of capital.
f. In alternative specification without dummy variables for size.
Source: SUDENE/World Bank survey.

farms appear to have lower levels of production than those they are apparently capable of achieving. This may be because small-scale farmers have restricted access to inputs other than labor; rely on family workers who have unequal skills; or have more difficulty than large-scale farmers in marketing their output. Small family farms do maximize expected income, if their use of labor is indeed regulated by the wages and chances of obtaining employment on the large farms. The small family farms' absorption of labor is also socially efficient: Although they use too much labor for optimum productive efficiency and its marginal product is low, the "extra" output they produce partially compensates for the underproduction on large farms. They thus help offset the effects on resource use of the skewed land distribution, the lack of well-developed land markets, and the only partially productive efficiency of the large farms.

Efficiency in Factor Allocation

For the great majority of Northeastern farms, land and labor are essentially the only two factors available. Labor is the only factor for which markets, delivery systems, and mobility are sufficient to balance demand and supply. Large (nonfamily) farms presumably have greater freedom to choose both land and labor intensities so as to maximize profits if they wish to do so, whereas family farms are more likely to be constrained by lack of financial resources, poor access to credit, and small land endowments. Even so, large farmers tend to employ less labor than they would require to maximize profits, even after proper account is taken of their relative abundance of land. Conversely, small farmers tend to employ more labor than profit maximization would warrant, probably in part because family members have difficulty in obtaining enough employment elsewhere.

Profit-Maximizing Behavior

There are strong suggestions that factors other than labor are not being allocated according to profit-maximization rules. The marginal productivity of land on large farms is far below reasonable opportunity costs, and for permanent land improvements (structures) and livestock the marginal rates of return are erratic and generally below those from comparable assets outside the Northeast. Modern inputs and credit are consistently associated with higher output, even for small, homogeneous groups of users. Utility maximization, and farmers' expectations about prices and yields, may account for the divergences from optimal behavior. But an alternative explanation may be that, in the use of factors other than labor, market conditions are such that the majority of Northeastern farmers have little freedom of choice.

The problems, development options, and policy choices facing agriculture in the Northeast are diverse and complex and demand that all available tools of analysis be brought to bear. The analysis presented thus far has permitted the description of statistical patterns and identified some hypotheses; some of the questions raised by the descriptive statistics have been addressed in a more systematic way by the econometric analysis in this chapter. One of the advantages of the econometric methods used is that they permit hypotheses to be tested with a minimum of assumptions about underlying behavioral and technical causes. Often, however, statistical analysis cannot go far enough in explaining the relations it reveals and indeed may simply reveal new hypotheses to be tested. For our purposes in this study, it has two other important drawbacks. First, when a large number of variables need to be considered simultaneously, the treatment of the data needs to be highly aggregative, and important aspects of farmers' behavior—for example, their responsiveness to price changes or their aversion to risk—are ignored as a consequence. Second, and even more limiting, is the fact that the statistical tables and tests can only provide a view of an existing situation: They do not permit us to analyze how that situation would change if its underlying causes were changed. The programming model to which we now turn is designed to complement and extend the statistical analysis, to reach a deeper understanding of the workings of the agricultural economy and the constraints on its productivity and expansion.

5

The Structure of
the Programming Model

The value of large quantitative models, which can bring many variables and constraints into focus simultaneously, has been demonstrated in many agricultural policy and project applications. Such models cannot adequately treat nonquantifiable social, political, and institutional influences on an economy. But otherwise their scope is limited only by the data at hand, the skills of the modelers in translating what they observe into a mathematical framework, and the algorithmic facilities available for deriving solutions.

The modeling exercise in this study was undertaken for two main reasons. First, a properly specified model can go beyond the "positive" or explanatory function: If it can adequately simulate the main characteristics of the economy and can identify the factors constraining growth and income, it can then be used in the normative sense to estimate the changes that would be induced by policy interventions or alterations in economic structure. We constructed the model with a view to simulating the effects of alternative actions, previously considered or hypothesized, that have a hope of alleviating the Northeast problem. The second reason was a desire to use an internally consistent quantitative framework of analysis, particularly in view of the inconsistency of existing data sources on the Northeast but also to evaluate the effects of policy interventions. Evaluating proposed interventions in a partial context, rather than tracing their effects through the economy as a whole, can give highly misleading results. The direct effects of a new policy may be desirable but may be lessened or nullified by its indirect effects, which are more difficult to predict and observe.

The model selected for this endeavor follows that popularized by the Duloy and Norton CHAC model for Mexico and applied to several other developing economies for the analysis of agricultural policies and identification and analysis of projects.[1] These models are linear programming models, though they can incorporate many nonlinearities. In the sense that their solution procedure depends upon a linear (or linearized) function to be optimized, they are optimizing models. The objective is usually specified, however, so as to yield a competitive equilibrium; for example, maximizing the sum of producers' and consumers' surplus will (approximately) equate market prices with the marginal costs of production. These models typically contain detailed representations of the production technologies being used in the different areas or the productive units they consider, based on Leontief assumptions. Thus, for each of the different areas it considers, such a model will yield a production pattern that conforms to competitive equilibrium criteria—that is, a pattern in which product prices are equated to marginal costs, assuming that producers maximize profits. The model will also yield aggregate welfare indexes for producers, consumers, and government, as well as tabulations of employment, land use, fertilizer demands, and such items ordinarily of interest to agricultural planners and policymakers.

Two considerations led us to design the Northeast model rather differently than such accepted models as CHAC. First, the diversity and complexity of agriculture in the Northeast pointed to the need for a model composed of individual models for different types of farms in different physiographic zones. Second, because the descriptive analysis suggested that many of the economic, social, and political problems of the Northeast are associated with the distribution of resources, the model contains an accounting framework for employment and income by type of agent: farmers of different types, sharecroppers, permanent workers, and temporary hired workers. Hence the solutions may be analyzed both in terms of their efficiency—as measured by aggregate output, income and employment, and the utilization levels of the basic factors of production—and in terms of their distributional characteristics—the patterns of employment and income over types of farms and types of agents.

Because readers will have different degrees of interest in the model structure, the first section of this chapter gives a general description intended for the layman. The following sections are more detailed, and purely technical material, including the algebraic statement of the model, is contained in the appendixes to the chapter.

1. John H. Duloy and Roger D. Norton, "CHAC: A Programming Model of Mexican Agriculture," in *Multi-Level Planning: Case Studies in Mexico*, ed. Louis M. Goreux and Alan S. Manne (Amsterdam: North-Holland Publishing Company, 1973).

An Overview of the Model

The individual farm models that are the microeconomic foundations of the sector model view the farm as a decisionmaking entity, endowed with resources and facing production possibilities and opportunities to augment its resources—for example, through hiring labor or borrowing on credit. In general, the farmer maximizes profits subject to the constraints on his production and a penalty on the riskiness of the farm plan chosen.

It is assumed that all farms face a common core of activities and constraints. Augmenting this core are features that distinguish farm models of different types in different zones: differences in resource endowments, constraints, production, and the supply of farm inputs; and different input parameters, such as the elasticities of demand for their particular products.

The typology of Northeastern farms used in the model is derived in Appendix A to this chapter. A brief description follows.

Family farms have an average size of 10–30 hectares, depending on the zone, and supply more than three-fourths of their own labor. Though many are subsistence farms (the majority in the West, Middle-North, Sertao, and Agreste), a third of them are commercially oriented, marketing 80–90 percent of their output. Family farms make up just under a third of all farms in the Northeast.

Estates, which average more than 500 hectares in most zones, are typically livestock fazendas in the West and Middle-North; fazendas with sharecroppers, livestock, and a feudalistic structure in the Sertao; and sugar or cacao plantations in the East or Southeast, relying on hired labor. The generic term "estates" is used for these large farms for the sake of convenience, but it should be borne in mind that many of them are not richly endowed; nor are their owners necessarily wealthy. As measured by the application of labor to land and by the proportion of land under crops, much of the land on estates is not intensively used. Estates account for about 6 percent of all Northeastern farms.

Medium-size farms have an average of 50–100 hectares, depending on the zone, and market more than half their output. Other characteristics vary from zone to zone. In the coastal areas they are mainly modern farms relying on hired labor and producing almost exclusively for the market. Medium-size farms make up roughly two-thirds of the farms in the Northeast.

The Core of the Farm Models

Table 5-1 presents the core matrix of each farm model, which comprises crop production and selling activities; the total use of labor and the hire of temporary or permanent labor; constraints on the availability of land of different types, working capital, and family labor; and balances on production and product distribution, and labor sources and use. The objective function is, in the core matrix, the maximization of the difference between the returns from product sales and the costs of labor use and other inputs.

The crops that can be produced and the possible ways of producing them obviously differ according to the zone; the derivation of production coefficients is described in Appendix C to this chapter. In all cases, a production activity is defined as the cultivation of one hectare of land, with corresponding requirements of labor by month and working capital (short-term financial capital). The outputs of the production activities, in physical terms, are registered in the output balance rows, which are linked to the product-selling activities. Labor requirements are linked to labor summation activities, which register the total labor requirements of the farm plan. These are linked to the labor balances from which the labor demands are supplied. The labor balance rows are constrained by the availability of family labor, on the assumption that family labor will be used before outside labor is hired.

The main constraints on the farm models are thus on land, family labor, and working capital. Land as represented in the models is of three types, good, medium, and poor, classified according to farmers' opinions of the value of their land, supplemented by estimates of its productivity. In general, "good" land is flat and near a water source or in a humid, low-lying area; "medium" land is hilly or more arid; and "poor" land is useful only for natural pasture or occasionally certain tree crops.

The average farm family is assumed to have five members, of whom 2.2 (man-equivalents) are workers. The family labor constraint can be relaxed by hiring temporary workers (on a monthly basis) or permanent workers (on an annual basis). All workers are assumed to be equally productive. Their wages differ, however; family workers have a reservation wage rate about half that of temporary workers. This was the rate for family workers estimated with production function analysis, and it corresponds quite closely to the expected wage in the Harris–Todaro sense (namely, the

Table 5-1. *Core Matrix of Farm Models*

Constraint block	Activity block					
	Crop production	Product selling	Total labor	Temporary labor hire	Permanent labor hire	
Objective function	– – – –	+ + + +	– – – –	– – – –	–	
Good land Medium land Poor land	1 1 1 1 1 1					≤L_G ≤L_M ≤L_P
Labor requirements	+ + + + + +	–1	–1			= 0
Output balances	+ + +	–1				= 0
Working capital	+ + +		–1	–1		≤WC
Labor balances			–1	–1	–1 ...... –1	≤Family labor

Note: A minus sign indicates a negative number, and a plus sign indicates a positive number, in Tables 5-1 through 5-5.

current wage rate multiplied by the probability of obtaining a job as a temporary worker),[2] as was seen in Chapter 4. Permanent workers, contracted on an annual basis, are cheaper per month than temporary for the same reasons but will be contracted only if the farm plan can use them fully over the course of the agricultural year. (Sharecropper labor is treated differently in the model and is discussed below.)

The availability of short-term financial capital, that is, the previous year's savings plus any available short-term credit, is very difficult to capture adequately in linear programming farm models. To do so would require detailed disaggregation of the production year, knowledge of the farms' budgetary constraints in different seasons and of their intertemporal utility functions, as well as assumptions about the operations of short-term credit markets, their lending criteria, and so forth. Such details are beyond the scope of this study, but because experience in other areas suggests that agricultural credit plays an important role in the adoption of modern techniques and the full employment of land and labor resources, we include a working capital constraint in each farm model. As a proxy for the short-term capital available, the model registers, on an annual basis, all the money costs of the activities undertaken by the farm, as reported by the survey. These costs include the wage payments to workers; the costs of seeds, fertilizer, and other inputs purchased for the cultivation of crops; and the costs of rations and veterinary services for maintaining a livestock herd. These expenditures are registered in the working capital row and are constrained by the average amount actually spent during the survey year by the farm type being represented (an amount reported separately in the survey).

This treatment does not explain farm expenditures; actual expenditures may depend on the perceived profitability of the enterprises farms could undertake or on individual preferences and attitudes toward risk, as well as on the amount saved from the previous years' operations or the restrictions of the credit market. Nonetheless, with such a formulation the model solutions can broadly indicate whether easier access to short-term credit would have beneficial effects and what interest rates farmers would, on the average, be willing to pay for it. It should be borne in mind that the use of cash outlays as a proxy for the available short-term capital can give the impression that the entire amount spent within a year is available to the farmer at any given point in the year—obviously an oversimplification. Hence, the average expenditure level that is used as a constraint in the

2. J. R. Harris and M. P. Todaro, "Migration, Unemployment, and Development: A Two-Sector Analysis," *American Economic Review*, vol. 60, no. 1 (March 1970), pp. 126–42.

model must be considered as an upper bound to the short-term funds effectively available to the farm. Moreover, because the sources of such funds are not differentiated in the model, any result that shows working capital is scarce will hold even more conclusively for the many real situations in which only a part of farm expenditures can be financed by a single, uniformly priced, outside credit source.

Two further aspects of crop production, not mentioned in Table 5-1, are reflected in the linear programming vectors. The first is the interplanting of two or more crops in the same field, which is more common than single-crop planting in the Northeast, partly for agronomic reasons and partly to reduce risks.[3] The model treats such a "consortium" much like a single crop—that is, joint production of the individual crops concerned—and uses the production coefficients estimated for those crops as though they were being grown separately. (The model's treatment of cropping activities is described in Appendix C.)

Second, many crops grown in the Northeast have a life cycle longer than one year, the time coverage of the model. The method adopted for this study divides these crops into two categories: medium-cycle crops (three to seven years) for which decisions in a one-year, comparative static model are relevant; and long-cycle crops, some of which have lives of 100 years or more, for which decisions to expand or contract the stock of trees have no effect on production in a one-period model. For the medium-cycle crops, tree cotton, sugar, and bananas, the stream of inputs and outputs is discounted and averaged, and where consortiated planting is possible in the first one or two years, rotation constraints are added. Cotton *moco*, for example, is a five-year crop that is interplanted with corn and beans in its first year. The rotation constraint requires that for every hectare of moco grown in consortium, as represented in the farm model, there must be four other hectares wholly of moco being grown on that farm. In this manner the model for a single year represents a steady state while capturing, to some extent, the investment nature of the medium-cycle crops.

It is beyond the scope of a one-period model to capture investment decisions on long-cycle tree crops such as cacao, coconut, oranges, and the oil palms babacu and carnauba. For these, the production activities in the model represent harvesting from the existing stock of trees. Because the size of the harvest is constrained by the actual stocks of trees, the decision is simply to harvest them fully or not. The shadow prices on these stock constraints are of interest, however; they can indicate the net return, for the

---

3. The spacing requirements of first- or second-year tree cotton, for example, are such that annual food crops can be grown in between the young trees.

year of the solution, from increasing the stock and may be compared, if data become available, with the costs of establishing new plantations.

Additional constraints on production activities not shown in Table 5-1 are proxies for agronomic characteristics that are not explicitly captured in the model. Rice, for example, can be grown only near rivers, whereas cotton *herbaceo* requires humidity and low-lying land, and the amounts of land on which these two crops can be grown are constrained by the estimates from the survey.

Characteristics of Individual Farm Models

The characteristics that distinguish the farm models and augment the core matrix common to all of them are discussed below in turn.

Farm Family Consumption

Most farms in the Northeast, except the large commercial farms and those situated near market centers, produce food for their own consumption. Corn, beans, manioc, and rice are the main crops produced for this purpose, though the combination varies according to the zone. Within zones, the survey data show that the market value of the bundle consumed varies little among different types of farms. To model on-farm consumption, for those farm types in which it is applicable, estimates are made for the average farm in each zone of the amount and value of consumption of the three principal self-produced foods. The farm is assumed to change its consumption mix according to movements in the relative prices of the three crops. (If corn prices rise, for example, it will be more profitable to sell corn and to reserve more rice for family consumption, as a substitute.) Three alternative consumption bundles are then derived for the farm, each dominated by one of the three main food crops in that zone and each with the market value already estimated for consumption on that farm. The three crops are substituted for one another, across bundles, at rates equal to the observed price ratios.[4] The part of the farm model matrix relevant to family consumption is shown in Table 5-2. The crux of this treatment is that the farms that are observed to supply their own food are required to do so in the model solutions, but they may vary the composition of the consumption

4. For a fuller description of this method, see John H. Duloy and Roger D. Norton, "Prices and Incomes in Linear Programming Models," *American Journal of Agricultural Economics*, vol. 57 (November 1975), pp. 595–98.

Table 5-2. *Family Consumption Tableau*

Constraint block	Activity block			
	Crop production	Product sales	Consumption	
Objective function	− − − −	+ + +	+ + +	

Output balances	+
	  +
	+ +
	  +
	      +
		− 1
		·
		·
		·
		        − 1
			− − −
			
			− − −
			
			− − −
				= 0

Consumption constraint			1 1 1	= C

bundle according to the relative prices of its components. Family consumption activities are included in the models for all the farms in the West, all farms except estates in the Agreste and Sertao, and family farms in the East and Southeast.

Risk

Rainfall varies widely from year to year throughout most of the Northeast, the coastal areas excepted, rendering crop production quite risky. Inadequate or untimely rainfall may destroy certain crops but have little effect on others. Furthermore, different crops may respond in opposite ways to climatic variations: Little or late rainfall may ruin a bean crop but induce high yields of some varieties of cotton.

A wide body of literature recognizes that farmers are responsive to such variations and generally adopt farm plans that are less than optimally efficient in order to reduce the risk of failure. The present study uses techniques developed by Hazell for farm models and by Hazell and Scandizzo for sector models that capture the influence of risk in linear programming applications.[5] As Table 5-3 shows, these techniques involve the inclusion in the model of a time series of actual deviations from mean

5. P. B. R. Hazell, "Farm Planning under Uncertainty," *American Journal of Agricultural Economics*, vol. 53 (February 1971), pp. 53–62; and P. B. R. Hazell and P. L. Scandizzo, "Competitive Demand Structures under Risk in Linear Programming Models," *American Journal of Agricultural Economics*, vol. 56 (May 1974), pp. 235–44.

Table 5-3. *Risk Tableau*

Constraint block	Activity block			
	Total production	*Sum of negative deviations*	*Risk penalty*	
Objective function			$-f(\phi)$	

Revenue deviations	+ − + −
	− − −
	   +
	+ + +
	− − + +
		1 ⋱
		      ⋱ 1
				≥ 0

Sum of negative deviations		1 ⋯⋯⋯⋯⋯ 1	− 1	= 0

revenues per hectare, summing the negative deviations, and charging a risk penalty to the objective function. This penalty varies directly with the riskiness of the combination of enterprises selected and thus provides a measure of the tradeoff between the expected profitability of the farm plan and the risk associated with it. Because different types of farms in different regions presumably have different attitudes toward risk taking, the penalty is scaled by a factor phi (ϕ): The lower the phi, the greater the weight of expected profit in the objective function; and the higher the phi, the more risk-averse the simulated farm plan. Phi is also taken to be larger, the smaller the farm: Subsistence farmers in drought-prone areas need to ensure survival, whereas large farms are undoubtedly more willing and able to gamble for higher expected profits. In the present study, phi varies from zero, for large farms near the humid coastal areas, to a value of 2.5 in the interior drought-prone areas. Risk considerations apply in all the farm models, though in the models where phi is zero they have no effect.

Livestock

The importance of cattle production and the proportion of agricultural land used for native and cultivated pasture (about 75 percent) do not allow us to ignore this subsector. In some places, cattle production competes with crop production for resources, particularly medium-quality land and working capital. The treatment of livestock in the model is designed to capture this competition as simply as possible.[6] It ignores small animals, even in the few instances of specialization in small-animal production (scattered chicken and pork enterprises near towns), and deals only with work animals, beef, and dairy cattle.

Because the survey reveals that the great majority of cattle enterprises do not specialize in different aspects of production such as breeding, dairying, or beef production, the model does not include differences in herd composition, either among zones or among farms of different types. It thus refers to the maintenance of an "average" animal. Inputs, by contrast, vary substantially, both among zones and among farms of different types. Those other than labor may be classified and represented as follows:

—Items that are necessary no matter what the feeding technology, such as veterinary services, vaccinations, and mineral supplements (particularly salt). For this class of inputs, the total average annual cost per animal is simply charged to the objective function.
—Native pasture, which is the poor-quality land in the model, requires no labor for its maintenance and is the basis for the lowest level of feeding technology.
—Planted pasture is land of either high or medium quality cultivated for grass. The model derives labor coefficients for planted pasture as it does for crop production, but the "output" of pasture enters directly into the livestock-feeding activities, as described below.
—Purchased rations are available in many different types, the nutritional content of which is to a large extent reflected in their prices, and those at a given price are close substitutes for one another. In the model the various types are denoted by their prices, in cruzeiros.

Because the amounts of native pasture, planted pasture, and rations per animal vary widely with and across zones, we assume they can be substituted freely for one another. Cobb–Douglas production functions were used to construct three alternative livestock maintenance technologies for each zone. These alternatives, shown in schematic form in Table 5-4, are in turn intensive in planted pasture, natural pasture, and purchased rations, and each represents a point on the three-dimensional Cobb–Douglas unit isoquant. The row *FAT* serves as a convex combination constraint permitting combinations of the three technologies. The labor rows register the total labor requirements, by month, for the technology employed, includ-

6. For a more detailed livestock model, see Wilfred V. Candler, "A Demonstration Model for the Dairy Industry of La Laguna," in *The Book of* CHAC: *Programming Studies for Mexican Agriculture*, ed. R. D. Norton and L. Solis M. (Baltimore, Md.: Johns Hopkins University Press, forthcoming).

Table 5-4. *Livestock Tableau*

Constraint block	Activity block			BEEF	RAT	
	Livestock feeding alternatives					
Objective function				+	− 1	
Working capital	+	+	+		+ 1	
Planted pasture	+	+	+			
Natural pasture	+	+	+		− 1	= 0
Rations	+	+	+			
FAT	1	1	1	− 1		= 0
Labor	+ +	+	+ +			

ing the cultivation and maintenance of planted pasture, if used. The activity *BEEF* registers the total number of animals maintained. It has an objective function entry equal to the average annual revenue per animal derived from sales of meat and dairy products, net of the technology-invariant costs (veterinary services, vaccinations, and mineral supplements). *RAT* charges the costs of the rations to the objective function and the working capital constraint.

This somewhat simple structure permits the size of the livestock herd to be determined endogenously, gives some flexibility as to production technology, and captures the competition between livestock and crops for land, labor, and working capital. Livestock activities are included in the models for all farms in the West and for medium-size farms and estates in all other zones, except the cacao plantations in the Southeast.

Sharecropping

Sharecropping is an important form of agrarian contract in the Northeast; it is concentrated in the cotton-growing regions of the Sertao and to some extent in the rice-growing areas of the West. Debate continues in the literature over the efficiency of resource allocation, impediments to innovation, and myriad other issues surrounding share contracts. These issues

Table 5-5. Sharecropping Tableau

Constraint block	Activity block				
	Sharecropper production	Sharecropper product shares	Sharecropper family consumption	Number of sharecroppers	
Good land Medium land	$+\cdots+$ $+\cdots+$				
Plot size	$1\cdots\cdots\cdots 1$			$-p$	$= 0$
Sharecropper labor balances	$+$ $+$ $+$ $+$			$-b$ $\vdots$ $-b$	$\leqq 0$
Landowner product balances	$s+\cdots\cdots s+$				
Sharecropper product balances	$(1-s)+\cdots (1-s)+$	$-1\cdots -1$			$= 0$
Sharecropper consumption level			$1\cdots\cdots\cdots 1$	-1	$= 0$

Note: The parameters are: p = average plot size; b = average size family in terms of labor available; and s = share of product accruing to the landowner.

cannot be ignored in a rural development study. Their complexity, and the lack of previous linear programming studies addressing them, forced us to undertake a background study of the economics of sharecropping in the Northeast before this form of contract could be incorporated in a framework that represents the farm in its entirety.[7]

That study focused on a single typical sharecropped plot in the Sertao, in a partial equilibrium frame not concerned with other aspects of farm behavior. It examined the nature of the share contract and the way changes in the contract would influence incomes of landowner and sharecropper, gross outputs, and efficiency of resource use. One of its principal features was the recognition that landowners and sharecroppers have different, and presumably opposing, objectives that must be reconciled in the share contract. The landowner is presumably concerned only with his money income from the sharecropped plot, whereas the sharecropper is interested in his own money income, his family's consumption, and his leisure. The principal conclusions of the study were that the observed pattern of crop shares reflected agreement on the farm plan between landowner and share-cropper and was Pareto-optimal, and that this condition held only for a small range about the actual shares. Any change in favor of the sharecrop-per might encourage the landowner to choose other methods, such as cultivating the land himself with hired labor or using it as pasture. At a minimum, imposing a farm plan on a tenant would require enforcement costs; it might also induce the sharecropper to seek alternative employment.

The treatment of sharecropping in the present model has the following elements: The shares accruing to the landowner are those actually observed; the plot size, which is largely determined by the size of the sharecropper's family and its ability to supply labor, is fixed at the average observed size; and the farm plan adopted must allow the sharecropper to supply his family's food at the average on-farm consumption level of the zone in question.

Though these assumptions are somewhat restrictive, they permit a fa-zenda model in which the number of sharecroppers and their levels of income are determined endogenously. They also permit an explicit choice between sharecropping and cultivation by the landlord with hired labor, and a choice of production pattern, including that between crops and livestock. Table 5-5 illustrates the treatment of sharecropping. Although this is not made explicit in the tableau, sharecroppers compete with owner-

7. Gary P. Kutcher and Pasquale L. Scandizzo, "A Partial Analysis of Sharetenancy Relationships in Northeast Brazil," *Journal of Development Economics*, vol. 3 (December 1976), pp. 343–54.

administered production for both good and medium-quality land and compete with livestock production for medium-quality land. Sharecropping,
however, requires no drawings on the landowner's working capital, unlike
other production strategies. We also assume that risks are shared between
the landlord and the sharecroppers, so that an indirect form of cost sharing
(through the sharing of the landlord's risk penalty) is introduced. Sharecropping activities are permitted in the models for all medium farms and
estates in the West and the Sertao.

Linkages among the Farm Models

The system of computer programs that generates, solves, and reports
solutions can handle a single farm model, a collection of farm models such
as those representing a zone, or all the farm models in the region. The
choice of the level (farm, zone, or region) on which to base particular aspects
of the analysis depends on the linkages among the farm models or the extent
to which they compete for the same resources. The economic relations
among farms in the Northeast are in general quite limited, so that farms can
be treated as independent self-sustaining units.[8] Most of the agricultural
resources in the Northeast are endowed at the farm level, and for other
inputs there is little competition among farms: For modern inputs, demand
is very limited; and for labor, unemployment and underemployment are so
extensive in the Northeast that the supply available for wage employment
can be assumed to be perfectly elastic.

Labor Markets

The treatment of labor markets thus focuses on the demand for labor
generated by the production activities. As was described above, the farm
models reveal the demand in any given month for hired labor after family labor has been exhausted. Farms can choose to employ temporary
(monthly), permanent (annual), or, in certain zones, sharecropper labor
from the common pool available in the zone in question. This pool is
defined as the number of rural residents economically active in the sector,

---

8. Small-scale farmers do offer their excess labor to large farms, but given the extent of
unemployment this form of interaction is not relevant for the design of the present model. For
an analysis of small/large farm interactions, see Gervasio Castro de Rezende, "Plantation
Systems, Land Tenure, and Labor Supply: An Historical Analysis of the Brazilian Case with a
Contemporary Study of the Cacao Regions of Bahia, Brazil" (Ph.D. dissertation, University of
Wisconsin, Madison, 1976).

adjusted to man-equivalents, less the estimated number of owner-operators and their family man-equivalent dependents. Unless otherwise noted, these labor pools are never exhausted, and considerations such as interzonal migration are not relevant.[9]

Product Markets

In the base case, the main linkage among farm models is effected through the product markets for food crops. Product markets in the Northeast have many complications, only some of which can be adequately handled in this type of model. First, given the isolation of most producers and a tendency toward "safety first" behavior, much of what is marketed is a residual. A large proportion of the food crops is consumed by farmers and their families, sharecropper families, and other farm workers who may be paid in kind. Second, the market outlets are structurally and spatially diverse. Of the food crop production not consumed locally in the interior, part is distributed through middlemen to market centers in the Northeast and, for some crops at some times, other market centers in Brazil. Some products, particularly meat and dairy products, cotton, and sugar, are processed locally, whereas others such as babacu, carnauba, and cacao are exported to the Center-South for processing. Third, supplies and hence prices of perishable food crops fluctuate seasonally. Unpublished SUDENE data reveal that the market prices of beans and corn, for example, have varied by as much as a factor of three during some twelve-month periods.

Though the model distinguishes on-farm from marketed consumption and disaggregates the demand for food crops by zone, its structure and the lack of data, particularly on trade flows, do not permit a complete consideration of such complications. There are taken to be two distinct product markets in the Northeast: that for export crops, of which the bulk of the output is sent abroad or out of the Northeast to other parts of Brazil; and that for other crops, which are almost entirely consumed within the Northeast. Demand for livestock products is assumed to be infinitely elastic.

The main export crops depicted in the model are cacao, cotton, babacu, carnauba, cashews, castor beans, and sisal. For all except cotton, supply is subject to the capital stock constraints on long-cycle crops described earlier, and demand is assumed to be infinitely elastic. The supply of cotton is

---

9. A certain amount of seasonal interzonal migration of temporary agricultural workers is observed, particularly from the interior to the cacao and sugar areas during harvest months. The available evidence suggests, however, that excess labor nevertheless remains in all zones and probably in all months.

subject to two other constraints: at the farm level, on the availability of suitable land and the rotation constraints described earlier; and at the sectoral level, on the ginning capacity of the region.[10] Export demand for cotton products is assumed to be infinitely elastic, whereas domestic demand for cotton, as for food crops, depends on price.

The principal food crops, rice, corn, beans, and manioc, are short-cycle crops whose supply is subject to risk penalties but not, in general, to additional constraints. The exceptions are rice in the West, which requires low-lying, moist land, and instances where these food crops are grown in consortium with cotton and hence face rotation constraints. Sugar, coconuts, and oranges, though occasionally exported, are almost entirely consumed within the Northeast. Two of these, being tree crops, are subject to the stock constraints described above. Sugar production is constrained by processing capacity, but since there is a good deal of excess capacity at the production levels recorded by the survey and entered in the model, this constraint does not become binding. The prices of all these food crops, and of bananas, are endogenous to the model.

It is assumed that the marketing and transport infrastructure in the Northeast is so limited that the model need not take account of interzonal trade in crops that are not exported. For all the crops for which price is endogenous to the model, the markets in different zones are thus assumed to be completely separate from one another. This assumption may not be entirely valid but was dictated by the lack of data on interzonal transfers and marketing and transport capacities and costs. A test of the full model permitting interzonal trade at transport costs derived from unpublished SUDENE data revealed that this assumption is not critical. Only about 4 percent of all crop production was traded, and this was chiefly rice from the West.

The Treatment of Demand

The treatment of price-endogenous demand is based directly on that of Duloy and Norton, though modified where appropriate by the risk considerations of Hazell and Scandizzo.[11] Its main elements are illustrated in Figure 5-1, a purely static picture of a single crop equilibrium. Though the

---

10. In the absence of detailed information on ginning capacity, this constraint was not activated.

11. Duloy and Norton, "Prices and Incomes," pp. 591–600; and Hazell and Scandizzo, "Competitive Demand Structures under Risk," pp. 235–44.

Figure 5-1. Demand, Output, and Price Relations: Model Structure

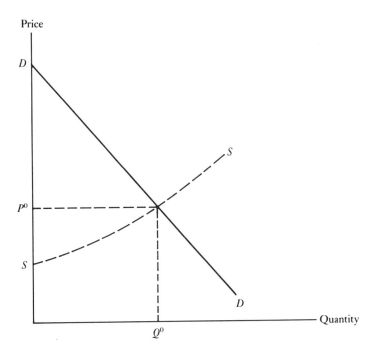

picture will vary with the different demand structures and supply constraints that characterize different crops, it is representative of the main Northeastern food crops. For each of these, an exogenous linear demand curve DD is specified, taking the quantity (Q^0) and price (P^0) from the survey data and estimating the price elasticity of demand so as to derive the slope.[12] The supply curve SS is endogenous and is determined by the costs of production (including opportunity costs). It slopes upward because at higher levels of output the resource costs are greater—for example, hired labor must be used, which is more expensive than family labor, and lower-quality land must be brought into production.[13] (For the special case

12. The estimation of the demand functions and price elasticities is described in Appendix C to this chapter.

13. This class of supply functions is analyzed for intercept, intersection, and elasticity in Gary P. Kutcher, "Agricultural Planning at the Regional Level: A Programming Study of Mexico's Pacific Northwest" (Ph.D. dissertation, University of Maryland, 1972).

of long-cycle crops, production of which is bounded from above by the level of stocks, the supply curve is of course vertical.)

The intersection of *DD* and *SS* is obtained by maximizing the sum of the area that is below the demand curve and above the supply curve. This maximization process may be used to measure consumers' and producers' surpluses, differentiated by the price line, or may be viewed simply as a device to ensure a competitive solution in which producers are assumed to equate marginal costs with prices for the commodity in question. The solution obtained in this way does not ensure the full use of resources; depending on the position of the demand curve, the equilibrium quantities produced could well result in idle land, labor, or other resources.

This treatment of demand is not without its limitations: The surpluses in the maximand can be interpreted in various ways, and agricultural price elasticities are notoriously difficult to estimate with confidence. Moreover, it needs to be assumed that markets clear instantaneously and that all farmers maximize profits, in the sense that they choose production patterns that equate market prices with the marginal costs of production. This last assumption in particular is open to question, since the cross-sectional analysis has strongly suggested that many farmers are not profit maximizers in this sense. The characteristics of these limitations will be investigated further in Chapter 6 to assess their importance for the conclusions to be drawn from the model. It can, however, be said at this juncture that the price-endogenous treatment appears to approximate quite closely the equilibrium conditions of Northeastern agriculture. The approach permits more realistic assumptions than do the obvious, simpler alternatives: Using a fixed-price objective function, one would need to assume that demand for *all* products is infinitely elastic; and a cost-minimization approach would eliminate the possibilities for expanding output, which is one of the key variables in experiments to increase employment and consumption.

Appendix A: Aggregation of Farm Types

Although the analysis in Chapter 4 gives a general idea of the diversity of farming systems in the Northeast, the distinctions it draws between different types of farms are insufficiently detailed to form the basis for a programming model of this highly diverse sector. This appendix describes the procedures used to classify farms into homogeneous groups, which are represented by the farm-level models described in Chapter 5. A combination of linear discriminant analysis and a multivariate sorting procedure is used to group the sample farms into mutually exclusive classes. The number and average size of farms in these classes are then estimated for each zone. The appendix concludes with a short note on linear discriminant functions.

The Approach Taken

Although necessary and sufficient conditions for the unbiased aggregation of programming models have recently been demonstrated by Paris and Rausser, Day's earlier homogeneity conditions maintain their appeal because of their simplicity and ease of application.[14] These conditions are: that the matrix of input–output coefficients be the same for all the farms to be aggregated (technological homogeneity); that the coefficients of the objective function of each farm differ from each other by the same factor of proportionality (pecuniary proportionality); and that the vector of binding constraints for each farm be proportional to the vector for the aggregate of farms (institutional proportionality).

As several studies have suggested, the most restrictive and yet the simplest way of interpreting Day's conditions is as a quest for homogeneity among the farms to be aggregated.[15] If we assume that the farm population can be divided into groups made up of members identical with each other except for a random component, not only will the aggregation conditions be respected "on average" but also the aggregates can be interpreted as average farms or representative farm types.

We also assume that Day's first condition is met; that is, that all farms face the same production possibility set. As noted in Chapter 4, production function analysis revealed no difference in the elasticities of substitution between capital and labor for farms of different types over all zones, and, as Chapter 2 reported, capital/output ratios are similar on farms of all sizes. This evidence is supported by the fact that yields of the major crops do not differ with farm size (Chapter 3). Given that land quality also appears to be homogeneous across farm size (Chapter 2), it appears that the input–output

---

14. Quirino Paris and G. C. Rausser, "Sufficient Conditions for Aggregation of Linear Programming Models," *American Journal of Agricultural Economics* (November 1973), pp. 659–66; and Richard H. Day, "On Aggregating Linear Programming Models of Production," *Journal of Farm Economics*, vol. 45 (November 1963), pp. 797–813.

15. See, for example, T. A. Miller, "Sufficient Conditions for Exact Aggregation in Linear Programming Models," *Agricultural Economics Research*, vol. 18 (1966), pp. 52–57; and A. E. Buckwell and P. B. R. Hazell, "Implications for Aggregation Bias for the Construction of Static and Dynamic Linear Programming Supply Models," *Journal of Agricultural Economics*, vol. 23, no. 2 (1972), pp. 119–34.

coefficients for land and capital do not vary for farms of different sizes and types.

In Chapter 4, following Nakajima, we drew a distinction between family and nonfamily farms according to the percentage of the labor used on the farm that is supplied by the farm family and the percentage of the farm's output that is marketed.[16] To obtain a more detailed and useful typology that satisfies Day's second and third conditions, the two Nakajima variables are now considered in conjunction with other aspects of farm organization and behavior: the degree of decentralization of farm management, which will be used to measure pecuniary proportionality; land value; and patterns of resource use, which will indicate institutional proportionality. The procedure has the following stages:

1. Construct an initial classification of groups of homogeneous farms, determine the number of groups, and tentatively assign to them the observations of farms with extreme characteristics.
2. Compute a set of discriminant functions and critical values to predict the membership of the groups.
3. If necessary, reclassify those observations with extreme characteristics in accordance with the criteria given by (2);
4. Classify the residual farms with intermediate characteristics, according to the criteria given by (2).

An Initial Farm Typology

The organizational characteristics of large farms are fundamental to their objectives. In the Northeast the plantation is typical of the sugar zone, where crop specialization and the traditions remaining from slavery require the landlord to be heavily involved in the administration, with a pyramidal structure to control hired labor. Fazendas, which are found mainly in the livestock areas of the Southeast and in the Sertao, are more diverse and often highly decentralized through permanent laborers (moradores) and sharecroppers. Although the centralized plantation is market-oriented and can be assumed to maximize its profits without regard to subsistence consumption, production on the decentralized fazenda, with its elements of both family farming and capitalistic enterprise, is likely to reflect a much more complex mixture of commercial and subsistence objectives.

---

16. Chihiro Nakajima, "Subsistence and Commercial Farms: Some Theoretical Models of Subjective Equilibrium," in *Subsistence Agriculture and Economic Development*, ed. C. R. Wharton, Jr. (Chicago: Aldine, 1970).

The presence of resident sharecroppers, as reported in the SUDENE/World Bank survey, is taken to indicate that a large farm shares some of the organizational and behavioral characteristics of small farms. An initial classification of farms can now be built up to take account of the proportion of family labor, the proportion of output marketed, and the type of institution regulating the relations among ownership, entrepreneurship, and labor.

Traditional farms
—Family farms: all farms where the family supplies more than 50 percent of the labor used
—Fazendas with sharecroppers: farms of at least 100 hectares, marketing less than 40 percent of their output
—Fazendas without sharecroppers
—Plantations: farms marketing more than 60 percent of their output, relying mainly on permanent, nonsharecropping workers (moradores) and with more than 40 percent of their land in nonintensive use

Transitional farms: farms with intermediate characteristics (40–70 percent of output marketed; 30–70 percent of labor supplied by the family), without openly declared sharecropping arrangements, mostly in the Sertao, the Semihumid Southeast, and the Agreste

Modern Farms
—Nonfamily farms: capitalistic enterprises based on wage labor, marketing 70 percent or more of output
—Family farms: farms marketing 70 percent or more of output, supplying over 70 percent of their own labor.

These tentative categories are established on the basis of the mean values, for each size class and zone, of the variables considered. Farms are assigned to categories according to their individual values of these variables.

Patterns of Resource Use

This initial classification leaves a sizable number of farms that fit none of its categories. To classify this residual group and to test whether the classification criteria are reasonable, new variables are now introduced: the proportion of farmland under crops; labor use (in man-years) per hectare; and the values per hectare of land, livestock, and farm structures and equipment.

Patterns of resource use are much more difficult to capture in any ad hoc classification than are market orientation or organizational structure. As Buckwell and Hazell show, however, Day's requirement of institutional

Table 5-6. *Man-years of Labor per Hectare, by Farm Size and Zone*

Zone	Farm size (hectares)						Zone average
	0–9.9	10–49.9	50–99.9	100–199.9	200–499.9	500+	
West	0.45	0.08	0.03	0.02	0.01	0.01	0.14
Middle-North	0.23	0.08	0.03	0.01	0.01	0.01	0.06
Sertao	0.23	0.08	0.04	0.02	0.02	0.01	0.11
Semihumid Southeast	0.23	0.08	0.04	0.02	0.01	0.01	0.09
Humid East	0.44	0.09	0.05	0.03	0.04	0.01	0.25
Humid Southeast	0.25	0.16	0.09	0.10	0.07	0.10	0.16
Agreste	0.51	0.10	0.05	0.04	0.03	0.02	0.33

proportionality can be expressed geometrically as the requirement that all farms in the same group lie along a ray through the origin in the resource space.[17] Table 5-6, which gives average ratios of land application to land, clearly shows some scope for aggregation based on institutional proportionality: Most average farms of the same size class appear to lie on the same ray through the origin.

When the analysis is extended to resources other than land and labor, and also to observations within the size classes of farms, visual inspection is no longer possible, and a multivariate technique becomes necessary. In a way similar to that suggested by Buckwell and Hazell, we use a clustering algorithm based on a combination of discriminant analysis and centroid sorting. In the following stages of the analysis, observations are shifted from one group to another so as to maximize a relative measure of similarity within the groups: λ = variation between groups/variation within groups. This measure, known as Wilks's lambda, is a multivariate statistic that summarizes the proximity of the individual observations in a group to the mean for the group for any number of classificatory variables. At each stage of the sorting process a value of λ is thus computed, which together with a set of linear equations (discriminant functions) permits the assignment of the observations that could not previously be classified and indicates the group to which each observation is most likely to belong. The value of λ is then varied by allowing observations to change groups in accordance with their predicted membership. After this, a new set of discriminant functions is computed to yield a new set of assignments to groups. The predicted membership is again compared with actual membership and, if λ appears to increase, a new shift of observations is allowed. The relocation of observations is stopped when the value of λ does not increase further. At this point, the coincidence of the actual membership of groups with their predicted membership will be near its maximum.

Results of the Classification Procedure

This procedure yields a complete classification of the sample farms. (It also shows that despite some variation among the zones 80 percent or more of the sample farms with extreme characteristics had been classified correctly on the basis of the degree of market orientation and organizational structure.) The majority of the farms with intermediate characteristics are categorized as plantations and transitional farms. Table 5-7 presents the

17. Buckwell and Hazell, "Implications," pp. 124–27.

Table 5-7. *Northeast Farm Characteristics, by Farm Type*
(sample means)

	Traditional					Modern	
Characteristic	*Family farm*	*Fazenda with share-croppers*	*Fazenda without share-croppers*	*Plan-tation*	*Transi-tional*	*Non-family farm*	*Family farm*
Farm size (hectares)	107.26	742.06	441.135	550.48	200.27	212.02	106.73
Farm value (cruzeiros)	5,031.60	28,978.55	26,610.19	51,853.01	9,990.79	43,721.04	17,507.21
Total labor[a]	0.01	0.01	0.01	0.02	0.06	0.08	0.11
Value of structures[b]	77.30	25.22	19.01	42.07	59.61	94.08	81.85
Value of livestock[b]	44.70	17.01	17.37	37.99	46.43	36.40	47.28
Value of equipment[b]	1.77	1.79	2.57	2.53	3.97	10.89	2.08
Percentage of output marketed	14.22	20.42	8.95	83.47	63.38	91.50	84.67
Family labor/total labor	89.15	13.41	10.28	27.14	55.04	10.20	91.12
Cropland/total land	16.92	20.24	5.82	6.69	21.59	50.41	23.82

a. Man-years per hectare.
b. Cruzeiros per hectare.
Source: SUDENE/World Bank survey.

mean values of key variables for the different farm types for the Northeast as a whole.

These mean values highlight the differences among the farm types. Family farms, whether traditional or modern, appear to have some similar physical and economic traits, with similar average sizes and similar values of equipment, livestock, and structures per hectare. Modern family farms, however, apply ten times as much labor per hectare as traditional family farms, have a higher proportion of their land under crops, market a far larger share of production, and have higher farm values. The average characteristics of fazendas appear to differ little whether or not they have sharecroppers, except in the proportion of land under crops and the percentage of output marketed. It is possible that a significant number of landlords did not declare their sharecropping arrangements when interviewed for the survey. Plantations differ sharply from other large estates. They market the bulk of their output, they have only a small proportion of their land under crops and relatively high values of livestock and of structures per hectare, and at least a fourth of the labor they use is supplied by the family. Transitional and modern farms are relatively small and labor-intensive, with one-fifth to one-half their land under crops, and generally have higher values of structures and equipment than traditional farms.

Tables 5-8 to 5-14 show the characteristics of the various farm types zone by zone and the number of observations of each type in the sample. They show that family farms and the two types of estates, fazendas and plantations, have the most distinct characteristics and that the prevalent type of estate varies according to the region. They also show that for farms of the same type there are very few large differences between the West and the Middle-North.

The Farm Typology for the Programming Model

For the final classification of farms used in the programming model, only three farm types and five zones are thus distinguished. The three farm types are: *family farms*, both traditional and modern; *estates*, combining, according to the zone, fazendas with and without sharecroppers, plantations and family estates; and *medium-size farms*, a residual group, dominated in the coastal regions by modern farms and in the interior by transitional farms. The seven zones used for the cross-sectional analysis are reduced to five by subsuming the Middle-North into the West and combining zones D and F into one zone, the Southeast.

Table 5-15 gives estimates for the Northeast of the number and average size of the groups of farms for the five zones used in the model. As the notes

Table 5-8. *West: Farm Characteristics, by Farm Type*
(sample weighted means; standard errors in parentheses)

Characteristic	Traditional					Modern		Total
	Family farm	Fazenda with share-croppers	Fazenda without share-croppers	Family estate	Transitional	Non-family farm	Family farm	
Total labor[a]	0.088	0.006	0.006	0.005	0.069	0.061	0.129	0.063
	(0.022)	(0.002)	(0.001)	(0.002)	(0.014)	(0.018)	(0.034)	(0.008)
Value of structures[b]	0.276	0.838	0.656	0.112	2.994	13.546	0.905	1.886
	(0.055)	(0.834)	(0.464)	(0.052)	(2.047)	(7.854)	(0.366)	(0.844)
Value of livestock[b]	48.016	29.761	11.574	28.918	76.067	40.146	146.139	58.769
	(14.364)	(16.852)	(3.452)	(15.881)	(25.746)	(25.967)	(57.756)	(11.817)
Value of equipment[b]	35.990	13.170	6.592	8.716	38.431	27.993	87.190	33.916
	(6.892)	(6.720)	(1.468)	(2.507)	(6.511)	(10.640)	(25.434)	(3.846)
Percentage of output marketed	13.234	5.488	6.589	79.829	61.767	91.994	86.082	41.390
	(1.243)	(3.439)	(1.177)	(3.759)	(1.052)	(2.008)	(1.356)	(1.434)
Family labor/total labor	0.880	0.120	0.087	0.253	0.561	0.103	0.901	0.544
	(0.014)	(0.056)	(0.014)	(0.067)	(0.022)	(0.023)	(0.017)	(0.017)
Cropland/total land	0.085	0.069	0.029	0.029	0.129	0.488	0.171	0.109
	(0.014)	(0.057)	(0.009)	(0.008)	(0.013)	(0.076)	(0.035)	(0.008)
Number of cases	134	8	107	17	209	17	45	537

a. Man-years per hectare.
b. Cruzeiros per hectare.

Table 5-9. *Middle-North: Farm Characteristics, by Farm Type*
(sample weighted means; standard errors in parentheses)

	Traditional					Modern		
Characteristic	Family farm	Fazenda with share-croppers	Fazenda without share-croppers	Family estate	Transi-tional	Non-family farm	Family farm	Total
Total labor[a]	0.076	0.004	0.007	0.012	0.038	0.061	0.027	0.035
	(0.018)	(0.001)	(0.001)	(0.003)	(0.008)	(0.015)	(0.008)	(0.004)
Value of structures[b]	0.542	0.326	0.720	0.815	3.280	7.548	0.576	2.027
	(0.214)	(0.205)	(0.213)	(0.455)	(1.236)	(2.685)	(0.344)	(0.493)
Value of livestock[b]	29.085	5.018	7.824	21.852	26.668	23.017	20.391	21.270
	(7.261)	(1.519)	(1.331)	(4.534)	(5.709)	(7.186)	(7.296)	(2.574)
Value of equipment[b]	38.735	5.957	6.906	12.790	21.711	52.352	33.207	22.754
	(9.010)	(1.175)	(1.057)	(2.905)	(3.893)	(23.885)	(12.676)	(2.744)
Percentage of output marketed	15.572	17.003	8.848	80.159	61.919	87.573	86.010	46.911
	(1.347)	(2.404)	(1.247)	(1.704)	(1.042)	(1.620)	(1.767)	(1.334)
Family labor/total labor	0.857	0.120	0.098	0.358	0.481	0.132	0.932	0.450
	(0.016)	(0.020)	(0.014)	(0.043)	(0.020)	(0.014)	(0.015)	(0.015)
Cropland/total land	0.177	0.218	0.048	0.045	0.156	0.578	0.143	0.157
	(0.025)	(0.042)	(0.010)	(0.006)	(0.016)	(0.045)	(0.033)	(0.010)
Number of cases	100	34	110	58	220	37	41	600

a. Man-years per hectare.
b. Cruzeiros per hectare.

Table 5-10. *Sertao: Farm Characteristics, by Farm Type*
(sample weighted means; standard errors in parentheses)

	Traditional					Modern		
Characteristic	Family farm	Fazenda with share-croppers	Fazenda without share-croppers	Family estate	Transi-tional	Non-family farm	Family farm	Total
Total labor[a]	0.078	0.014	0.014	0.013	0.054	0.055	0.080	0.057
	(0.007)	(0.002)	(0.001)	(0.001)	(0.003)	(0.006)	(0.009)	(0.002)
Value of structures[b]	1.409	1.997	1.449	1.857	3.230	8.832	2.403	2.996
	(0.290)	(0.527)	(0.528)	(0.515)	(0.468)	(3.326)	(0.922)	(0.360)
Value of livestock[b]	40.230	21.238	21.685	26.408	36.589	40.077	35.496	35.672
	(4.387)	(2.821)	(2.966)	(3.634)	(1.928)	(5.737)	(4.444)	(1.458)
Value of equipment[b]	53.362	35.971	21.333	21.965	49.285	61.335	44.656	47.351
	(4.832)	(5.718)	(2.548)	(2.930)	(4.169)	(10.769)	(3.600)	(2.416)
Percentage of output marketed	15.905	24.905	11.881	79.868	61.903	87.660	83.115	54.321
	(0.786)	(1.521)	(1.538)	(1.444)	(0.507)	(0.801)	(0.615)	(0.696)
Family labor/total labor	0.900	0.147	0.126	0.308	0.558	0.119	0.909	0.588
	(0.008)	(0.019)	(0.016)	(0.040)	(0.011)	(0.008)	(0.007)	(0.008)
Cropland/total land	0.180	0.216	0.073	0.071	0.241	0.442	0.256	0.230
	(0.008)	(0.019)	(0.016)	(0.040)	(0.011)	(0.008)	(0.007)	(0.008)
Number of cases	326	59	95	62	826	125	218	1,711

a. Man-years per hectare.
b. Cruzeiros per hectare.

Table 5-11. *Semihumid Southeast: Farm Characteristics, by Farm Type*
(sample weighted means; standard errors in parentheses)

Characteristic	Traditional					Modern		Total
	Family farm	Fazenda with share-croppers	Fazenda without share-croppers	Planta-tion	Transi-tional	Non-family farm	Family farm	
Total labor[a]	0.075	0.004	0.008	0.013	0.047	0.084	0.055	0.052
	(0.021)	(0.003)	(0.001)	(0.003)	(0.006)	(0.012)	(0.014)	(0.006)
Value of structures[b]	6.981	0.137	0.438	0.771	1.542	5.921	0.665	2.924
	(6.447)	(0.135)	(0.288)	(0.380)	(0.681)	(2.184)	(0.245)	(1.649)
Value of livestock[b]	49.234	15.010	36.166	70.690	45.708	48.133	45.013	47.197
	(11.116)	(4.678)	(12.957)	(16.737)	(6.638)	(16.480)	(9.944)	(4.445)
Value of equipment[b]	141.558	66.202	27.151	47.095	65.173	107.980	76.650	84.971
	(57.220)	(45.993)	(4.716)	(9.984)	(9.130)	(15.346)	(18.758)	(15.263)
Percentage of output marketed	8.620	29.700	6.214	88.044	69.324	95.906	88.383	54.486
	(1.533)	(2.600)	(2.488)	(2.380)	(2.076)	(1.803)	(1.323)	(2.439)
Family labor/total labor	0.905	0.141	0.138	0.254	0.626	0.101	0.893	0.630
	(0.020)	(0.045)	(0.031)	(0.076)	(0.030)	(0.020)	(0.016)	(0.023)
Cropland/total land	0.081	0.151	0.010	0.039	0.141	0.403	0.135	0.125
	(0.012)	(0.129)	(0.004)	(0.010)	(0.017)	(0.032)	(0.022)	(0.010)
Number of cases	60	2	22	16	78	18	42	238

a. Man-years per hectare.
b. Cruzeiros per hectare.

Table 5-12. *Humid East: Farm Characteristics, by Farm Type*
(sample weighted means; standard errors in parentheses)

	Traditional					Modern		
Characteristic	Family farm	Fazenda with share-croppers	Fazenda without share-croppers	Planta-tion	Transi-tional	Non-family farm	Family farm	Total
Total labor[a]	0.186	—	0.037	0.025	0.134	0.081	0.108	0.108
	(0.037)		(0.014)	(0.003)	(0.028)	(0.012)	(0.003)	(0.012)
Value of structures[b]	1.883	—	3.638	2.627	14.698	16.602	1.086	9.569
	(1.268)		(1.769)	(0.843)	(5.960)	(5.908)	(0.419)	(2.439)
Value of livestock[b]	76.023	—	24.227	44.052	54.100	37.491	26.714	46.036
	(29.302)		(9.394)	(9.582)	(17.882)	(6.961)	(8.785)	(7.368)
Value of equipment[b]	323.706	—	35.918	47.668	185.651	111.691	69.949	144.832
	(135.333)		(11.517)	(12.608)	(54.393)	(35.759)	(20.160)	(26.370)
Percentage of output marketed	13.803	—	11.879	88.300	68.324	93.479	87.721	69.734
	(2.404)		(4.138)	(2.131)	(2.148)	(1.070)	(1.569)	(1.909)
Family labor/total labor	0.909	—	0.021	0.192	0.422	0.106	0.928	0.444
	(0.025)		(0.009)	(0.053)	(0.032)	(0.012)	(0.015)	(0.024)
Cropland/total land	0.299	—	0.204	0.112	0.323	0.503	0.249	0.321
	(0.054)		(0.074)	(0.009)	(0.029)	(0.030)	(0.041)	(0.017)
Number of cases	33	0	14	29	91	62	43	272

— Not applicable.
a. Man-years per hectare.
b. Cruzeiros per hectare.

Table 5-13. *Humid Southeast: Farm Characteristics, by Farm Type*
(sample weighted means; standard errors in parentheses)

	Traditional				Modern			
Characteristic	*Family farm*	*Fazenda with share-croppers*	*Fazenda without share-croppers*	*Planta-tion*	*Transi-tional*	*Non-family farm*	*Family farm*	*Total*
Total labor[a]	—	—	—	—	0.103	0.116	0.134	0.117
					(0.069)	(0.011)	(0.035)	(0.010)
Value of structures[b]	—	—	—	—	2.451	3.886	0.112	3.496
					(2.424)	(1.089)	(0.067)	(0.962)
Value of livestock[b]	—	—	—	—	11.272	8.982	4.881	8.725
					(5.354)	(1.940)	(4.079)	(1.731)
Value of equipment[b]	—	—	—	—	270.332	234.135	90.303	223.202
					(203.011)	(27.105)	(26.258)	(25.223)
Percentage of output marketed	—	—	—	—	100.000	99.325	99.775	99.393
					(0)	(0.204)	(0.225)	(0.180)
Family labor/total labor	—	—	—	—	0.541	0.031	0.969	0.134
					(0.155)	(0.008)	(0.019)	(0.042)
Cropland/total land	—	—	—	—	0.772	0.722	0.651	0.718
					(0.028)	(0.017)	(0.094)	(0.017)
Number of cases	0	0	0	0	2	40	4	46

— Not applicable.
a. Man-years per hectare.
b. Cruzeiros per hectare.

Table 5-14. *Agreste: Farm Characteristics, by Farm Type*
(sample weighted means; standard errors in parentheses)

Characteristic	Traditional					Modern		Total
	Family farm	Fazenda with share-croppers	Fazenda without share-croppers	Planta-tion	Transi-tional	Non-family farm	Family farm	
Total labor[a]	0.226	0.020	0.028	0.034	0.102	0.117	0.241	0.140
	(0.052)	(0.005)	(0.008)	(0.004)	(0.011)	(0.021)	(0.051)	(0.014)
Value of structures[b]	2.672	9.902	18.711	5.924	4.769	15.598	3.730	6.322
	(0.693)	(8.911)	(9.892)	(1.346)	(0.958)	(2.841)	(1.036)	(0.775)
Value of livestock[b]	53.664	27.114	39.425	92.420	71.264	49.605	51.350	61.865
	(6.650)	(14.621)	(7.004)	(11.097)	(8.538)	(6.290)	(8.287)	(3.882)
Value of equipment[b]	114.002	31.106	78.545	95.669	98.600	91.623	196.627	113.313
	(23.197)	(16.853)	(26.709)	(16.335)	(11.884)	(9.145)	(41.737)	(9.365)
Percentage of output marketed	12.809	12.533	9.062	87.808	67.226	92.865	83.302	58.827
	(1.136)	(6.343)	(2.392)	(1.504)	(1.186)	(0.869)	(1.002)	(1.341)
Family labor/total labor	0.898	0.104	0.115	0.199	0.606	0.095	0.909	0.585
	(0.013)	(0.042)	(0.024)	(0.031)	(0.019)	(0.008)	(0.010)	(0.015)
Cropland/total land	0.225	0.182	0.088	0.081	0.240	0.485	0.296	0.250
	(0.023)	(0.057)	(0.031)	(0.007)	(0.018)	(0.026)	(0.032)	(0.011)
Number of cases	142	6	34	61	230	75	92	640

a. Man-years per hectare.
b. Cruzeiros per hectare.

to the table show, the organization and product specialization of estates vary according to the zone. The estimates of the number of farms of each type are obtained by extrapolating the sample results to the population, taking account of the farm size distribution: The estimated percentage of farms of each type in each size class is multiplied by the estimated number of farms in that size class (shown in Table 2-5). Farm sizes are derived in the same way, so that the areas quoted are averages weighted by the number of farms in each size class. Last, to maintain a close correspondence between farm size and the classification, a small number of farms exhibiting the characteristics of family farms, but larger than 200 hectares, were shifted into the category of medium-size farms.

A Note on Linear Discriminant Functions

To illustrate the use of linear discriminant functions,[18] we consider for simplicity the classification of a sample of two variables (say, X_1 and X_2) into two groups. The procedure used in discriminant analysis is to search for a linear combination of the two variables such that the distributions of the two groups display the least overlapping. The linear discriminant function can be indicated as:

$$(5.1) \qquad Y_{it} = \beta_1 X_{i1t} + \beta_2 X_{i2t}, \quad i = 1, 2$$
$$t = 1, 2, \ldots, n_i$$

where i denotes the group and t the number of observations within each group. Unlike the case in regression analysis, the variable Y_i is endogenous, resulting from the linear combination of the observed variables X_{i1} and X_{i2t}.

The discriminant function in equation (5.1) can be generalized to the case of j variables:

$$(5.2) \quad Y_{it} = \beta_1 X_{i1t} + \beta_2 X_{i2t} + \ldots + \beta_0 X_{ijt} + \ldots \quad i = 1, 2$$
$$t = 1, 2, \ldots, n_i$$

where X_{ijt} denotes the value of the jth variable for the tth observation in the ith group.

The problem of discriminant analysis is to obtain an optimum discriminant plane—or hyperplane in the case of equation (5.2)—according to some prespecified criterion. A popular method consists of maximizing the ratio:

$$(5.3) \qquad \lambda = \frac{\text{variation within groups}}{\text{variation between groups}}.$$

18. For a more detailed treatment, see B. W. Bolch and C. J. Huang, *Multivariate Statistical Methods for Business and Economics* (Englewood Cliffs, N.J.: Prentice-Hall International, 1974).

Table 5-15. *Northeast: Estimate of Number and Size of Farms, by Type*

Zone	Family farms	Medium farms		Estates
West (zones A, B)				
Number	37,001	113,551		14,569[a]
Average size (hectares)	18.43	108.72		794.57
Sertao (zone C)				
Number	62,599	252,912		11,221[b]
Average size (hectares)	16.92	81.21		676.43
East (zone E)				
Number	11,964	17,623		1,314[c]
Average size (hectares)	9.42	60.06		1,086.50
Southeast (zones D, F)				
Number	26,824	76,574	4,766[d]	5,208[e]
Average size (hectares)	26.82	47.72	763.47	441.27
Agreste (zone G)				
Number	69,580	68,545		5,168[f]
Average size (hectares)	8.97	60.06		634.56

a. Mainly livestock fazendas.
b. Mainly fazendas with sharecroppers.
c. Mainly sugar plantations.
d. Mainly livestock fazendas.
e. Mainly cacao plantations.
f. Mainly diversified fazendas.

For the case of two groups and two variables, the above ratio is given by

$$(5.4) \qquad \lambda = \frac{1}{n_1 + n_2 - 2} \frac{\beta'(\overline{X}_1 - \overline{X}_2)(\overline{X}_1 - \overline{X}_2)'\beta}{\beta'S_*\beta},$$

where β is the vector of coefficients to be estimated; $\overline{X}_i$ = vector of average sample values for the ith group; and S_* = variance–covariance matrix for the sample data.

The maximization in equation (5.4) requires a normalization rule, generally given by

$$(5.5) \qquad c = \beta'(\overline{X}_1 - \overline{X}_2)/D^2 = 1,$$

where D^2, known as Mahalanobis's D^2 or generalized distance, is equal to $(\overline{X}_1 - \overline{X}_2)'S_*^{-1}(\overline{X}_1 - \overline{X}_2)$.

Under the constraint (5.5), the first-order conditions for the maximization of λ yield the result:

$$(5.6) \qquad \hat{\beta} = S_*^{-1} (\overline{X}_1 - \overline{X}_2).$$

Once the discriminant function parameters are estimated from equation (5.6), it is necessary to determine a critical value in order to classify new observations (or to determine how well the old ones have been classified) into groups 1 and 2.

If the costs of misclassification are equal for the two groups, and there is an equal probability that an observation is drawn from either of them, the critical value of Y^* is given by

$$(5.7) \qquad Y^* = \frac{1}{2} \beta(\overline{X}_1 - \overline{X}_2).$$

The discrimination rules can then be expressed as follows: Given a new observation Y_{jt}, not included in the sample, classify it into group 1 if $Y_{jt} \geq Y^*$; classify it into group 2 if $Y_{jt} < Y^*$. Given an observation Y_{it} of the sample used to construct the classification, consider it well classified if $Y_{it} \geq Y^*$ and Y_{it} in group 1 or $Y_{it} < Y^*$ and Y_{it} in group 2; consider it misclassified otherwise.

Appendix B: Algebraic Statement of the Programming Model

Indexes

z Physiographic zone

    (A = West
    C = Sertao
    D = Southeast
    E = East
    G = Agreste)

s Farm type

    (1 = family farm
    2 = medium-size farm
    3 = livestock fazenda if $z = A$
    3 = sharecropped fazenda if $z = C$
    3 = diversified fazenda if $z = D$ or G
    3 = sugar plantation if $z = E$
    4 = cacao plantation if $z = D$ only)

i Commodities

    (04 = cotton moco
    05 = cotton herbaceo

    06 = cotton verdao
    11 = rice
    13 = bananas
    14 = sweet potatoes
    16 = babacu
    19 = cacao
    21 = cashews
    22 = sugarcane
    25 = carnauba
    30 = coconuts
    34 = beans de arranca
    35 = beans de corda
    43 = oranges
    48 = manioc
    51 = corn
    54 = castor beans
    69 = sisal)

m Month ($1 =$ January, . . . , $12 =$ December)

k Production activity ($= 01, 02, \ldots , 80$)

t Year ($= 60, 61, \ldots , 70$)

ℓ Demand segment (quantity axis) ($= 01, 02, \ldots , 20$)

q Land quality

    (G = good cropland
    M = medium cropland or cultivated pasture
    P = poor cropland or native pasture)

j Livestock feeding alternative

    (1 = cultivated pasture-intensive
    2 = native pasture-intensive
    3 = rations pasture-intensive)

n Family consumption alternative, explained in Chapter 5 ($= 1, 2, 3$)

Activities (variables)

$D_{zi\ell}$ Demand for commodity i, segment ℓ of demand function in zone z (measurement units, SU in thousands, typically metric tons)

Z_{yzs} Negative deviation counter for risk penalty, year y, farm type s (in thousands of cruzeiros)

CP_{kzsq} Proprietor-managed cropping activity k, on land quality q (in thousands of hectares)

CS_{kzsq} Sharecropped cropping activity (in thousands of hectares)

P_{izs} Marketed production of proprietors' crop output (in thousands of SU)

S_{izs} Marketed production of sharecroppers' crop output (in thousands of SU)

TP_{zsm} Total labor use, month m (in thousands of man-months)

LF_{zsm} Family labor use (in thousands of man-months)

LT_{zsm} Temporary labor hire (in thousands of man-months)

LP_{zs} Permanent labor hire (in thousands of man-years)

NS_{zs} Number of sharecropping plots (in thousands of plots)

EP_{zsm} Proprietor consumption, bundle m (in thousands of bundles)

ES_{zsm} Sharecropper consumption (in thousands of bundles)

LSF_{zsj} Livestock feeding alternative j (in thousands of bundles)

$BEEF_{zs}$ Number of cattle maintained (in thousands of cattle)

RAT_{zs} Rations demanded (in thousands of cruzeiros)

VET_{zs} Veterinary services demanded (in thousands of cruzeiros)

TGM_{zs} Good-quality land used as medium-quality land (in thousands of hectares)

TMP_{zs} Medium-quality used as poor-quality land (in thousands of hectares)

Parameters/data

$d_{zi\ell}$ Area under demand function in segment ℓ

p_{zs} Risk penalty

c_{zk} Cost of purchased inputs for cropping activities

r_{iz} Price of export crop i

v_z Value of average consumption bundle

e_z Value of average annual livestock product sales

c^v Average annual cost of veterinary services per animal

w^F Family reservation wage rate per month

w^T_z Temporary labor wage rate per month

w^P_z Permanent labor wage rate per year

y^i_{kzq} Yield (kilograms per hectare) of ith product from kth activity

α_i Share of product i accruing to proprietor from sharecropping activities

u Marketing margin retained by proprietor from sharecroppers' product sales

f_{izn} Quantity of ith product in consumption alternative n

g_k Land requirements per unit level of cropping activity ($= 1$, except for long-cycle crops [$= 0$], and manioc [$= 1.5$, as average cycle is one and a half years])

w_{zkm}^c Labor requirements (man-days per hectare), cropping activity k, zone z, month m

w_{yjm}^L Labor requirements, livestock feeding activity j (includes maintenance of cultivated and native pasture and herd supervision)

x_{1j} Medium-quality land requirements, livestock feeding technology j

x_{2j} Poor-quality land requirements, livestock feeding technology j

θ_z Sharecropping plot size (hectares per family)

$a_{zi\ell}$ Quantity sold, product i, segment ℓ.

Objective function (OBJ)

$$\sum_z \sum_i \sum_\ell d_{zi\ell} D_{zi\ell} \qquad + \sum_z \sum_i \sum_s r_{iz} P_{izs} \qquad + \sum_s \sum_n v_z EP_{szn}$$

[area under demand   + [revenue from   + [value of on-farm
 functions]   export crops]   consumption]

$$+ \sum_z \sum_s e_z BEEF_{zs} \qquad\qquad - \sum_z \sum_t \sum_s p_{zs} Z_{tzs}$$

+ [revenue from livestock − [risk penalty]
  product sales]

$$- \sum_z \sum_k \sum_s \sum_q C_{zk} (CP_{zksq} + CS_{zksq}) \quad - \sum_z \sum_s RAT_{zs} \qquad - c^v \sum_z \sum_s BEEF_{zs}$$

− [purchased input costs   − [cost of livestock   − [cost of veterinary
   of cropping activities]   rations]   services]

$$- w^F \sum_z \sum_s \sum_m LF_{zsm} \qquad - \sum_z \sum_s \sum_m w_z^T LT_{zsm} \quad - \sum_z \sum_s w_z^P LP_{zs}.$$

− [family reservation   − [temporary labor   − [permanent
   wages]   costs]   labor costs]

Commodity balances

Proprietors (BP_{zis})

$$\sum_k y_{kzq}^i CP_{kzsq} \qquad\qquad + \alpha_i \sum_k \sum_q y_{kzq}^i CS_{kzsq}$$

[yield from pro-   + [proprietors' direct share
 prietors' crop-   of sharecroppers' cropping
 ping activities]   activities]

$+ u\, S_{izs}$ $- P_{izs}$

$+$ [marketing margin $-$ [product sales][19]
      from sharecroppers'
      sales]

$- \sum_{n} f_{izn}\, EP_{szn}$ $= 0$ for all i, z, s.

$-$ [on-farm consumption]

Sharecroppers (BS_{zis})

$(1 - \alpha_i) \sum_{k} \sum_{q} y^{i}_{kzq}\, CS_{kzsq} - S_{izs}$

[sharecroppers' retained $-$[sharecroppers'
      production]   "sales"]

$- \sum_{n} f_{izn}\, ES_{szn}$ $= 0$ for all i, z, s.

$-$ [sharecroppers'
      consumption]

Demand balances (price-endogenous crops) (Q_{zi})

$- \sum_{\ell} a_{zi\ell}\, D_{zi\ell}$ $+ \sum_{s} P_{zis}$ ≥ 0 for all z, i.

[quantity sold] + [quantity
                        supplied]

Demand convex-combination constraints (CC_{zi})

$\sum_{\ell} D_{zi\ell} \leq 1$ for all i, z.

Consumption levels (EP_{zs}, ES_{zs})

$\sum_{n} EP_{zsn}$ $= N_{zs}$ for all z, s,

[number of $=$ [number of farm
  bundles]   families][20]

$\sum_{n} ES_{zsn}$ $= NS_{zs}$ $= 0$ for all z, s.

[number of $=$ [number of
  bundles]   sharecroppers]

19. Or transfers to market demand functions for price-endogenous crops.
20. If on-farm consumption is applicable.

Deviation constraints (for risk) (DEV_{tzs})

$$\sum_k \theta_{kzsq} \, CP_{kzsq} \qquad\qquad + \sum_k \theta^*_{kzsq} \, CS_{kzsq}$$

[revenue deviations of + [adjusted[21] revenue
proprietors' cropping deviations of
activities] sharecropping activities]

$+ Z_{tzs}$ $\qquad\qquad\qquad \geq 0$ for all t, z, s.

+ [negative deviation
counters]

Land constraints

Good cropland (HG_{zs})
$$\sum_k g_k \, (CP_{kzs}G + CS_{kzs}G) \qquad + TGM_{zs}$$

[good land used for crops] + [good land used as medium land]

$\leq \overline{HG}_{zs}$ for all z, s.

$\leq$ [net (of long-cycle stocks)
good land available]

Medium cropland (HM_{zs})
$$\sum_k g_k \, (CP_{kzs} \, M + CS_{kzs}G) \qquad + \sum_j x_{1j} \, LSF_{zsj}$$

[medium land used for crops] + [cultivated pasture use]

$- TGM_{zs} \qquad + TMP_{zs} \qquad \leq \overline{HM}_{zs}$ for all z, s.

$-$ [good $\quad$ + [medium $\quad \leq$ [net medium land
land used $\quad$ land used $\quad$ available]
as medium] $\quad$ as poor
$\qquad\qquad$ land]

Poor cropland (HP_{zs})
$$\sum_j x_{2j} \, LSF_{zsj} \qquad\qquad - TMP_{zs}$$

[native pasture use] − [medium land used as poor]

$- \frac{1}{4} \sum (CP_{k*zsq} + CS_{k*zsq}) \qquad\qquad \leq HP_{zs}.$

$-$ [residual pasture available in $\qquad \leq$ [poor land
fourth year of cotton moco cycle][22] $\quad$ available]

---

21. To reflect proprietors' component of risk ($\theta^* < \theta$ since $s_i < 1$).
22. k^* implies the activity contains crop $i = 04$ (cotton moco).

Labor Constraints

Proprietors' labor balances (RP_{zsm})

$$\sum_q \sum_k w^c_{zkm} CP_{zksq} \quad + \sum_j w^L_{zjm} LSF_{zjs}$$

[labor required for + [labor required for
cropping activities   livestock maintenance
(man-days)]   (man-days)]

$- 25TP_{zsm} \qquad\qquad\qquad = 0$ for all z, s, m.
− [total labor required
(man-months)]

Proprietors' labor constraints (RC_{zsm})

$$TP_{zsm} \qquad - LF_{zsm} \qquad - LT_{zsm} \qquad - LP_{zs} \quad \le 0 \text{ for all } z, s, m.$$

[total labor − [family labor − [temporary − [permanent
required]   supply]   hire]   hire]

Note: LF_{sz} is bounded at farm family labor availability.

Sharecroppers' labor balances (RS_{zsm})

$$\sum_k \sum_q w^c_{zkm} CS_{zksq} \; - 55NS_{zs} \le 0.$$

[labor required in − [labor supplied by
sharecropping   each sharecropper's
activities]   family per month]

Regional labor constraints (LAB_{zm})

$$\sum_s (LT_{zsm} \quad + LP_{zs} \quad + 2.2NS_{zs}) \quad \le LAB_{zm} \text{ for all } z, m.$$

[temporary + [permanent + [share-   ≤ [landless
workers]   workers]   croppers]   labor
                                      available]

Sharecroppers' plot size (θ_z)

$$\sum_k CS_{zksq} \qquad - \theta_z NS_{zs} \qquad = 0 \text{ for all } z, s.$$

[total area   − [plot size
sharecropped]   times number
                 of sharecroppers]

Livestock rations balance (RAT_{zs})

$$\sum_j x_{3j} LSF_{zsj} \qquad - RAT_{zs} \qquad = 0 \text{ for all } z, s.$$

[rations required − [total rations]
in feeding alter-
natives]

Livestock maintenance balance (FAT_{zs})

$$\sum_j LSF_{zsj} \quad - BEEF_{zs} \quad = 0 \text{ for all } z, s.$$

[number of − [number of
feeding   animals
alternatives] maintained]

Working capital (WC_{zs})

$$\sum_k \sum_q C_{zs}(CP_{zksq} + CS_{zksq}) + RAT_{zs} + c^v BEEF_{zs}$$

[crop purchased inputs] + [livestock purchased inputs]

$$+ w_z^T \sum_m LT_{zsm} \quad + w_z^P LP_{zs} \quad \leq \overline{WC}_{zs} \text{ for all } z, s.$$

+ [temporary   + [permanent ≤ [annual
labor wage   labor wage   working
costs]   costs]   capital
                                 availability]

Bounds[23]

$$LF_{zsm} \leq \overline{LF}_{zsm} \text{ for all } z, s,$$

[farm family labor availability]

$$CP_{zksq} \leq \overline{CP}_{zksq} \text{ for all } z, s, q, k \, \varepsilon \, K^L \text{ (where } K^L \text{ is the}$$
subset of cropping
[long-cycle crop stocks]   activities comprising
long-cycle crops).

23. Bounds are convenient ways of constraining individual activities without recourse to additional rows in the problem.

Appendix C: Estimation and Testing of Parameters

Little theoretical guidance is available on the problem of incorporating statistical information from cross-sectional data into a mathematical programming model. Although there is a considerable body of literature on the stochastic programming aspects of the problem, no significant theory has been developed that explains the properties of a model's solution as a function of the statistical characteristics of its parameters.[24]

The matrix of production coefficients used in the model is, with several exceptions described below, composed of means computed from the survey data.[25] These have a number of possible sources of error. Despite the large size of the sample, the number of observations of the production relations for any individual crop is quite small, because crops are so frequently interplanted. The frequency of observations varies widely among crops and consortiums, and the coefficients estimated for those with only a small number of observations may be significantly biased. Moreover, although the sample points are scattered over large areas, it is possible that the observations of particular crops were spatially concentrated and thus give a distorted impression of their average distribution and also, perhaps, of their average production relations, because local weather, soil quality, and other ecological factors may significantly affect yields, labor requirements, and so forth. Finally, some of the survey data are better than others, because of differences among the survey teams and the degree of understanding of the informants.

In view of these problems, the reliability and consistency of the numerical values of the parameters estimated were analyzed before they were incorporated in the model. The analysis had the following parts:

—calculation of the distribution statistics of the basic input–output relations
—where the same crop is produced in more than one activity, that is, alone or interplanted with other crops, or both, tests for significant differences in yields

---

24. As Hadley puts it, "when some of the technological coefficients are made random variables, the problem becomes nonlinear and assumes a form for which, at present, there does not exist any general technique for finding an optimal solution." See George Hadley, *Non-Linear and Dynamic Programming* (Reading, Mass.: Addison-Wesley Publishing Co., 1964).

25. The full technology data set has been published by SUDENE, as *Coeficientes tecnicos do Nordeste* (Recife, 1976).

—comparison of the empirical with estimated theoretical distributions of the parameters for different activities (generally normal) and rejection of outliers.

Three of the principal parameters in the model required additional information and background analysis:

—the yield (output in kilograms per hectare) coefficients for the various cropping activities
—the risk-aversion factors of different types of farms
—the demand activity coefficients that are the basis for the determination of price and quantity of nontraded crops.

Later, tests were also made of the robustness of the model by varying the values of its parameters. Some of these tests are described in Chapter 6.

The Stratified Yield Estimator

The model treats each combination of land (of good or medium quality) and crop (or consortium of interplanted crops) as a separate activity. Each farm model thus has pairs of cropping activities whose nonzero values are identical (in magnitude and by rows) except insofar as they draw from different resources (good or medium-quality land) and their yield coefficients are different. (It is assumed that the variable inputs, labor and purchased inputs, are identical.) The yields from both sets are carried into a single set of commodity balances.

The yield coefficients are derived from two mutually independent samples. The first of these has a wide coverage but gives yields irrespective of land quality; and the other, smaller and subject to more measurement error, gives yields stratified by good and medium land quality. To incorporate the greater accuracy of the results from the first (y) and the greater detail of those from the second (y_i), the estimates (y^*) are computed by minimizing

$$\sum_{i=1}^{n} \left(\frac{y_i^* - y_i}{s_i}\right)^2 + \sum_{i=1}^{n} \left[\frac{w_i(y_i^* - y)}{s}\right]^2$$

where $y_i =$ the stratified mean yields from the second sample

$s_i =$ the standard error of y_i

$y\ =$ the mean yield (unstratified) from the first sample

$s =$ the standard error of y

$w_i = a_i / \Sigma_i^n a_i$, a weight with respect to y_i

a_i = the land area devoted to the activity generating y_i

n = the number of land types.

This equation maps the information contained in the two samples (y_i and y) into our estimates and takes into account their sampling variance (s_i and s, respectively).[26]

After a little algebra, the first-order condition yields

$$y_i^* = g\, y_i + (1 - g)y, \text{ where } g = s^2/(s^2 + w_i^2 s i^2),\ i = 1, 2, \ldots, n.$$

In practice, only two land types (high- and medium-yield land) are used: The yield coefficients for each are determined according to the above equation.

Treatment of Risk

The treatment of risk is based on that described by Hazell and Scandizzo.[27] The risk penalty charged to the objective function in each farm model depends upon the riskiness of the farm plan chosen, as estimated from past downward deviations from average yields, scaled by a factor phi, which indicates the ability or willingness of the farm type in question to bear risk.

Revenue Deviations

A time series exists for 1960–69 of the revenues generated by single crops, state by state.[28] These data are mapped into a regional series using a rough weighting scheme. They are then made applicable to crops grown in consortiums, which is more usual than plantings of single crops, using the following procedure.

A weight (w_i) corresponding to the contribution of the crop in question to the total revenue of the activity is computed by

---

26. The underlying statistical model can be expressed as:

$y_i = \mu_i + \epsilon_i,\ E(\epsilon_i) = 0,\ \text{Var}(\epsilon_i) = \sigma_i^2,\ \text{Cov}(\epsilon_i, \epsilon_j) = 0\ (i = 1, 2, \ldots, n, j = 1, 2, \ldots, n)$

$y = \sum_i \omega_i \mu_i + \epsilon,\ E(\epsilon) = 0,\ \text{Var}(\epsilon) = \sigma^2,\ \text{Cov}(\epsilon, \epsilon_i) = 0\ (i = 1, 2, \ldots, n).$

27. Hazell and Scandizzo, "Competitive Demand Structures under Risk," pp. 235–44.
28. Unpublished SUDENE data.

$$(5.8) \qquad w_i = \frac{y_i \, p_i}{\sum_i y_i \, p_i}$$

where y_i = the yield of the ith crop in the activity and p_i = the base-year price of crop i.

A new revenue series is then generated by

$$(5.9) \qquad r_t^* = \sum_i w_i \, r_{it}$$

where r_t^* = the new revenue series (on an activity basis); and r_{it} = the single-crop series.

Two mean revenues are then generated by

$$(5.10) \qquad \bar{r}^* = \sum_t r_t^*/T \text{ and } \bar{r}^{**} = \sum_i y_i \, p_i.$$

Then the adjusted revenue deviation series is generated by

$$(5.11) \qquad d_t = \frac{r_t^* \, \bar{r}^{**}}{\bar{r}^*} - \bar{r}^{**}.$$

The above procedure maintains the proportionality of the original series, $d_t/\bar{r}^{**} = (r_t^* - \bar{r}^*)/\bar{r}^*$. It assumes, first, that factors causing revenues to vary operate homogeneously (that is, there is a proportional effect with respect to some expected mean revenue); and, second, that revenue varies according to the crop mixture of an activity and not according to the activity itself.

The risk-aversion parameters (phi) were first posited intuitively; small-scale farmers facing the possibility of starvation in a bad year were given a high phi of 2.5 and large-scale farmers, a low phi of 0 to 0.5. Values of phi in this range were confirmed by the results of a special study of 200 farmers and sharecroppers.[29] The risk parameters finally used were determined through sensitivity tests of the phi's in solutions of individual farm models. That is, the posited values for phi were varied upward and downward to see if these variations would greatly change the farm model's ability to reproduce observed farm plans for the different farm types. The results of these tests suggested that, for estates in the West, a phi of 1.0 was more appropriate than 0.5 and that, throughout the East, for all practical purposes, risk could be ignored (phi=0), because of the high reliability of rainfall there. Otherwise, the tests revealed no basis for rejecting the phi's originally posited.

29. See John L. Dillon and Pasquale L. Scandizzo, "Risk Attitudes of Subsistence Farmers in Northeast Brazil: A Sampling Approach," *American Journal of Agricultural Economics*, vol. 6, no. 3 (August 1978), pp. 425–35.

Demand Activity Coefficients

Following Duloy and Norton, the demand activity coefficients are formed from the base-year prices and quantities marketed and from price elasticities.[30] The procedure adopted is straightforward except for the price elasticities, for which direct estimates were lacking. These were calculated from Engel elasticities and budget shares, using a procedure derived by Feder and Scandizzo:[31]

$$\eta_{ii} = - E_i(\alpha_i - \frac{1 - \alpha_i E_i}{\omega})$$

and

$$\eta_{ij} = - E_i\, \alpha_j\, (1 + E_j/\omega),$$

where E_i = Engel elasticity

η_{ii} = own-price elasticity of the ith good

η_{ij} = cross-price elasticity

α_i = budget share of the ith good of the average consumer of Northeastern products

ω = Frisch parameter.

30. Duloy and Norton, "Prices and Incomes," pp. 591–600.
31. See Gershon Feder and P. L. Scandizzo, "A Two-Region Multisectoral Model for Brazil" (World Bank, Development Research Center, 1977; processed). The budget shares are taken from studies by the United Nations Food and Agriculture Organization and the Federal University of Pernambuco.

6

Results from the Base Solution

Before the model can be used to simulate the effects of policy interventions, its results for the base year, 1973, must be validated against those obtained from the tabular and cross-sectional analyses. This "base case" version of the model can also be used to investigate the structural and resource-related constraints on development in the region. As will become clear in the course of this chapter, the validation process itself reveals useful insights into the workings of the model. When these insights are examined in the light of the survey data, results from the cross-sectional analysis, and other prior information, they often lead to new hypotheses and explanations of farm behavior.

Validation Considerations

For economic planning models, the rather small body of literature on validation criteria and testing procedures permits only three general conclusions: that testing and validation *are* important; that the validation criteria must depend on the uses of the model; and that the validation procedure must instill confidence in the model, on the part of both the analyst and the user of the results. Though there are no rules for accepting or rejecting a model of the type used in this study, which is designed to explore a wide range of hypothetical situations for which no benchmarks exist, it is worthwhile briefly to review some precedents.

Nugent explored the possibility of validation tests in the context of a multisector, multiperiod linear programming model of the Greek economy.[1] In that study, he indicated three reasons a model may not

---

1. Jeffrey B. Nugent, "Linear Programming Models for National Planning: Demonstration of a Testing Procedure," *Econometrica*, vol. 38, no. 6 (November 1970), pp. 831–55.

perfectly simulate an actual economy: The model's constraint set may have been inaccurately specified; the underlying structure of the economy may be incorrectly represented (functionally or numerically); and it may be incorrect to assume that agents are strict optimizers with a singularity of purpose—either because some of their behavior is nonoptimal or because the objective function does not capture all their objectives. Departures from simple optimization behavior remain exceedingly difficult to handle in a linear programming framework. Where the observed production and price levels differed from "optimal" levels, Nugent used regression analysis to distinguish the differences owing to incorrect representation of the underlying market structure (using tests of the model's structure and objective function) from those owing to omissions of variables from the model. Kutcher proposed and undertook several validation tests for an agricultural model of Mexico's Pacific Northwest region.[2] These tests, however, were applicable only to the production/technology part of the model and were undertaken primarily because, unlike in the present study, no primary data on technology were at hand. Egbert and Kim, in a study of Portuguese agriculture, employed Theil U_2 coefficients to test their model's ability to simulate aggregate production levels before conducting aggregation experiments and using the model to indicate areas of priority for investment.[3]

Although this background is helpful, it is not sufficient to define an appropriate rigorous testing procedure, particularly in the present case where farm-level behavior is embedded in a sectorwide, market-clearing framework. Our approach will be, first, to compare the model simulations of aggregate production, output prices, and levels of employment with the available survey and census data and then to undertake sensitivity analysis, varying the model parameters, to investigate the possible sources of bias. We then examine whether the bias can be traced to the simulation of particular farm types.

2. Gary P. Kutcher, "Agricultural Planning at the Regional Level: A Programming Study of Mexico's Pacific Northwest" (Ph.D. dissertation, University of Maryland, 1972).

3. Alvin C. Egbert and Hyung M. Kim, *A Developmental Model for the Agricultural Sector of Portugal*, World Bank Staff Occasional Paper no. 20 (Baltimore, Md.: Johns Hopkins University Press, 1975). The model and its validation are also described, in condensed form, in "Analysis of Aggregation Errors in Linear Programming Planning Models," *American Journal of Agricultural Economics*, vol. 57, no. 2 (May 1975), pp. 292–301. Coincidentally, Leuthold, in the same issue, argued that such uses of Theil coefficients are inappropriate and are likely to give misleading results. His alternative, however, is to use "more sophisticated techniques." Raymond M. Leuthold, "On the Use of Theil's Inequality Coefficients," *American Journal of Agricultural Economics*, vol. 57, no. 2 (May 1975), pp. 344–46.

Table 6-1. *Model Performance: Crop Production and Prices*

	Production[a]		Prices[b]		Demand price elasticity
Crop	Q^o *Observed*	Q^s *Simulated*	P^o *Observed*	P^s *Simulated*	
Cotton moco	427,531	575,246	2.10	1.60	$-0.4, -\infty$
Cotton herbaceo	214,367	290,005	2.00	1.50	$-0.4, -\infty$
Cotton verdao	120,127	161,348	1.90	1.40	$-0.4, -\infty$
Rice	308,767	318,711	0.76	0.68	-0.3
Bananas	12,156	13,462	3.80	1.80	-0.2
Sweet potatoes	14,225	14,437	0.23	0.22	-0.3
Babacu	621,852	619,814	1.00	1.00	$-\infty$
Cacao	203,098	208,896	5.00	5.00	$-\infty$
Cashews	11,002	10,765	1.00	1.00	$-\infty$
Sugarcane	35,488	42,809	36.00	17.50	-0.4
Carnauba	836,746	852,652	0.80	0.80	$-\infty$
Coconuts	4,544	5,314	40.00	14.18	-0.27
Beans de arranca	68,901	83,605	2.50	0.52	-0.26
Beans de corda	126,006	128,513	1.60	1.49	-0.26
Oranges	8,600	10,094	10.00	5.60	-0.4
Manioc	3,546,204	3,847,328	0.18	0.09	-0.17
Corn	632,123	635,521	0.51	0.49	-0.14
Castor beans	23,428	23,449	1.50	1.50	$-\infty$
Sisal	103,766	83,095	1.00	1.00	$-\infty$

Note: $\Sigma Q^o P^o = \text{Cr\$}7,175,456$
$\Sigma Q^s P^o = \text{Cr\$}8,156,485$
$\Sigma Q^o P^s = \text{Cr\$}5,450,249$
$\Sigma Q^s P^s = \text{Cr\$}6,074,674$

a. In metric tons, except for sugarcane, which is in thousands of metric tons, and coconuts and oranges, which are in thousands of fruits.

b. In cruzeiros per kilogram, except for sugarcane, which is in cruzeiros per metric ton, and coconuts and oranges, which are in cruzeiros per hundred fruit.

Production and Prices

Because the model's full solution involves the summing of solutions for five zones and three to four farm types, depending on the zone, our first concern is whether this summation yields realistic totals for production levels and the associated (endogenous) market prices. The simulated production totals by crop and average Northeast-wide prices are reported in Table 6-1.[4] The simulated gross value of production of all crops, at

4. Weighted average prices are reported because for most crops and livestock there are price differentials based on distances and access to markets.

observed prices, is Cr$8,157 million, or 13.67 percent more than the observed total at observed prices.

The crops in the table are grouped into three categories: the price-endogenous food crops that are, according to the best information available, consumed almost entirely within the Northeast; the cotton varieties that face both a price-responsive domestic demand and a perfectly elastic export demand for their processed products; and the long-cycle crops, which face either price-endogenous or perfectly elastic export demands but whose production is subject to stock constraints.

For most of the food crops, the simulated production levels are close to, though slightly above, the observed levels. The total simulated value of these crops, at observed prices, is Cr$3,274 million, compared with an observed value of Cr$3,078 million, a discrepancy of 6.4 percent. The only dramatic difference in this group is for sugar production, the simulated value of which is 20 percent higher than that observed, even though this crop is generally considered to have long lost its comparative advantage in the Northeast. Most of the overestimation of sugar production occurs in the Agreste, not in the Zona da Mata.

The simulated production of all varieties of cotton is about one-third greater than that observed; indeed, the simulated total of just over 1 million tons is about 10 percent greater than production in any of the previous ten years. (Although from 1962 to 1972 there were moderate increases in the area under cotton, output virtually stagnated because of declines in yields.) There are several possible reasons for this discrepancy. First, a static model cannot account for historical considerations: Farmers may have expected the previous declines in yields to continue and hence have planted less than the optimal (in a comparative-static sense) number of hectares. Second, cotton production may be subject to constraints not considered in the model. (Processing capacity, constraints on which were excluded from the model, could be a limiting factor; but knowledgeable sources have assured us that sufficient capacity exists to handle the volume of production simulated, and capacity expansion has historically kept pace with output growth.) Either of these explanations may be valid to some degree, but the principal reason, discussed more fully below, is that the fazendas in the Sertao, where the bulk of cotton is produced, use labor and land far more intensively in the simulations than they are observed to do.

The production levels of the constrained long-cycle crops are, of course, generally extremely close to those observed. The deviations are due either to numerical (round-off) errors in tabulating the survey data and organizing them for linear programming, or to the use of stocks of trees, by area, as the constraint on production, rather than a simple limitation on the volume of output.

Table 6-2. *Regression Results: Goodness-of-Fit Tests for Production Volumes of Price-Endogenous Crops Simulated by the Model*

Zone	Parameter a (95 percent confidence interval)	Parameter b (95 percent confidence interval)	R^2
West	−0.247	1.012	
	(−1.010, 0.515)	(0.943, 1.082)	0.998
Sertao	−0.142	0.998	
	(−0.584, 0.299)	(0.958, 1.037)	0.997
Southeast	0.155	0.983	
	(−1.618, 1.928)	(0.828, 1.138)	0.993
East	0.207	0.979	
	(−1.183, 1.597)	(0.817, 1.142)	0.992
Agreste	−0.117	1.000	
	(−1.134, 0.899)	(0.904, 1.097)	0.993
Northeast	0.058	0.985	
	(−0.208, 0.324)	(0.960, 1.010)	0.995

The fact that for almost every price-endogenous crop the simulated volume of production is above the observed requires closer inspection. As an alternative to Theil inequality coefficients—which may be inappropriate and are also difficult to interpret—and simple correlation tests—which would not capture systematic deviations that may be present here—we use the following regression test: $\log Q^s = a + b \log Q^0$, where Q^s is the simulated volume of production of a given crop at observed price levels, Q^0 the observed production, and a and b are parameters to be estimated by regression. If, apart from random error, the model perfectly simulated the production levels, a, the intercept, should not differ from unity. The log transformation is used to abstract the b coefficient (though not the constant) from the scale and unit differences among the crops. The R^2 from the regression will indicate the goodness of fit.

The divergences in production levels across farm types are discussed later, but first it is worth investigating whether there are zonal patterns. The results of these regressions for each zone and the entire Northeast are shown in Table 6-2. For all zones and for the Northeast as a whole, a is not significantly different from zero and b is not significantly different from unity at the 95 percent level.

As with most crops, the simulated value of output from livestock is higher than that observed. Although livestock production faces perfectly elastic demands in the model and no restraints other than those on the production factors (pasture, labor, credit for purchased inputs) and hence might be expected to dominate a solution of this type of model, the simulated herd sizes are within 20 percent of those observed and the value of production is only 18.3 percent greater. About 60 percent of the total difference between the observed and simulated livestock output occurs in the Southeast, where the model nearly doubles the existing herd sizes. Interestingly, knowledgeable sources indicate that since 1973 stock raising has indeed shown rapid growth in this region of Bahia. Thus, the model may have captured a latent comparative advantage at about the same time producers began to expand.

The volume of total crop and animal production simulated by the model is only 15 percent larger than that observed, and its composition is very similar. The survey tabulations indicate that 33 percent of gross output originates from animal sources. If all outputs in the model are valued at observed prices, livestock's share is slightly more than 28 percent; when these outputs are valued at model (endogenous) prices, its share is about 34 percent.

The model gives a much less satisfactory representation of prices than of production volumes. Indeed, as Table 6-1 shows, most crops with downward-sloping demand functions have equilibrium prices significantly below those observed. The exceptions are beans de corda, corn, rice, and sweet potatoes. The simulated prices of several crops (bananas, beans de arranca, coconut, manioc, and sugar) are at least 50 percent below their observed prices. For all crops, including those with fixed prices, the Laspeyres price index is 76, and the Paasche index 74, the observed price level being 100. For the price-endogenous crops alone, both indexes are about 60. A regression test for prices, similar to that for output volumes reported in Table 6-2, failed at the 95 percent confidence level for the Sertao and for the Northeast as a whole and gave positive results for these two cases only when the confidence level was lowered to 90 percent.

These prices are of concern inasmuch as they correspond to marginal costs of production, averaged over zones and farm types. Thus, if we have confidence in the model's treatment of production technology and in the other input parameters estimated from the survey data, the results indicate that for several important products it would pay to expand production up to the point where market prices have fallen to 50 percent of present prices or lower. Either there are substantial disincentives to such expansion, or the observed operations of many farms are far below economically optimal levels. We return to these questions later in this chapter.

Table 6-3. *Persons Occupied in Agriculture: Model Results*

Type of worker	West	Sertao	South-east	East	Agreste	North-east
Farmers and family workers	309,435	827,010	173,747	52,168	388,919	1,751,279
Sharecroppers and family workers	—	969,714	—	—	—	969,714
Permanent workers	126,756	3,837	17,938	63,485	45,213	257,229
Temporary workers	426,608	147,318	643,613	66,608	235,994	1,520,141
Total	862,799	1,947,879	835,248	182,261	670,120	4,498,363

— Not applicable.
Note: The derivation of these estimates is described in the text.

Employment and Labor Utilization

The model provides several alternative measures of employment and labor utilization. The number of persons occupied in agriculture (the definition used by IBGE for the 1970 agricultural census) is one such measure. Table 6-3 reports the simulated totals by zone for the four broad categories of agents: farmers and their family workers, sharecroppers and their family workers, permanent workers, and temporary workers. For these totals an occupied person is defined as follows. Because, in the model solution, all farms are operational to some degree, all the farm family workers are assumed to be occupied (though not necessarily fully employed). Thus, the farm family entries in Table 6-3 are simply the sum of the number of farms of each type multiplied by the corresponding survey estimates of family workers; for sharecroppers, the number of sharecropped plots simulated by the model is multiplied by the average size of the sharecropper's occupied family (2.2 persons). The number of occupied permanent workers is measured as the number of annual contracts (whether or not these workers were fully used throughout the year), and the number of temporary workers as the peak monthly hirings in each zone. Thus, the totals in Table 6-3 are in fact upper bounds on the amount of labor actively engaged.

Even so, the Northeast total of about 4.5 million persons occupied in agriculture derived in this way contrasts sharply with labor force estimates in the neighborhood of 6 million (see Chapter 2) and indicates unemployment rates of 25 percent or more. Almost 40 percent of those occupied are farmers and their family workers (1.75 million), and only 27 percent of the remaining occupied persons have permanent or share-tenant contracts. The

Table 6-4. *Labor Requirements: Model Results*
(man-years)

Labor	West	Sertao	South-east	East	Agreste	North-east
Farmers and family workers	174,571	487,111	148,605	34,920	292,349	1,137,557
Sharecroppers and family workers	—	420,688	—	—	—	420,688
Permanent workers	126,756	3,837	17,938	63,485	45,213	257,229
Temporary workers	96,599	23,061	149,535	28,368	61,898	359,463
Total (1)	397,927	934,698	316,078	126,773	399,461	2,174,938
Survey estimates (2)	336,434	754,751	222,570	77,562	376,861	1,768,178
Percentage deviation (1)/(2)	+ 18.3	+ 23.8	+ 42.0	+ 63.4	+ 6.0	+ 23.0

— Not applicable.
Note: The derivation of these estimates is described in the text.

other 33 percent of the occupied persons are temporary workers receiving a minimum of one month's employment a year. Because the typical *employed* temporary worker receives an average of two to three months' employment a year and most family farms and sharecropped plots exhaust half or less of the family's labor, it appears that well over half the agricultural labor force is either unemployed or unquestionably underemployed, if we ignore nonagricultural employment.

To derive more precise measures of un- and underemployment from the model, actual labor requirements were tabulated from the crop and livestock production activities. The results are shown in Table 6-4 along with the survey estimates of labor requirements reproduced from Table 2-4.

For all zones and the Northeast as a whole, the model uses labor more intensively than was recorded by the survey. This squares with the model's tendency to overestimate production: The simulated labor requirements are 23 percent greater, whereas production is 15 percent greater. The discrepancies between actual and simulated labor use are largest in the Southeast, which is dominated by cacao plantations (42 percent), and in the East, which is dominated by sugar plantations (63 percent), whereas they are smallest in the Agreste. It seems clear that there is considerable scope for more intense employment even under existing farming systems. The labor requirements simulated by the model are substantially higher than in actual practice but may be used to investigate unemployment questions further if it is borne in mind that the employment rates they suggest are likely to be upper bounds.

Table 6-5. *Employment Rates, by Month and Zone: Model Results*
(percent)

Month	West	Sertao	South-east	East	Agreste	North-east
January	53.90	63.70	66.15	62.48	47.78	58.80
February	46.55	61.25	37.98	75.95	44.10	51.45
March	25.73	72.28	24.50	56.35	40.43	47.78
April	19.60	61.25	14.70	60.03	40.43	40.43
May	18.38	52.68	15.93	44.10	44.10	36.75
June	20.83	40.43	20.83	75.95	53.90	36.75
July	26.95	26.95	20.83	51.45	50.23	30.63
August	25.73	40.43	23.28	90.65	53.90	37.98
September	39.20	49.00	22.05	77.18	35.53	40.43
October	37.98	39.20	26.95	95.55	36.75	37.98
November	69.83	58.80	88.20	98.00	69.83	69.83
December	78.40	46.55	100.45	89.43	63.70	67.38
Annual average	39.20	51.45	39.20	73.50	49.00	46.55

Source: Based on survey estimates of total labor available reported in Table 2-4.

Table 6-4 shows that full-time equivalent employment is generated for only 2.17 million, or 48 percent, of the 4.5 million persons occupied. Of the actual labor absorbed, 52 percent is supplied by farmers and their families, with sharecroppers and permanent and temporary workers supplying 19 percent, 12 percent, and 17 percent, respectively. For a nonpropertied labor force approaching 5 million, only slightly more than 1 million man-years of employment are generated.

A good part of the underemployment problem can be traced to the seasonality of agricultural labor requirements. Table 6-5 reports the monthly use of labor by zone from the model results as a percentage of the labor force available. Of the nearly 6 million available in the work force, only 31 percent are engaged during July, and no more than 70 percent are ever engaged (during November). This variation is partly due to the model's exclusion of activities not directly related to cropping and stock raising (such as maintenance and postharvest processing of some products), but it nevertheless stresses the importance of seasonality in the underemployment problem. The likelihood that workers will be idle or assigned to marginal tasks for several months during the year probably also explains, in part, estate owners' reluctance to hire workers on annual contracts.

Thus far, comparisons with the survey data have shown that the model slightly overestimates production, as might be expected of an optimization model; that it more strongly underestimates prices; and that it overestimates the intensity of labor use. The following three sections examine some sources of bias and test the model's sensitivity to changes in parameters.

Family Reservation Wage

The model's deviation in labor use may be due partly to an incorrect assumption about the family reservation wage rate. This parameter determines the minimum return to family labor, below which the farm would not be operated. Its value, in relation to the wages that must be paid to nonfamily workers, will in general influence the combination of the various labor sources employed on the farm; other things being equal, the higher (lower) the family's reservation wage, the more (less) attractive it will be for them to employ other workers.

The reservation wage used in the model, Cr$3 a day, is about half the average daily wage of hired laborers. The probability that a farm family worker could find alternative agricultural employment is about 0.5. In varying the reservation wage to test the model's sensitivity, little leeway was possible: Cr$2 a day is probably the bare subsistence minimum, and in the West and the Sertao even permanent laborers earn little more than Cr$4 a day. Table 6-6 reports the effects on the model solutions of varying the reservation wage.

These sensitivity tests reveal that aggregate output, income, and employment rise somewhat but are largely insensitive to the reservation wage. Though the use of Cr$2 as the wage rate gives the most accurate representation of these aggregates, it causes some misrepresentation of the composition of employment, because family labor is substituted for permanent hired labor and, in particular, sharecropper labor. Indeed, sharecroppers all but drop out of this solution, leading us to reject the Cr$2 figure on these grounds alone. The Cr$4 figure must also be rejected because it leads to an unrealistically high use of sharecroppers and permanent workers and further departs from the output, price, and total employment levels of the Cr$3 case. Though this test does not establish Cr$3 as the correct reservation wage, it allows us to conclude that it is more appropriate than Cr$2 or Cr$4.

The increases in aggregate output and employment shown in Table 6-6 are in fact confined to the Sertao and can be explained by the model's treatment of sharecropping in that zone: The landowner is assumed to be the decisionmaker (the producer in the objective function), with the proviso that the production plan he selects for each sharecropped plot will permit a minimum consumption bundle for the sharecropper's family, who supply

Table 6-6. *Effects on Model Results of Variations in the Family Labor Reservation Wage*
(percentage changes from Cr$3 a day)

Category	At Cr$2 a day	At Cr$4 a day
Sector income	− 1.9	+ 1.6
Price index	+ 1.1	− 1.3
Gross output		
Livestock	− 1.7	+ 1.5
Crop	− 0.4	+ 1.6
Total	− 1.1	+ 1.6
Labor use		
Farm family	+ 8.4	− 15.8
Sharecroppers	− 81.6	+ 51.9
Temporary	+ 5.6	− 5.5
Permanent	− 14.4	+ 50.1
Total	− 2.8	+ 3.8

the labor to produce this bundle for themselves at no cost to the landowner. Thus, any labor employed for sharecropper family consumption is costless to the model, and because this production for own consumption does not enter the market it does not provide utility to the model in the form of consumers' surplus. Under the lower reservation wages, when the landowner produces a good portion of the cash crop, cotton, he produces cotton alone because the additional labor required for interplanting food crops is not warranted. When the family reservation wage rate is increased, however, and sharecroppers are substituted for family labor, the consumption requirements of the sharecropper, still of no concern to the landowner, induce greater labor use and more output.

Price Elasticities of Demand

The model's underestimation of food crop prices may be due partly to the low price elasticities of demand used for these crops, particularly when combined with the model's overestimation of production. These elasticities were shown in Table 6-1. They are short-run elasticities, because the base case of the model refers to a single point in time. Though they were estimated as rigorously as possible (see Chapter 5, Appendix C) it is important, for several reasons, to assess how strongly they affect the model results. First, the model results suggest that Northeastern agriculture is constrained by demand—a hypothesis on which the demand elasticities obviously have a direct bearing. Second, the magnitudes of the elasticities are particularly important in the evaluation of simulated policies to shift supply—for example, technical progress, employment subsidies, and policies to promote land use. The structure of the model is such that unless demand is infinitely elastic (as it is assumed to be for export crops) increases in supply will depress prices, benefiting consumers but potentially harming farmers. The distribution of the benefits from supply-augmenting interventions thus depends partly on the magnitude of the demand elasticities. Finally, there is room to argue that the elasticities that have been estimated are too low in absolute value for a framework that will be used primarily for comparative-static analysis of equilibrium points several years apart. This topic will be addressed more fully in Chapter 7, but it should be pointed out here that longer-term demand schedules are likely to be more elastic (higher in absolute value).

Higher elasticities yield less steep demand functions and—given the supply functions in the base case of the model—higher output levels and higher prices. In Figure 6-1, D_1D_1 is a typical demand schedule under the rather low elasticities used in the base case, and SS is a typical supply function. Because D_1D_1 and SS intersect to the right of the base period quantity Q^0 (as is the case for most of the food crops considered), the new solution price P^1 is lower than the base price P^0. Increasing the elasticity (D_2D_2) has the effect of rotating the demand schedule about the point (P^0, Q^0), *not* about the price intercept of D_1D_1, raising both quantity (to Q^2) and price (to P^2). It can also be surmised from Figure 6-1 that the opposite directional changes would result from an increase in elasticity if in the base case SS intersected D_1D_1 to the left of Q^0 and that no changes would occur if all supply functions intersected demand functions exactly at Q^0.

A sensitivity test was undertaken in which the demand elasticities were doubled, with all other aspects of the base case kept constant. The results of this test are not reported in their entirety, simply because there were no dramatic changes. Crop output rose by 3.2 percent, and livestock output fell by 0.8 percent, as some medium-quality land was shifted from pasture use to crops. Employment rose by only 1.3 percent, and incomes of all agents rose by 0.8 percent. Such magnitudes demonstrate that the key lessons from the base solution do not depend entirely on the demand elasticities, although the latter are of obvious importance for the distribution of gains between consumers and producers under different policy conditions. The model's representation of prices and quantities cannot be made more accurate by manipulating the elasticities, because a closer fit of prices will correspond to a poorer fit of quantities. It remains, then, to

Figure 6-1. Effects of More Elastic Demand Schedules:
Model Structure

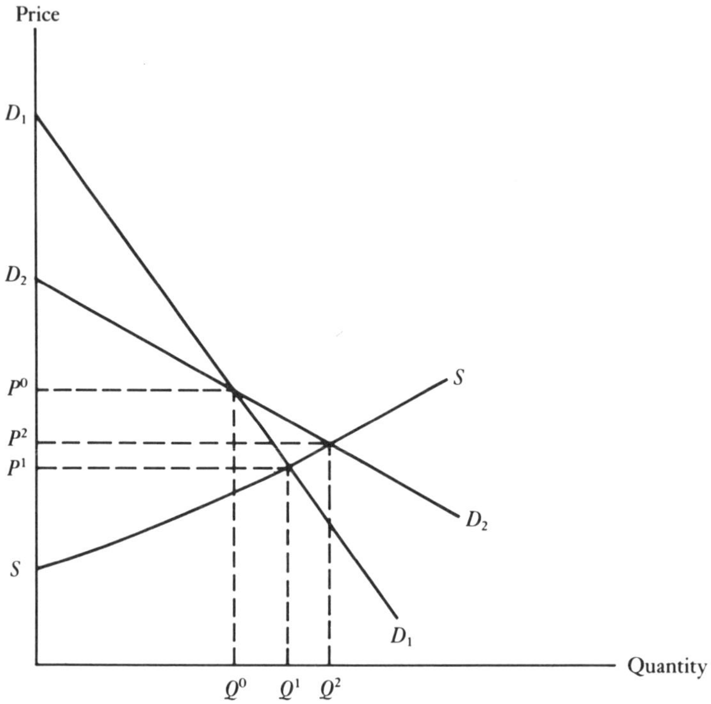

investigate the causes of the model's overestimation of production and resource use.

Optimality Assumptions

Much of the overestimation of production and the underestimation of product prices that is directly related to it may lie in the optimality assumptions embedded in the linear programming framework. In virtually all known examples based on reliable production and resource-endowment data, linear programming models are more "efficient" than the reality they are designed to depict.

The cross-sectional analysis of the performance of farms of different sizes, reported in Chapter 4, strongly suggested that large-scale farmers do

Table 6-7. *Output Generation and Labor Use, by Farm Type:*
Survey Data and Model Results
(cruzeiros of gross output per hectare of farm size; man-years of labor per hectare of farm size)

Category	West	Sertao	South-east	East	Agreste	North-east
			Family farms			
Output per hectare						
Survey averages	231	246	280	417	506	344
Model results	140	124	347	375	480	288 (− 10 percent)
Labor per hectare						
Survey averages	0.090	0.085	0.088	0.102	0.130	0.102
Model results	0.042	0.036	0.095	0.108	0.175	0.095 (− 7 percent)
			Medium-size farms			
Output per hectare						
Survey averages	85	157	147	376	273	162
Model results	79	176	283	348	180	175 (+ 8 percent)
Labor per hectare						
Survey averages	0.024	0.032	0.025	0.056	0.046	0.032
Model results	0.016	0.036	0.046	0.074	0.052	0.036 (+ 12 percent)
			Estates			
Output per hectare						
Survey averages	24	69	68	75	153	63
Model results	50	84	85	150	103	83 (+ 32 percent)
Labor per hectare						
Survey averages	0.004	0.010	0.008	0.101	0.028	0.010
Model results	0.015	0.020	0.019	0.026	0.023	0.019 (+ 90 percent)

not equate marginal costs and prices; that is, they do not maximize profits with respect to their productive land resources. Given the attention paid to the complexities of Northeastern agriculture in the design of the model and the painstaking analysis that lies behind the technical parameters used, the estate subsector is the most obvious of the remaining possible sources of bias.

The comparisons in Table 6-7 of survey data and results from the model show that the model's overestimation of production and employment is indeed almost entirely traceable to its simulation of the estate subsector; on family and medium-size farms aggregate output and employment are much more precisely simulated. In all zones save the Agreste it would be optimal for the estates to employ far more labor and produce substantially more than they do currently. If they were to employ their fixed and variable resources so as to equate marginal costs with market prices (taking account of risk penalties, and so forth), they would on average employ 90 percent more labor and attain about one-third more production.

Table 6-7 also shows that the simulated characteristics of family and medium-size farms are biased in opposite directions, or that the behavior of these farms departs from the optimal in different ways. First, the typical family farm not only makes fuller use of family labor and produces more per hectare than other types of farm but actually uses more labor and produces more output (by about 10 percent in both cases) than the model indicates would be optimal. Second, the medium-size farm uses less labor than would be optimal and produces slightly below optimal levels (again in the range of 10 percent).

These identified biases do not render the model inappropriate for most conceivable policy and project uses, as long as they are kept in mind in reviewing the results.

The Pattern of Constraints

Part of the power of linear programming lies in its ability to identify constraining factors and to provide marginal valuations (shadow prices) of those that are binding. The present model permits us to examine the constraints on output and the employment of resources at two levels: the farm and the sector.

Constraints at the Farm Level

The constraints at the farm level are family labor, which may be augmented by hiring permanent or temporary labor (and sharecroppers in the Sertao); land of three types (good and medium-quality cropland and pasture); working capital; and the existing stock of tree crops. Family labor is seldom a binding constraint on family farms, but on large farms, once family labor is exhausted, the expense of hiring additional workers often leaves gross margins on crops too small to warrant the cultivation of the whole farm.

This pattern of behavior shows up vividly in the land constraints; see Table 6-8, which reports shadow prices for good and medium-quality cropland and native pasture. For cropland of both qualities, family farms generally show much higher shadow prices. An exception is the Southeast, where cropland is not exhausted for any of the farm types; all the excess is used as either planted or native pasture. Within zones, the differences in land shadow prices are the counterpart of farm employment patterns. Land

Table 6-8. *Shadow Prices of Land, by Farm Type and Zone: Model Results*
(cruzeiros per hectare)

Farm type	West	Sertao	South-east	East	Agreste
			Good cropland		
Family farms	83	90	16	850	531
Medium-size farms	6	42	16	511	44
Estates	10	58	16	477	28
			Medium quality cropland		
Family farms	83	87	16	717	288
Medium-size farms	6	42	16	378	42
Estates	6	53	16	344	28
			Native pasture		
Family farms	6	42	16	—	—
Medium-size farms	6	42	16	67	28
Estates	6	35	16	72	28

— Not applicable.

shadow prices are highest on the family farms, reflecting the abundance of idle family labor, and generally decline as farm size increases, in direct relation to the higher percentage of hired labor used.[5] The differences in shadow prices further indicate distortions in the land market. Why is a land rental market not operating when family farmers in, say, the Agreste would pay up to Cr$531 a year for the use of one hectare of good cropland while the fazendas are realizing an annual marginal return of only Cr$28? The across-zone differences in land shadow prices closely follow the pattern expected from consideration of location (access to markets), soil quality, and the volume and timing of rainfall. The shadow prices are highest in the East, which has abundant rainfall and lies near the major coastal cities; are next highest in the Agreste, just inland from the East and not subject to periodic droughts; and are lowest (apart from the Southeast) in the drought-prone and more remote Sertao and West.

Another constraint at the farm level is the stock of previously planted or native long-cycle tree crops: babacu, cacao, carnauba, cashews, castor beans, coconut, and sisal. The model harvests the entire stock of all except

5. The decline in shadow prices as farm size increases is not always monotonic; in several cases the largest farms have land shadow prices slightly greater than the medium-size farms. This result is due to different technologies employed in the livestock activities. Because average labor is more expensive for large farms, they tend to use labor-saving techniques, which results in a higher opportunity value of land.

Table 6-9. *Shadow Prices of Tree-crop Stocks, by Zone: Model Results*

Crop	West	Sertao	South-east	East	Agreste
Babacu	399	—	—	—	—
Cacao	—	—	3,568	—	—
Cashews	92	123	—	—	—
Carnauba	510	3,782	—	—	—
Coconuts	—	—	—	1,008	—
Castor beans	—	333	96	—	—
Sisal	—	—	—	—	0

— Indicates that the crop is not grown in the particular zone.

sisal, and the shadow prices on the stock constraints may be interpreted as the net income that would accrue from an additional hectare of the crop under consideration. Table 6-9 reports these shadow prices averaged over farm types and land qualities.

In all but two of the farm models the simulated use of working capital is less than the actual use, as measured by farm expenditures taken from the survey data. Credit is a binding constraint for the livestock fazendas in the West and the cacao plantations in the Southeast. This finding appears to be completely unrealistic, inasmuch as these plantations have vastly larger capital stocks and vastly higher income levels (both actual and simulated) than any other type of farm. The shadow price of short-term capital for the fazendas in the West indicates that they would borrow at a real rate of interest of up to 30 percent. There are two possible reasons the other farm types, as simulated by the model, consistently use far less working capital than the expenditures recorded by the survey. Though it is likely that the model has failed to capture fully items such as maintenance and construction materials that require working capital, it is also quite probable that farmers' responses during the survey did not make a sharp enough distinction between the working capital required for agricultural production and that required for family consumption and services. Indeed, the discrepancies between actual and simulated expenditures are largest for the family farms. These results do not allow us to conclude that credit for working capital is not a constraining factor in the Northeast; we may conclude only that the model is not an appropriate tool for investigating the credit problem. The working capital constraint was therefore transformed into an accounting row for crudely monitoring those simulations that might pose severe cash flow problems.

The constraints that are binding at the farm level can now be summarized quite simply. For all farms in the applicable zones, the stock of most exportable tree crops is a binding factor. For family farms, the overwhelming constraint is land, particularly land suitable for crops. Medium-size farms appear to be constrained partly by land—though much less critically than are the family farms—and partly by the availability of relatively cheaper family labor. For large farms, with the possible exception of the livestock fazendas in the West, which may lack sufficient credit, there are no clearly evident constraints, either in reality or in the model's representation.

Constraints at the Sectoral Level

Possible constraints at the sectoral level are labor, processing capacity, credit (already dismissed), and the level of market demand for the price-flexible crops. As was evident from the earlier discussion, the stock of available labor is never exhausted, but the supply of labor at wage rates low enough to induce the full utilization of land may be a binding constraint. Temporary workers' wages are probably already at the bare subsistence level,[6] and those of permanent workers and sharecroppers are not far above that level. Processing constraints on cotton and sugar are not enforced, although they might become important for cotton if production expanded dramatically.

Although the level of demand for price-endogenous crops is not a constraint comparable to the availability of fixed resources, the model clearly shows it to be an important element of the stagnant low-level equilibrium. As was noted earlier, in all zones the prices of these crops are equated to marginal costs at levels that are far too low to induce full utilization of the available land and labor, and at levels of output and employment that imply extremely low income levels for the millions of landless and small farmers.

The treatment of demand in the model is discussed at some length in the following chapters, but here we investigate whether export sales could relieve the demand constraints for crops not currently being exported. A simple exercise, reported in Table 6-10, reveals this is not likely.

Table 6-10 shows the orders of magnitude and the components of domestic resource cost (DRC) coefficients, which are computed as the ratios between the shadow prices given by the model (base year solution) and data on weighted f.o.b. border prices, again for 1973. Clearly, without consideration of marketing margins, transport losses, or quality, and even with

---

6. The observed wage rate for temporary labor is at most Cr$10 per day of employment. The minimum subsistence-level income is about Cr$2 a day. If paid US$2.13 a day a worker would earn US$100 a year working 300 days. Because most temporary workers are engaged for only 50–60 days a year, Cr$10 a day is probably the *effective* subsistence wage.

Table 6-10. *Domestic Resource Cost Coefficients of Food Crops, 1973*

Crop	Border price[a] (U.S. dollars per metric ton)	Farm-level domestic resource cost[b] (cruzeiros per kilogram)	Transport cost[c] (cruzeiros per kilogram)	Domestic resource cost (cruzeiros per kilogram)	Domestic resource cost coefficient[d]
Rice	126.62	0.68	0.40	1.08	1.15
Beans	202.53	1.50	0.25	1.75	1.16
Manioc	74.08	0.45	0.30	0.75	1.36
Corn	76.76	0.49	0.25	0.74	1.30

a. Instituto Brasileiro de Geografia e Estatistica, *Anuario estatistico do Brasil* (Rio de Janeiro, 1975).

b. From base-year solution of the model.

c. *Conjuntura economica* (June 1974), p. 61, table XXXI.

d. Based on a shadow exchange rate of Cr$7.44:US$1.00. The domestic resource cost coefficient is computed as the ratio between the shadow cost of foreign exchange and the cost of generating foreign exchange by producing export crops—indicated by the border prices of those crops.

allowance for Brazilian currency overvaluation, Northeastern food crops do not show potential for export. In comparison, the DRC coefficients for the Northeast's traditional exports, apart from sugar, are all below or equal to one.[7]

The market prospects of traditional exports as of 1973 were not particularly encouraging. The model results suggest that it would have paid to expand production of cacao and cotton, diversify out of sugar, and moderately expand beef production. For both cotton and cacao the long-term demand prospects were good. The lack of suitable land, however, would have severely limited the expansion of high-quality cotton production. With the prevailing pattern of land tenure and high subsidies for sugar production, financial incentives tended to favor beef and sugar production rather than cotton on large farms. Small-scale farmers, for their part, may have been discouraged from expanding cotton production by the margins exacted by the marketing intermediaries and the gins. For cacao, the land tenure and marketing situation would not have presented such problems, but prospects for growth were confined to small areas of Bahia and, according to government expansion plans, selected areas of the Amazon.

7. For example, the coefficients are 0.6 for cocoa, 0.8 for cotton, 1.0 for beef, and 1.2 for sugar.

7

Policy and Project Options
for Northeastern Agriculture

In this chapter the model is used to explore alternative ways of promoting growth in agricultural production, employment and incomes, and improvements in income distribution. Despite the wealth of detail the model contains, it should be emphasized at the outset that the model is not a tool for detailed planning. It is suitable for the simulation of broad policy or project options and can roughly estimate their effects on the agricultural sector, but it is not suitable for the detailed specification of policies or individual projects. Costs, in particular, can be made explicit in only a few cases. Furthermore, some of the simulated experiments may not have counterparts in any readily defined intervention or policy instrument, even though their effects may be of great interest. Exogenous shifts in demand for food crops, or accelerated technical progress, for example, are difficult to induce directly. Nonetheless, the nature and size of the consequential changes identified by the model can help provide a perspective for the analysis of possible indirect measures to achieve these ends, such as investment in marketing and transport infrastructure, agronomic research, or improved extension services.

The analytical framework used is comparative-static. Most, if not all, of the simulated changes would require considerable time to make their effects felt, and hence the model's base case is projected forward five years to 1978. This projection suggests how Northeastern agriculture might have changed over time without interventions and provides a reference point against which the results of experiments can be contrasted. Though the five-year time span is inevitably arbitrary, it is judged long enough for most adjustment to be completed, but not long enough for the basic structure of the economy to be substantially altered.[1]

After the changes in parameters necessary to make this projection, as well as the main features of the 1978 base solution, are described, five types of simulated interventions are analyzed, alone and in combination: promotion of technical progress, reduction of risk, labor policies, promotion of demand, and agrarian reform. The promotion of technical progress is selected because it is emphasized in current policy toward the Northeast, both in Brazil and in World Bank operations. Farmers' ability and willingness to bear risk have an important influence on existing production patterns in the Northeast; farmers' attitudes toward risk are also an important factor in the spread of technical progress. Labor policies are simulated because employment is probably the single most important problem in the rural Northeast. Demand-related programs, often ignored in sector analyses, are considered because the model has suggested the hypothesis that the low-level stagnation may be due to limited access to markets. Agrarian reform is considered because it has been strongly advocated by others and has been legislated and funded, but we feel its potential effects on the agricultural sector at large have not been adequately evaluated.

The Agricultural Economy Projected to 1978

In projecting the model's base from 1973 to 1978, three types of changes must be taken into account: behavioral, technical, and demographic.

Behavioral changes occur on the part of both consumers and producers. Consumers respond to growth in their incomes and to price changes. The treatment of demand shifts caused by income growth will be described later. For food crops, price elasticities of demand are assumed to be higher in the long run than in the short, primarily because consumers take time to adjust their tastes and habits to changes in relative prices.[2] Empirical verification of this phenomenon is scant, though Houthakker and Taylor were able to estimate both short- and long-run elasticities for several

---

1. Duloy and Norton, in the CHAC study, chose a six-year horizon for their comparative-static analyses of Mexican agriculture, but they were not explicit about the reasons for this choice. See John H. Duloy and Roger D. Norton, "CHAC: A Programming Model of Mexican Agriculture" and "CHAC Results: Economic Alternatives for Mexican Agriculture," in *Multi-Level Planning: Case Studies in Mexico*, ed. Louis M. Goreux and Alan S. Manne (Amsterdam: North-Holland Publishing Company, 1973), chaps. IV.1 and IV.3.

2. See George J. Stigler, *The Theory of Price*, rev. ed. (New York: Macmillan Company, 1952).

products.[3] In many cases, they found long-run elasticities to be about twice as high in absolute value as short-run elasticities. For want of information to the contrary, we shall, as in the parametric exercise described in Chapter 6, take the price elasticities for the longer-run case as double those estimated for the base case.

Producers are assumed to adjust their output patterns and the intensity and use of resources so as to continue to maximize their annual profits, that is, to continue to equate marginal costs (including the risk penalty costs) to prices for each commodity.[4] Thus, for them, projections to the 1978 base require no structural or parameter changes to the model.

Agricultural practices in the Northeast have stabilized over perhaps centuries, and there is no available evidence to suggest that they would change much in the course of five years. But though progress in irrigation, mechanization, and the like can thus be ignored in the model, two other changes affecting output must be considered: the time trend in the yields of many crops, and the changes in the stocks of long-cycle or tree crops.

The IBGE data in Table 7-1 reveal that yields of several important crops declined in the decade before 1973. (The possible upward bias in the IBGE data, discussed in Chapter 3, probably does not distort the time trends of the variations in yields.) Several students of the Northeast suggest that this decline was due to the expansion of cultivated area to less productive land, unaccompanied by technical progress.[5] Although the expansion of cultivated area was much faster than that of population or income, the declines in yields left gross production growing at about the same rate as population. Indeed, virtually identical changes occurred in overall crop production growth and population growth over the twenty years preceding 1973.

Because the model can represent demand shifts between different points in time, as well as different land qualities that permit different crop yields, these effects are treated endogenously. Expansion of demand should induce a more than proportional expansion of the cultivated area and declines in average yields per hectare.

3. Hendrik S. Houthakker and Lester D. Taylor, *Consumer Demand in the United States: Analyses and Projections* (Cambridge, Mass.: Harvard University Press, 1970).

4. To the extent that farms do not optimize over the variables we consider, the results will be misleading; if, indeed, many large farms are held as status symbols or inflation-hedging assets, the simulated effects of, say, wage subsidies will be overestimated. But since the base case shows large farms as more efficient than they actually are, the model will underestimate the efficiency gains from structural changes, such as land reform, affecting these farms.

5. See, for example, George F. Patrick, "Efeitos de programas alternativos do governo sobre a agricultura do Nordeste," *Pesquisa e planejamento economico*, no. 1 (February 1974), pp. 43–82.

Table 7-1. *Time Trends in Yields and in Area Harvested,*
Principal Crops, 1961–63 to 1971–73

Crops	1961–63	1964–66	1967–69	1971–73
	Yield (kilograms per hectare)			
Cotton	339	293	292	276
Rice	1,504	1,332	1,360	1,295
Sugar	41,068	42,897	44,441	44,898
Beans	539	495	572	548
Manioc	11,833	12,058	12,528	12,143
Corn	784	743	814	724
	Area harvested (thousands of hectares)			
Cotton	2,268	2,586	2,923	3,187
Rice	553	669	766	878
Sugar	562	566	604	698
Beans	1,022	1,247	1,548	1,638
Manioc	706	788	976	1,036
Corn	1,482	1,743	2,084	2,184

Note: Three-year averages tabulated from IBGE data; 1970, a drought year, is omitted.

The area under long-cycle or tree crops is taken as exogenous to the model, and we assume that the time trends in the areas under these crops obtained from 1973 to 1978 are the same as were estimated by IBGE for 1968–73. Thus, for the 1978 solution the area under coconuts is assumed to have increased by 16.67 percent, that under oranges by 26.35 percent, and that under castor beans by 13.2 percent; and the area under all other long-cycle crops is assumed to be the same as in 1973.

Demographic changes concern the expansion of population and related growth in the labor force and in consumer demand. World Bank estimates place the Northeast's rural population growth rate between 1973 and 1978 at 1.2 percent a year, net of migration, and we assume that the labor supply also grows at this rate. This assumption has little consequence for the structure of the model because no conceivable policy changes would result in a labor shortage within the time period considered. Nevertheless, it is necessary for assessing the extent of unemployment, on the assumption that labor force participation rates do not change. The additional workers are assumed to join the pool of landless labor available for permanent, temporary, and sharecropping employment. The principal effects of population growth in the model are on product demand. Population and income growth and changes in income distribution will raise the demand for different commodities by different factors, depending on the characteristics of the consuming groups and the Engel elasticities assumed. An unpub-

Table 7-2. *Percentage Shifts in Demand for Price-Endogenous Crops, 1973–78*

Crop	Shift
Cotton	21.71
Rice	18.04
Bananas	21.71
Sugar	17.03
Coconuts	21.71
Beans	15.87
Oranges	20.14
Manioc	14.20
Corn	15.49

lished study by the United Nations Food and Agriculture Organization and the Superintendency for Planning, Ministry of Agriculture, projects demand for the principal agricultural products of the Northeast on the basis of the income shares of different consuming groups, and these estimates imply the shifts reported in Table 7-2.

In summary, the changes made to project the model to 1978 are as follows: Product demand functions are shifted rightward, depending on the growth of population and income and Engel elasticities, and are made more elastic; labor availability is increased in line with population growth; the stocks of some long-cycle tree crops are shifted according to changes observed in the previous five-year period.

The 1978 Base Case Solution

Table 7-3 compares key indicators at the sectoral level from the 1978 solution and the 1973 base. Farmers' and workers' incomes and employment rise, but consumers appear to suffer: Over the five years, the increase in total output (14.9 percent) is slightly below that of population (16 percent), and real prices rise by 3.2 percent. The substantial growth in the value of crop output (24.3 percent) is largely confined to the exportable crops, production of which expands by 46.2 percent. Output of food crops grows by only 7.7 percent. This minimal growth in food crop production combined with a decline of 11.5 percent in livestock output implies that the per capita agricultural consumption of Northeasterners would have declined over the five years considered, unless imports from outside the Northeast had increased substantially.

The income gains accruing to farmers are quite skewed. Family farms attain only a 2 percent increase, which is wholly due to the rise in the price

Table 7-3. *Output, Income, and Employment: 1973 and 1978 Base Cases*

Category	1973	1978	Percentage change, 1973/1978
Gross output[a]			
Crops	8,965	11,146	+ 24.3
Livestock	3,180	2,813	− 11.5
Total	12,145	13,959	+ 14.9
Price index[b]	91.4	94.3	+ 3.2
Income[c]			
Family farms	749	764	+ 2.0
Medium-size farms	4,991	5,707	+ 14.4
Estates	1,161	1,287	+ 10.9
Sharecroppers	633	935	+ 47.7
Temporary workers	962	923	− 4.1
Permanent workers	454	776	+ 70.9
Total	8,949	10,392	+ 16.1
Employment[d]			
Farm family	1,138	1,222	+ 7.4
Sharecroppers	421	630	+ 49.6
Hired workers	617	770	+ 24.8
Total	2,175	2,622	+ 20.6
Peak month	3,259	3,386	+ 3.9

Note: The number of farms, and their family workers, remains constant from 1973 to 1978; the number of nonpropertied workers has increased by 6 percent.
a. Thousands of cruzeiros in constant prices.
b. Laspeyres index, 1973 observed price = 100.
c. Money incomes in thousands of cruzeiros, at model-endogenous prices.
d. Thousands of man-years; peak month in thousands of men.

level. Without technological progress, small-scale farmers simply do not have enough land to expand their production to take advantage of expanding product markets. At 14.4 percent, the medium-size farm sector shows the highest growth in incomes. Because this rate closely compares with the growth in total output, the model suggests that this subsector is the most flexible and responsive to expanding markets. Although the estates show an income increase of 10.9 percent, virtually all this growth occurs in the Agreste and East in response to the shift in demand for cotton and sugar. In the other zones, the West, Sertao, and Southeast (cacao region excepted), output, employment, and income on estates grow very little. This is probably because of the inferior and less income-elastic crops grown there, and the general remoteness of the region from expanding markets.

Employment and incomes of nontenured labor improve substantially. Sharecroppers' employment grows by 49.6 percent, although their per capita incomes decline by about 2 percent. The growth in sharecropper employment occurs almost entirely on medium-size farms in the Sertao where the average number of sharecroppers per farm doubles, almost perfectly in accordance with the expansion of cotton production (up 53 percent in the Sertao from the 1973 solution). The 70 percent growth in the employment and incomes of permanent laborers is greater than for any other population group. This growth occurs in all zones but is greatest in the Agreste where it triples. Temporary labor employment decreases slightly.

Overall, the simulated employment situation in 1978 remains poor, however. The number of "fully" employed, nontenured workers (share-croppers and permanent workers) increases by 380,000 over the five-year period, but temporary employment declines and the rural labor force grows by about 350,000. Thus, in spite of substantial emigration from the Northeast and in spite of the model's assumption that farmers optimize, these results suggest that the net increase in employment over the five years would have affected only about 1 percent of the un- and underemployed. A highly important first conclusion is that the employment problem will not be alleviated through time alone.

The 1978 solution of the model reflects a continuing expansion of cultivated area as revealed by the census data for preceding years, but it does not indicate a growing pressure on the availability of land. In the 1973 solution, 9.64 million hectares appear to be underused, of a total of about 79 million hectares of all types of land contained on agricultural properties. In the 1978 base solution, this falls only to 7.08 million hectares. In both solutions, the good and medium-quality lands are underused in roughly equal proportions. Even with the expansion of markets over time, in the 1978 solution 3 million hectares of good cropland are not cropped at all. This permits a second conclusion: Time and the expansion of markets cannot be expected, in the foreseeable future, to induce full utilization of the Northeast's land resources.

Other features of the 1978 solution will be brought out in the comparisons of alternative policy and project options that follow.

Technical Progress: The Effects of Improvements in Crop Yields

The promotion of technical progress—increasing crop yields through better agricultural practices and the use of so-called modern inputs—is a central component of most rural development programs and agricultural development plans. Technical progress on small farms is the principal

Table 7-4. *Technical Progress Experiment*

Category	1978 base case (1)	25 percent increase in crop yields (2)	Percentage change (2)/(1)
Gross output[a]			
Crops	11,146	11,812	+ 6.0
Livestock	2,813	3,080	+ 9.5
Total	13,959	14,892	+ 6.7
Price index[b]	100.0	87.7	− 12.3
Income[c]			
Family farms	764	977	+ 27.9
Other farms	6,994	7,439	+ 6.4
Hired labor	2,634	1,992	− 24.4
Total	10,392	10,407	+ 0.1
Employment[d]			
Farm family	1,222	1,283	+ 5.0
Sharecroppers	630	210	− 66.7
Temporary workers	342	386	+ 12.9
Permanent workers	427	333	− 22.0
Total	2,622	2,211	− 15.7

a. Thousands of cruzeiros in constant prices.
b. Laspeyres index, 1978 base case = 100.
c. Money incomes in thousands of cruzeiros at model-endogenous prices.
d. Thousands of man-years.

objective of a newly formed government agency, the Brazilian Agricultural Research Company (EMBRAPA), and is a key component of the World Bank's numerous state-level rural development programs in the Northeast. Because the model is based entirely on observed technological practices, it cannot address the question of how to improve yields as such: The survey simply did not reveal enough instances of advanced cultivation practices or of use of modern inputs to model such technologies. Nonetheless, the model can indicate the effects of increasing yields even if not the mechanisms and costs of doing so.

This experiment assumes that the yields of all crops rise by 25 percent over the five-year period or by 4–5 percent a year, a rate at the lower end of the range (4–7 percent a year) specified by a recent agricultural research program in Brazil financed in part by the World Bank. The results are shown in Table 7-4. Consumers clearly benefit, as the gross output of crops and livestock products rises by 6.7 percent and the overall price index falls by 12.3 percent. Crop output increases by only 6 percent, which implies that market restrictions may severely limit the benefits of technical progress. The 9.5 percent rise in livestock production is surprising; though one might have expected some of the land under pasture to be brought into use for crops, technical progress appears in fact to release land from crops for the expansion of livestock activities. That technical progress is land-augmenting is attested by a significant increase of 2.24 million hectares in underutilized land, mostly on estates.[6]

The simulation also reveals that, on balance, technical progress is labor-augmenting as well. Overall labor use declines by 15.7 percent; use of farm family labor rises by 5 percent, but there is a 66.7 percent drop in sharecropper employment and a 22 percent drop in permanent labor employment. Declines in sharecropping have occurred in most regions of the world where there have been significant advances in agricultural technology (either yield improvements or mechanization that is directly labor-augmenting). The fall in permanent labor employment of 22 percent simply reflects the labor-saving nature of the technical progress we have simulated and is perhaps by coincidence almost as large as the percentage increase in yields.

If it is assumed that yields improve equally on all farms, the income gains are greater for small farms: In the simulation, family farms realize income gains of 27.9 percent, whereas the medium-size farms realize a 5.2 percent gain and the large farms, 3.5 percent.

In sum, the simulation suggests that technical progress produces substantial gains in consumers' welfare and in small farmers' incomes but that on large farms land is used less intensively, fewer sharecroppers and permanent workers are contracted, and only moderate income gains are realized. If all disadvantaged groups are to benefit from technical progress, then other means of protecting the employment of nontenured labor or of inducing large farms to increase output and employment must be taken into account.

The Influence of Risk

It has long been conjectured that risk is an important factor limiting the volume of crop production and the adoption of new varieties and tech-

6. The 1978 base solution recorded 7.08 million hectares of underutilized land, down from the 9.64 million hectares of the 1973 base. The introduction of technical progress, which brings the amount back to 9.32 million hectares, virtually eliminates this gain in land-use intensity.

niques. The periodic droughts, some of which have been catastrophic, are the most vivid reminders of the effects of unpredictable and untimely rainfall in the Northeast, and they undoubtedly induce safety-first, subsistence-ensuring behavior on the part of many farmers of small plots in much of the Northeastern interior. The riskiness of crop production elicits the following tendencies: The more risky the crop, that is, the higher the coefficient of variation in a time series of revenues per hectare, the less important the crop will be in the farm plan; other things being equal, two (or more) crops whose output has typically deviated from the norm in opposite directions will be likely to appear in the same farm plan and jointly to form an important part of it; and the more risky the environment for most or all crops, the less intensely will most or all resources be employed.

The first of these tendencies is easy to understand. The second is common in the Northeast in the form of consortiated planting, particularly on small farms. Corn and beans require timely and sufficient rainfall, for example, whereas some varieties of cotton can still produce an acceptable yield in arid years; hence, this combination is one of the most prevalent in the interior of the Northeast. The third tendency, toward a less intense use of resources, can be explained if one considers risk as a form of costs. The Hazell–Scandizzo formulation, in which these costs are made explicit as a penalty on more risky farm plans, yields a supply function higher than might otherwise be supposed and an equilibrium with lower output and higher prices.[7]

It is possible to quantify the influence of risk on farm plans, aggregate output, and resource use by setting the risk penalties in the model to zero. The implication is that farmers will consider only the expected values of revenue per hectare and will ignore their experience of deviations from normal yields and the correlations among deviations. Short of a fully guaranteed income based on the farm plan, there are no readily definable interventions that could induce such behavior, though price supports would presumably assist. The results of the simulation should thus be viewed as the maximum potential gains from risk-reduction policies in general.

These gains are unremarkable. Aggregate crop output, livestock output, and employment all change by 1 percent or less. Some medium-quality

---

7. It is doubtful, however, that farmers' aversion to risk accounts for more than a small part of the underutilization of resources in the Northeast. The smallest farms, which are theoretically and observedly the most risk-averse, use their land and labor resources very intensively, whereas the bulk of the underutilized land is on the estates, many of which are large and wealthy enough virtually to ignore risk considerations.

land (about 4 percent) was transferred from pasture to crops, a shift that very slightly raised crop output and employment at the expense of livestock production. Possible reasons for this lack of response include the low price elasticities of demand, which restrain increases in food crop production under most supply-augmenting experiments with the model, and the insensitivity to risk of production on estates. A more important reason, however, appears to be that the evolution of crop varieties and cropping methods has gone so far in reducing the effects of risk that the behavioral aspects of farming have little remaining scope for improvement.

These results should not be taken to mean that risk in general can be ignored in the Northeast. Even if catastrophic droughts are ignored, year-to-year variations in yields owing to the vagaries of the weather do cause substantial fluctuations in income, which can be devastating for small-scale farmers. Changes in cropping patterns and resource use will not reduce these fluctuations sufficiently. Short of a complete income guarantee program, the best hope for reducing the risks faced by small-scale farmers lies in the identification of varieties and crops less susceptible to insufficient rainfall, combined with provision of sufficient land to cushion the effects of poor years.

Employment Policies

Severe agricultural underemployment coexists with extensive underuse of land. Before examining the role of demand we investigate whether labor policies could significantly reduce the employment problem. If land on large farms is underused because labor is too expensive relative to the marginal returns from cropping and livestock activities, then making labor cheaper should promote employment and output growth. Labor policies in the Northeast cannot be considered without addressing sharecropping, so this section also examines the implications of abolishing share contracts.

We first consider subsidies on the wages of permanent laborers who, apart from sharecroppers, appear to be the only nontenured workers with a chance of earning a reasonable income. Temporary workers are not considered because subsidies on their wages, which are paid on a daily or monthly basis, would be extremely difficult to administer. Table 7-5 shows the results of subsidizing permanent laborers' wages by 10 percent and 20 percent. Even under the 20 percent subsidy, crop output is virtually unchanged, and gross output rises less than 2 percent. Livestock output rises by about 9 percent—a result that reflects the relationships in the model; the workers employed for livestock maintenance typically have

Table 7-5. Alternative Employment Policies

Category	1978 base case (1)	10 percent wage subsidy (2)	Percentage change (2)/(1)	20 percent wage subsidy (3)	Percentage change (3)/(1)	No share-cropping (4)	Percentage change (4)/(1)	No share-cropping, 20 percent wage subsidy (5)	Percentage change (5)/(1)
Gross output[a]									
Crops	11,146	11,158	+0.1	11,165	+0.2	10,145	-9.0	10,660	-4.4
Livestock	2,813	2,919	+3.8	3,059	+8.8	3,018	+7.3	3,194	+13.5
Total	13,959	14,078	+0.9	14,224	+1.9	13,163	-5.7	13,854	-0.8
Output index[b]	100.0	100.9		101.9		94.3		99.2	
Price index[b]	100.0	99.7		96.9		104.6		97.1	
Income[c]									
Family farms	764	754	-1.3	748	-2.1	831	+8.8	802	+5.0
Other farms	6,994	7,011	+0.2	7,006	+0.1	6,803	-2.7	6,890	-1.5
Hired labor	2,634	2,786	+5.8	2,935	+11.4	2,189	-16.9	2,849	+8.2
Total	10,392	10,551	+1.5	10,689	+2.9	9,823	-5.5	10,542	+1.4
Cost of wage subsidy	0	243		271		0		461	

Employment[d]								
Farm family	1,222	1,161	−5.0	1,133	−7.3	1,289	+5.5	1,119	−8.4
Sharecroppers	630	629	−0.1	604	−4.1	—	−100.0	—	−100.0
Temporary workers	342	330	−3.5	360	+5.3	411	+20.2	380	+11.1
Permanent workers	427	542	+26.9	609	+42.6	640	+49.9	1,107	+159.3
Total nontenured workers	1,399	1,501	+7.3	1,573	+12.4	1,051	−24.9	1,487	+6.3
Total	2,622	2,661	+1.5	2,706	+3.2	2,340	−10.8	2,606	−0.5
Employment index	100.0	101.5		103.2		89.2		99.4	
Average number of full-time workers on estates								
West	8.13	8.35		8.52		8.13		8.52	
Sertao	12.94	13.06		12.82		10.93		12.47	
Southeast	0.83	0.80		0.80		0.83		0.80	
East	20.53	20.53		20.57		20.53		20.57	
Agreste	27.72	27.62		27.24		27.72		27.24	

— Not applicable.
a. Thousands of cruzeiros in constant prices.
b. Laspeyres index, 1978 base case = 100.
c. Money incomes in thousands of cruzeiros at model-endogenous prices.
d. Thousands of man-years.

permanent contracts, there being little seasonal variation in labor demand for this activity. Sector income also shows little change, rising by 1.5 and 2.9 percent under the respective subsidy rates of 10 and 20 percent.

The distributional effects of the wage subsidies are substantial. Permanent workers' employment and incomes rise by 26.9 and 42.6 percent under the 10 and 20 percent subsidies, and consumers gain somewhat because of the increase in output, which reduces the price index by 3 percent in the 20 percent subsidy case. Farmers' income as a whole is virtually unchanged. That of family farms declines slightly because they, not using hired permanent labor, are not much affected by the subsidy yet receive slightly lower prices.

The overall effects on the agricultural sector, although disappointing, show that wage subsidies probably have a positive cost/benefit ratio. Although the administrative costs cannot be estimated, the gains in sector income alone roughly offset the direct cost of the subsidies, leaving the gains in consumers' welfare as net benefits. The lower part of Table 7-5 shows nonetheless that wage subsidies cannot be relied upon to improve the performance of estates. Permanent employment increases slightly on estates in the West and the Sertao; in the other zones it remains the same or declines. On fazendas in the Sertao, where sharecropping predominates, there are no net additions to employment; about three sharecroppers per fazenda simply have their share contracts transformed into permanent worker contracts. Although wage subsidies reduce the marginal costs of production on larger farms, the effect on output from family and medium-size farms induces price declines that are large enough to continue to equate the marginal value product of labor with (subsidized) wage rates at about the same level of employment as before. Hence, wage subsidies alone will not significantly affect performance and employment in the region.

The treatment of sharecropping in the model, described in Chapter 5, depends on the agreement of landowners and sharecroppers on existing farm plans, which are considered to be Pareto-optimal. It is not possible to simulate enforced changes to share contracts, but it is possible to simulate the abolition of these contracts. The changes that follow from so doing, reported in Table 7-5, take place almost exclusively in the Sertao, the main sharecropping zone. Crop output in the Northeast as a whole falls by 9 percent; crop output in the Sertao falls by 20 percent. Livestock replaces sharecroppers; average livestock output and herd size increase by 15 percent in the Sertao and by 7.3 percent in the Northeast as a whole. Prices rise by 4.6 percent, making consumers worse off and family farmers marginally better off. About 22,000 fully employed workers in the Sertao would lose their jobs if sharecropping were abolished. In the base case, fazendas in the

Sertao employ an average of 12.28 sharecroppers and 0.66 permanent workers; when sharecropping is abolished they replace them with an average of only 10.93 permanent workers.

The far-right column of Table 7-5 reports a simulation combining the abolition of share contracts with the 20 percent subsidy on permanent laborers' wages. Permanent workers replace almost all the sharecroppers, which results in much the same aggregate output, income, and employment levels. The only significant change from the base case is the substitution of livestock for crops, mainly in the Sertao. These results reinforce the conclusion that intervention in share-tenancy arrangements would have no perceptible benefits. They also indicate that consumers' and hired laborers' welfare would almost certainly decline as a consequence.

The Promotion of Demand

Analysis of the base case solution suggested the hypothesis that the Northeast is a demand-constrained economy. The model can be used to give a broad idea of the effects on the sector at large of increases in demand for the principal crops consumed in the Northeast and of the distribution of gains that would result. Before undertaking such experiments, however, we must clarify what we mean by a demand constraint: It is easy—and naive—to recommend that a depressed economic region find unrestricted outlets for its products at higher prices.

Interpretations of a Demand Constraint

To review the analytics of the maximization procedure used, see Chapter 5, which describes how the model maximizes the sum of consumers' and producers' surpluses, such that the equilibrium price is equal to the marginal cost of production (Figure 5-1). First, it is clear from Figure 5-1 that the economy would be better off either from a rightward (upward) shift in the demand schedule or from a rightward (downward) shift in the supply schedule. On the face of it, there is no reason to assume that either a demand constraint or a supply constraint is operating to prevent this. Second, the magnitude of the demand elasticity assumed, which fixes the slope of the demand schedule about the point P^0Q^0, has no relevance to producers' welfare in this static case: Variations in the elasticity will not alter the measure of producers' surplus defined as the area below the P^0 price line and above the supply curve. Third, where the supply schedule represents an aggregation of different producers, the maximand acts as an allocation

Figure 7-1. Supply Schedules for Price-Endogenous Crops
of Different Classes of Farms: Model Structure

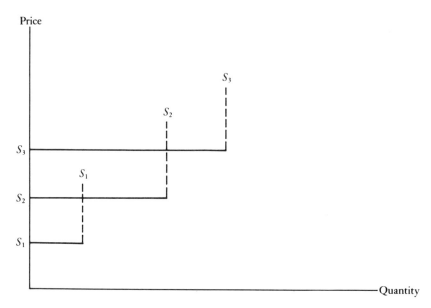

device. The most "efficient" producers—those with the lowest average
costs, including shadow costs of resources—supply the early portions of the
aggregate demand schedule until their capacity is exhausted, and they are
followed by the next most efficient producers, serially, until the surplus is
exhausted and prices are equated to marginal costs. (It is important to note
that this use of the term "efficiency" need have nothing to do with traditional optimality conditions; differences in their supply schedules may
simply reflect differences in producers' resource endowments and in their
access to input markets.)

Figures 7-1 and 7-2 show stylized representations of the Northeastern
supply schedule for the price-flexible crops. In the first of these, S_1S_1 is the
supply schedule of family farms; S_2S_2 that of medium-size farms; and S_3S_3
that of the estates. S_1S_1 has a low price intercept, because the family farms
rely largely or totally on "cheap" family labor, and a very short run on the
quantity axis until land is exhausted, at which point the supply schedule
becomes vertical. S_2S_2 has a somewhat higher price intercept, because
family labor must be supplemented by more expensive hired labor, and it
also has a longer run on the quantity axis before land is fully used. S_3S_3 has

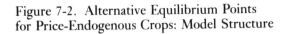

Figure 7-2. Alternative Equilibrium Points
for Price-Endogenous Crops: Model Structure

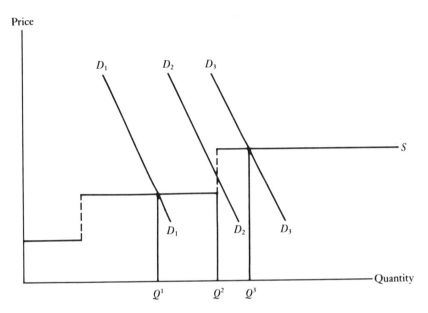

the highest price intercept, because the estates have the highest expenditures on hired labor, and a much longer run on the quantity axis, given their abundance of land. These three supply schedules are aggregated in Figure 7-2. A less simplistic view would result in a rising schedule that was smoother but still discontinuous in places because of the blending of different sources and types of labor contracts, different qualities of land, and so forth.

Also shown in Figure 7-2 are three demand schedules. If D_1D_1 applies, the static equilibrium quantity will be Q^1. This quantity is supplied by small farms up to the limit of their land, and the remainder by medium-size farms. The position of D_1D_1 in relation to the quantity axis results in a static equilibrium price too low to induce the medium-size farms to use all their land, and at which it is not profitable for the estates to produce these crops at all. If D_2D_2 applies, the equilibrium quantity will be Q^2, which occurs at the discontinuous point where the resources of medium-size farms are fully utilized but the resultant price is still too low to bring the estates into food crop production. D_3D_3 appears to typify the Northeast equilibrium for many crops: The resultant price is just high enough to bring some, but not all, of the large farms' land into crop production. A demand constraint, in the static sense considered so far, thus refers to a position of the demand curve in relation to the quantity axis at a point that yields a price too low to induce full utilization of the land and labor resources available.

Before we discuss demand constraints in a less restrictive framework, it is worthwhile to compare the effects of price supports with those of demand shifts in the static framework. If D_1D_1 or D_3D_3 in Figure 7-2 applies, very small supported price increases will cause fairly large increases in supply (with risk and other factors that might be constraining ignored). If D_2D_2 applies, however, even a quite substantial supported increase in price may have no effect at all on the quantity supplied; it could indeed be equivalent to an income subsidy to those farmers currently producing the crops in question (with the usually substantial costs of administration, product collection, and disposition ignored). A shift in demand, by contrast, will almost always raise the quantity supplied,[8] and thus the intensity with which resources are used, but will not necessarily raise price.

When the model is solved for different points in time, the price elasticities assume critical importance. Most agricultural projects are designed to increase production of agricultural commodities, and the elasticities of demand have a direct bearing not only on the gains to the economy as a whole but also on the gains to the producers concerned. The relevance of price elasticities can readily be seen from Figure 7-3, which portrays a supply-augmenting intervention in the face of three demand functions, differentiated solely by their elasticity (slope).

In this figure, S_0S_0 represents the prevailing supply curve of all producers combined,[9] and S_1S_1 applies after the intervention, once all responses by producers have been worked through to a new static equilibrium. The three demand curves all correspond to the same equilibrium price and quantity conditions in the static case, represented by the point P^0Q^0.

Depending upon which demand curve is applicable, the effects of augmenting supply will differ dramatically. If the demand for the product is highly inelastic (D_1D_1), the intervention reduces prices substantially but

8. The exception is a small range on the quantity axis around Q^2. Although it is accepted procedure to value incremental outputs at border prices (which implies infinite elasticity of demand), it must be realized that this theoretically attractive approach is of little relevance for the price-flexible crops considered here, which for a variety of reasons noted earlier are almost entirely consumed within the Northeast.

9. The reader may wish to examine the results of this analysis under alternative supply functions, such as those shown in Figure 7-2, and under alternative supply-oriented interventions, such as one that affects only output at the margin and does not affect the supply curve intercept, unlike the case illustrated in Figure 7-3.

Figure 7-3. Effects of Augmenting Supply
under Alternative Elasticities of Demand: Model Structure

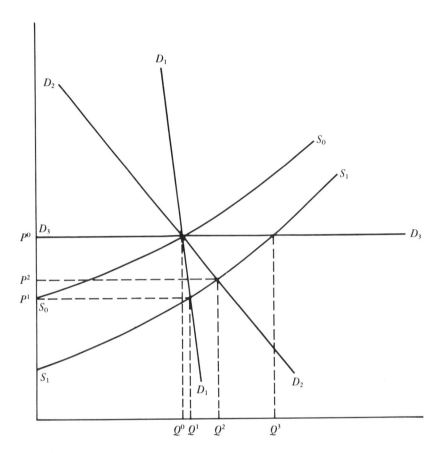

increases the quantity supplied only slightly. This may be a desirable
developmental strategy (at the extreme, it corresponds to taxation of farmers and subsidization of consumers), but it is not appropriate where the
overriding considerations are to stimulate the use of resources and raise
production and producers' incomes. If the intermediate, relatively elastic
curve D_2D_2 applies, the intervention results in both moderate production
increases and declines in price. Depending on the *shape* of the supply
curves, producers may or may not be better off. As they are drawn,
producers' surplus is about the same both before and after the intervention.
If demand is perfectly elastic as depicted by D_3D_3, all of the gains consid-

ered accrue to the producers (the increase in producers' surplus is greatest), and the gains in production (and, other things being equal, in resource utilization) are the highest.

These relations have no direct implications for policy, not only because it is difficult to influence demand elasticities through policy measures but because interpersonal utility comparisons between producers and consumers are required. Even in the case of an export crop, represented by the perfectly elastic curve D_3D_3, the gains from increasing supply may accrue largely to the wealthier farmers, who are the main producers of the crop, whereas small-scale farmers, lacking access to the investment capital needed to establish stocks and arrange marketing, are relegated to the production of locally consumed food crops, demand for which is represented by D_1D_1.

To sum up, when the effects of interventions to increase supply are being evaluated in a comparative-static framework, a demand constraint means that price elasticities of demand are so low as to restrain the response of production, and price declines are large enough to negate expected increases in producers' incomes.

The final meaning of a demand constraint that we wish to consider is only partly relevant to the time frame of this study but could be extremely important over the longer run. This concerns the role of income elasticities. In projecting the model to a 1978 base, the position of the demand curves was shifted rightward on the basis of population growth, income trends, and income elasticities. If higher income elasticities had been assumed, the production increases and the gains in producers' incomes over the projection period would have been larger. Although this effect is probably of only slight importance in a relatively short planning period, it is of substantial importance in the long run. As population and incomes grow, the resultant demand "pull" will have a direct bearing on how resources are employed to meet those demands and on the welfare of the producers employing those resources. Again, it is not a policy option to alter income elasticities, but interventions affecting production possibilities must be made in awareness of the longer-term demand for the products produced or producible in the region.

Demand Interventions

With this background we now turn to two experiments for the promotion of demand for the price-flexible crops: rice, beans, corn, manioc, sugar, and cotton, which together account for about two-thirds of the gross value of crop production in the Northeast. The first involves guaranteeing or sup-

Figure 7-4. Effects of Augmenting Demand: Model Structure

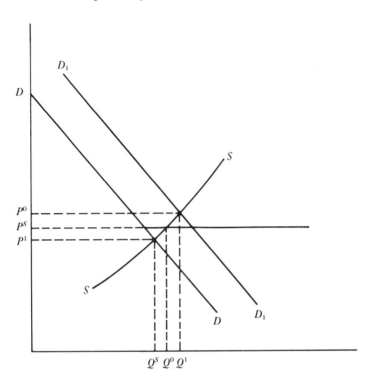

porting the prices of these crops at their observed levels of the base period (1973). In Figure 7-4, this is represented by making the demand curve perfectly elastic at the observed price P^0. The simulated price in the base solution, P^s, is slightly lower than P^0 as was noted in Chapter 6; making demand perfectly elastic at P^0 should simultaneously raise both output and prices above the levels simulated in the base case. This experiment is reported in column (2) of Table 7-6. The directions of the resulting changes are as predicted, but the magnitudes are disappointing; crop output and employment grow by only 1.4 percent. In most zones, only beans and manioc are affected; output of both types of beans rises by 9.3 percent, and that of manioc by 7.8 percent. These increases are, however, sufficient to induce a 5.2 percent increase in the overall price level, which accounts for most of the increase in farmers' incomes: 17.3 percent for small-scale farmers and 12.5 percent for others (mostly medium-scale farmers).

Whether such a price guarantee program would be desirable depends upon how one values increases in farmers' income as opposed to consumers'

Table 7-6. *Results of Promoting Demand*

Category	1978 base case (1)	Guaranteed prices for food crops (2)	Per- centage change (2)/(1)	25 percent demand shift (3)	Per- centage change (3)/(1)
Gross output[a]					
Crops	11,146	11,301	+ 1.4	12,466	+11.8
Livestock	2,813	2,785	− 1.0	2,566	− 8.8
Total	13,959	14,086	+ 0.9	15,032	+ 7.7
Output index	100.0	100.9		107.7	
Price index[b]	100.0	105.2		111.2	
Income[c]					
Family farms	764	896	+17.3	849	+11.1
Other farms	6,994	7,871	+12.5	7,801	+11.5
Hired labor	2,634	2,678	+ 1.7	3,057	+16.1
Total	10,392	11,444	+10.1	11,706	+12.6
Employment[d]					
Farm family	1,222	1,239	+ 1.4	1,292	+ 5.7
Sharecroppers	630	642	+ 1.9	615	− 2.4
Temporary workers	342	342	0.0	345	+ 0.1
Permanent workers	427	437	+ 2.3	600	+40.5
Total	2,622	2,659	+ 1.4	2,853	+ 8.8
Peak month	3,178	3,382	+ 6.4	3,457	+ 8.8
Employment index	100.0	101.4		108.8	

a. Thousands of cruzeiros at constant prices.
b. Laspeyres index, 1978 base case = 100.
c. Money incomes in thousands of cruzeiros at model-endogenous prices.
d. Thousands of man-years, except peak month, which is thousands of men.

welfare. The costs of such a program in the Northeast would undoubtedly be prohibitive, however; effective price stabilization requires control of sizable storage stocks and a substantial administrative structure, neither of which exists in the Northeast or indeed in most developing countries.[10] Furthermore, the resources required to establish these prerequisites would very probably yield a much higher return if used for other programs in the Northeast. For these same reasons, we shall not investigate direct measures to raise prices.

The other demand promotion experiment considered is the more round-about one of inducing shifts in the demand functions; this is also illustrated

10. John W. Mellor, *The Economics of Agricultural Development* (Ithaca, N.Y.: Cornell University Press, 1966), pp. 208–09.

in Figure 7-4. The demand curve shifts from DD to D_1D_1, inducing a supply response to Q^1 and raising the price level to P^1. Such a shift, which we take as exogenous, could be caused by various interventions, such as nutrition programs, urban incomes policies, and even those agricultural policies designed to raise the employment and incomes of hired laborers. The results of this experiment, in which all of the price-endogenous demand functions are shifted rightward by 25 percent, are reported in column (3) of Table 7-6. Total crop output rises by 22 percent, on the average, implying quite high supply elasticities. The supply of the affected crops, however, increases partly at the expense of livestock production, which falls by 8.8 percent. Overall land use is much more intense; underutilized land falls from 9.64 to 4.81 million hectares.

The effects on crop output realized through this shift in demand are much larger than those achieved with the price guarantee experiment. The two instruments are not comparable means of augmenting output, however, because they have very different effects on prices: The crop price index rises by 0.9 percent under the price guarantees but by 8.8 percent under the demand shift. Nevertheless, the results of the demand shift experiment do suggest the magnitude of the changes in demand and prices that would be needed for significant gains in output and welfare.

As regards the distribution of those gains, it is not possible strictly to compare consumers' welfare before and after the shift. The increase in crop production implies greater consumption, but overall prices rise by 11.2 percent. The major beneficiaries of demand promotion are farmers and permanent workers. Of these groups, the land-constrained family farmers gain the least, 11.1 percent, entirely because of increases in price, not output. Sharecroppers and temporary workers are little affected, but permanent workers' employment rises by more than 40 percent.

The effects of the simulated shifts in demand strongly support the hypothesis that the agricultural economy of the Northeast is constrained by demand. Better outlets for Northeastern production would mean substantial gains in farm incomes and wage employment, although how outlets can be improved is another question.

Development Strategies in the Absence of Agrarian Reform

The model results thus far suggest that at least in the medium term the Northeast problem will not take care of itself; intervention is required. Before addressing the question of land reform, we simulate alternative

Table 7-7. *Alternative Development Strategies in the Absence of Agrarian Reform*

	Solution						
Category	1978 base case (1)	(2)	(3)	(4)	(5)	(6)	(7)
Instrument[a]							
Technical progress		X			X		X
25 percent demand shift			X		X	X	X
20 percent wage subsidy				X		X	X
Gross output[b]							
Crops	11,146	1,812	12,466	11,165	13,727	12,668	13,631
Livestock	2,813	3,080	2,566	3,059	2,806	2,736	3,103
Total	13,959	4,892	15,032	4,224	16,533	15,404	16,733
Output index	100.0	106.7	107.7	101.9	118.4	110.4	119.9
Price index[c]	100.0	87.7	111.2	96.9	92.5	104.9	87.3
Income[d]							
Family farms	764	977	849	748	1,001	809	974
Other farms	6,994	7,439	7,801	7,006	8,267	7,759	8,118
Hired labor	2,634	1,992	3,057	2,935	2,613	3,455	3,005
Total	10,392	10,407	11,706	10,689	1,880	12,023	12,097
Employment[e]							
Farm family	1,222	1,283	1,292	1,133	1,288	1,164	1,105
Sharecroppers	630	210	615	604	422	530	175
Temporary workers	342	386	345	360	377	341	374
Permanent workers	427	333	600	609	485	954	1,012
Total	2,622	2,211	2,853	2,706	2,573	2,989	2,667
Peak month	3,178	3,281	3,457	3,675	3,950	3,802	3,957
Employment index	100.0	84.3	108.8	103.2	98.1	114.0	101.7

a. As defined in the text.
b. Thousands of cruzeiros at constant prices.
c. Laspeyres index, 1978 base case = 100.
d. Money incomes in thousands of cruzeiros at model-exogenous prices.
e. Thousands of man-years, except peak month, which is thousands of men.

packages of the development measures so far considered to examine whether, under the existing agrarian structure, they could induce substantial growth in production, employment, and the incomes of the poor.

The simulations reported in Table 7-7 show the results of different combinations of technical progress (that is, a 25 percent increase in crop yields), a 25 percent rise in demand, and a 20 percent subsidy on the wages of permanent labor.[11] The 1978 base case and the results of the interventions simulated individually are repeated for reference. The results of the packages are difficult to evaluate without a social welfare function and, indeed, without an account of the costs involved. If, for example, the employment and incomes of nontenured workers are the main concern, then solution (6), combining demand shifts and wage subsidies, is the best set of instruments. If Northeastern consumers are the principal target group, then solution (2), involving only technical progress, is the best strategy. For family farmers, solution (5), combining technical progress and demand shifts, results in the highest levels of income (up 31 percent from the base solution).

When all three instruments are combined, all the agents—consumers, farmers of all types, and nontenured workers—are better off than in the base case. Output in solution (7) is nearly 20 percent higher, prices are about 13 percent lower, and farm incomes rise by between 10 and 20 percent. Nonpropertied labor income increases by 14 percent, and about 800,000 more jobs are created in the peak month. Though these benefits are substantial, they are quite inadequate in the face of the employment problem: Overall labor use increases by less than 2 percent, and about 2 million people are still left unemployed even in the peak month.

A package of measures such as solution (7) cannot be recommended without examining the performance of the estates before and after its introduction. Given their control of about half the agricultural land and their much less intense use of land and labor than that of family and medium-size farms, it is safe to conclude that a developmental strategy can be successful only if this sector responds dramatically to the interventions or is otherwise restructured. Table 7-8 reports the gross production and labor use on estates in each zone in the 1978 base case and in solution (7), in which all three instruments are applied. Except for the fazendas in the Sertao, the results are not encouraging: Estates in the Northeast as a whole increase production by an average of 14 percent (compared with 20 percent for the region if all types of farms are included) and labor use by about 9 percent (above the regionwide average but far short of what is needed). The vastly improved performance of the fazendas in the Sertao reflects changes in the profitability of cotton, the predominant crop and one of the most

---

11. It should again be stressed that the model is not a suitable tool for investigating other potentially powerful instruments such as agricultural credit, irrigation, marketing improvements, and additions to on-farm capital in the form of structures, equipment, storage facilities, or long-cycle crops.

Table 7-8. *Responses of the Estate Subsector to Policy Interventions*

Category	1978 base case (1)	Technical progress, demand shifts, and 20 percent wage subsidy (2)	Percentage change (2)/(1)
Production[a]			
West	40,010	45,606	+ 14.0
Sertao	39,502	67,106	+ 69.9
Southeast	65,334	65,317	− 0.1
East	243,993	267,900	+ 9.8
Agreste	108,875	125,231	+ 15.0
Northeast average			14.0
Employment[b]			
West	11.62	12.67	+ 9.0
Sertao	13.43	15.74	+ 17.2
Southeast	14.75	14.71	− 0.3
East	35.05	36.65	+ 4.5
Agreste	33.49	36.48	+ 8.9
Northeast average			9.0
Net full employment increase[c]			
West		7,430	
Sertao		17,168	
Southeast		191	
East		1,734	
Agreste		7,339	
Northeast total		33,480	

a. Cruzeiros per farm.
b. Man-years labor use per farm.
c. Aggregate increase in number of permanent workers plus sharecroppers for all estates in the zone.

labor-intensive grown in the Northeast. Both the yield of cotton and the demand for it increase by 25 percent, and labor is subsidized.

Table 7-8 shows that the number of those fully employed (permanent workers and sharecroppers) on estates in the Northeast grows by only 33,480—an average increase of less than one worker per estate, which is insignificant compared with the aggregate employment problem. Whether the managers of estates optimize in practice appears doubtful. Even if they did so, however, and even with the substantial policy interventions considered, these simulations reveal that the estates cannot be relied upon to solve the employment problem.

8

The Land Reform Alternative

Land reform in the Northeast has been studied intensely, debated widely, legislated strongly, funded sufficiently, and all but abandoned. We did not set out to address the land reform issue in this study, and indeed we do so reluctantly. Agrarian reform has had mixed results in various parts of Latin America and the issue has had a stormy history in Brazil. A reform on the scale suggested by the sheer dimensions of the Northeast problem would undoubtedly tax the administrative capacity of the agencies involved, and disruption costs would be large, though difficult to measure.

Nevertheless, the analysis has indicated that the land reform issue cannot be dismissed. Land and labor markets have failed to compensate for unequal distributions of resources. Land rental markets are not operating—only 3 percent of the agricultural land is under rental contract, when vast differences in the shadow values of land indicate that this market should be vigorous. Estates, in particular, employ labor far below optimal levels in the face of widespread underemployment. Sharecropping, a contractual relation used throughout the world to alleviate land and labor distortions in a manner that satisfies both parties, is common only in the cotton-producing interior of the Northeast and is largely rejected by landowners in all other regions. Given the unequal distribution of assets in the Northeast, such market failures are severely impeding agricultural development. The changes in employment and income that could be wrought by the traditional policy instruments so far considered are wholly inadequate to meet the problem. Structural interventions to reduce the distortions in land and labor markets may in fact be a prerequisite for agricultural development in the Northeast.

The model's representation of farms of different types and sizes and its incorporation of aggregate constraints on demand make it possible to estimate both the aggregate and the distributional effects of agrarian reform. Though it cannot directly address questions of costs or trace the dynamics of adjustment over time, the model gives more realistic results than could be obtained, for example, by extrapolating microeconomic studies. Before the model's simulation of land reform is presented, it is necessary to review the legislative experience and briefly describe the official plans that have been put forward.

Legislative History

The current Brazilian land reform law, the Estatuto da Terra (Law no. 4504), was introduced in November 1964 and is an elaborate extension of Article 146 of the 1946 Federal Constitution, which enables the president of the republic to decree land reform measures.[1] Among its stated goals is to develop and strengthen efficiency and equity in the agricultural sector. Its features include: commitment to private enterprise; recognition of a need for government intervention; creation of instruments to implement agricultural change on privately held properties; establishment of performance norms for such properties; isolation for remedial action of regions in which a large proportion of the properties fail to meet these norms; planning and implementation of agricultural colonies to absorb the potential surplus population; creation of agencies to administer the above programs; and establishment of a land inventory. The statute's aims are to be achieved through progressive land taxation and curtailment of the right to private property.

All farms are to be taxed, depending on their size, location, production relationships, and social conditions, so that large and inefficient farms are taxed progressively. The highest potential tax rate, however, is only 3.45 percent of a property's unimproved land value, and the lowest is 0.02 percent. Ludwig and Taylor recognize that this range is "probably too low to evoke a response from affected land holders."[2]

The statute recognizes four types of holding, which are defined in terms of *modulos rurais* (land reform modules), a concept of fundamental importance. A module is a unit of land capable of providing the equivalent of four minimum annual salaries or requiring the labor of four working adults and of supporting them at a standard of living consistent with overall goals of

---

1. The section "Legislative History" was originally written by Maria Helena de Castro Silva. The principal source in English is Armin K. Ludwig and Harry W. Taylor, *Brazil's New Agrarian Reform* (New York: Praeger, 1969). A more recent study focusing on the political aspects of the topic is Marta Cehelsky, *Land Reform in Brazil: The Management of Social Change* (Boulder, Col.: Westview Press, 1979).

2. Ludwig and Taylor, *Brazil's New Agrarian Reform*, p. 81.

economic and social progress. The types of holding are: *minifundia*, of less than one module; "*latifundia* by size," that is, greater than 600 modules;[3] "latifundia by use," according to the degree of inefficiency with which the land is used and ranging between 1 and 600 modules; and *empresas rurais*, or rural enterprises, which may also be between 1 to 600 modules and which are distinguished on performance criteria. Holdings of the first three types lie under threat of expropriation or abrogation of the right of free disposal.

Land that is expropriated is to be redistributed into modules and given preferentially to landless workers. Recipients need only be twenty-one years of age or over, sane, and of good background or demonstrating the potential for rehabilitation. Recipients are eligible to borrow an amount up to one minimum annual salary for infrastructure investment and initial working capital at a 6 percent rate of interest (presumably nominal and thus highly negative) for up to twenty years. The statute authorizes funds with which to compensate landowners and delineates priority areas for reform, which in the zonal delineation used in this study are in the Sertao and the East.

The agencies initially established under the statute were 'absorbed into INCRA (National Institute of Colonization and Agrarian Reform) in 1970; since then this agency has been largely responsible for implementing the land reform law. By its third year, INCRA had a budget of US$100 million and 7,000 employees. Cline has documented a series of ill-fated or half-hearted attempts by INCRA to establish family farms (only 563 of 8,000 target families were resettled in 1973, mostly in colonized Amazonian areas).[4] INCRA has, however, completed two of the prerequisites of a land reform: a comprehensive cadastral survey, which is periodically updated,[5] and detailed specifications of land reform modules.

The Land Reform Module

As defined by INCRA, the module farm should be of sufficient size and capital endowment to fully employ four adults and yield each of them a net annual income equal to the minimum wage,[6] plus a return of 15 percent on

---

3. In most areas of the Northeast, this criterion implies a farm larger than 20,000 hectares.

4. William R. Cline, *Economic Consequences of a Land Reform in Brazil* (Amsterdam: North-Holland Publishing Company, 1970).

5. The INCRA cadastral survey of 1972 provided the basic information on landholdings used for the SUDENE/World Bank survey (see Appendix B to this volume).

6. About US$450 in 1974.

the capital invested in it.[7] The SUDENE/World Bank survey shows that in most of the Northeast existing farms need to be around 150 hectares before they can fully employ four adult workers, whereas the average productivity per fully employed worker is only around US$400 annually. Nevertheless, INCRA applied the module definition in great detail to each of the 1,365 municipios in the Northeast, taking account of population density in the locale (as a proxy for access to markets), existing patterns of land use and production, soil quality and other ecological conditions, and overall potential productivity. The module farm sizes that resulted from that exercise range from less than five hectares (sometimes as small as two) in the coastal areas near large urban markets, to more than 100 hectares in areas of the sparsely populated West where stock raising is the main activity.

Potential for Redistribution of the Estate Subsector

The five physiographic zones used for the model in this study certainly cannot match the very detailed disaggregation used by INCRA; nor can the very broadly defined farm types in the model be used as a proxy for INCRA's classifications. But it is at least possible to simulate the interpolation of average-size INCRA module farms into the existing agrarian structure, zone by zone, because the model is capable of reallocating land into different farm sizes and types. The average size of the INCRA module is calculated for each state and the figures are then transformed to average sizes for the zones used in the model: West, 63.15 hectares; Sertao, 31.30; Southeast, 19.90; East, 35.90; and Agreste, 23.20. In the experiments reported below, the land composing our estate subsector is divided into farms of these sizes.[8] Though this is a somewhat crude procedure, the results of the cross-sectional analysis reported earlier revealed that very few of the existing estates would not be classified as latifundia, either by use or size, if the criteria in the land statute were applied to them.[9]

Table 8-1 shows that nearly 800,000 module farms could be formed from the land on existing estates; this would yield a total of about 1.5 million

7. Ludwig and Taylor, *Brazil's New Agrarian Reform*, p. 16.
8. Estates in the Humid Southeast, comprising about 5,000 plantations in Bahia and less than 3 percent of total Northeastern agricultural land, are ignored throughout the land reform simulations because they were inadequately covered by the survey.
9. Although the majority of minifundia are too small by almost any criterion, we do not address the question of farm consolidation; administrative attention to the 1.4 percent of the land contained in properties smaller than ten hectares could only detract from the required attention to the 50 percent of the land on farms larger than 500 hectares.

Table 8-1. *Potential Number of Module Farms in the Estate Subsector*

Item	West	Sertao	South-east[a]	East	Agreste	North-east
Number of existing estates	14,569	11,221	4,766	1,314	5,168	37,038
Average size (hectares)	794.57	676.43	763.47	1,086.50	634.56	742.80
Total area (thousands of hectares)	11,576	7,590	3,639	1,428	3,279	27,512
Module size (hectares)	63.15	31.30	19.90	35.90	23.20	34.84
Potential number of module farms	183,310	242,492	182,864	39,777	141,336	789,779

a. Cacao plantations are excluded, as explained in note 8 to the text.

farms (family, medium-size, and module), or nearly double the present number.

Performance of the Module Farms

Table 8-2 summarizes the characteristics of the average module farms when they replace the existing estates. Because these performance figures are from the solution for the whole agricultural sector, reported in Table 8-3, all the sectorwide constraints in the model are operating. By contrast, when a model of a single farm (or farm type across the zones) is solved in isolation, the behavior of the farm does not affect any market equilibrium relations, and hence the solution is apt to give an unrealistically favorable impression of its performance.[10]

The results of the module experiment confirm that, with existing technology, practices, and markets, farms of this size range cannot provide full employment for four working adults. In all zones, the average modules barely absorb the labor of one family, assumed to be equivalent to 2.2 adults, and do so for a maximum of only one or two months a year. The modules in the East use the most labor on a year-round basis, at two man-years (600 days) a year, but the amounts they absorb vary from month to month; a maximum of 2.54 men are employed in the peak month. In the West, family labor is fully occupied in only one month of the year and never needs to be supplemented with temporary hired labor. In none of the zones

10. For example, another simulation of a comprehensive land reform that ignored demand constraints and other factors revealed a scope for expanding output up to 80 percent as opposed to our figure of about 15 percent, reported below. See R. Albert Berry and William R. Cline, *Agrarian Structure and Productivity in Developing Countries* (Baltimore, Md.: Johns Hopkins University Press, 1979), p. 130.

Table 8-2. *Characteristics of Land Reform Modules*

Characteristics	West	Sertao	South-east	East	Agreste
Size (hectares)	63.15	31.30	19.90	35.90	23.20
Good cropland	5.37	5.49	7.40	4.17	4.33
Medium cropland	5.82	8.23	4.36	5.10	6.23
Native pasture	15.64	10.48	2.53	6.70	11.28
Output and incomes (cruzeiros)					
Crop sales	3,519	1,927	3,758	7,762	3,699
Livestock sales	759	2,229	1,272	1,238	2,046
Head (number)	7.37	11.98	11.78	3.99	9.70
Value of consumption	518	767	770	785	934
Gross output	4,796	4,922	5,800	9,785	6,679
Money costs	191	520	464	362	805
Net money income (gross output minus money costs)	4,605	4,402	5,336	9,423	5,873
Net real income	3,302	3,336	4,397	7,676	4,256
Labor use					
Total labor use (man-years)	1.45	1.20	1.09	2.00	1.86
Peak month family labor use (man-equivalents)	2.20	2.20	2.20	2.20	2.20
Peak month temporary labor hire (man-equivalents)	0.00	0.15	0.52	0.34	0.43
Shadow prices (cruzeiros)					
Good cropland	126	52	38	510	104
Medium quality cropland	83	52	38	394	65
Native pasture	6	42	38	67	28
Performance (cruzeiros)					
Output per hectare	76	157	291	273	288
Output per man	3,308	4,102	5,321	4,893	3,591
Labor per hectare (man-years)	0.023	0.038	0.055	0.056	0.080

do the modules need to hire permanent workers, even though the observed annual wage for permanent workers that is used in the model is less than half the minimum individual income as specified by INCRA. Very little temporary labor is hired, the maximum being about two man-weeks in the peak month on module farms in the Southeast.

Even if the modules do not meet INCRA's stated employment objectives, they are quite consistent across zones in the amount of family labor they absorb. Family labor is fully employed in all zones in at least one month and supplies the following proportions of total labor use: West, 100 percent;

Table 8-3. *Results of a Land Reform in the Estate Subsector*

Category	1978 base case (1)	Land reform (2)	Percent- age change (2)/(1)
Number of farms	779,519	1,532.260	+ 97.0
Number of farmers and family workers	1,751,279	3,914,476	+124.0
Output[a] *and income*[b]			
Crop output	11,146	12,630	+ 13.3
Livestock output	2,813	3,361	+ 19.5
Gross output	13,959	15,991	+ 14.6
Farm income	7,758	10,531	+ 35.7
Nontenured labor income	2,634	1,462	− 44.5
Sector income	10,392	11,994	+ 15.4
Employment			
Man-year equivalents	2,622	3,034	+ 15.7
Peak month (thousands of men)	3,178	4,274	+ 34.5
Trough month (thousands of men)	1,868	2,119	+ 13.5
Sector performance			
Price index	100.0	94.7	− 5.3
Output per hectare (cruzeiros)	177.1	202.9	+ 14.6
Output per man-year (cruzeiros)	5,324	527.1	− 1.0
Labor per hectare (man-years)	0.033	0.039	+ 16.6
Underutilized land (millions of hectares)	7.08	3.90	− 45.0

a. In thousands of cruzeiros at constant prices.
b. Money incomes in thousands of cruzeiros at model-endogenous prices.

Sertao, 99 percent; Southeast, 96 percent; East, 97 percent; and Agreste, 97 percent.

The simulated income levels of the module farms are also far short of those specified by INCRA. As Table 8-2 shows, the highest money income is realized in the East and is equivalent to only about two, rather than four, INCRA minimum salaries (with the "return on capital" requirement ignored). Total money incomes from the module farms in all other zones average about the INCRA minimum individual salary. Even though much lower than the INCRA standard of CR$20,000, these incomes are substantially above those currently earned by Northeastern family farmers, sharecroppers, and permanent workers and are thus acceptable.

Although they do not meet INCRA's standards for absorbing labor and generating income, the modules perform very well as family farm units.

They are capable of providing acceptable levels of income and employment for rural families, and they are large enough to take advantage of improving markets and advances in technology. We can find no reason to alter the INCRA farm-size specifications for a potential land reform and can offer no better criteria for defining module farms.

Potential Effect of Land Reform

Apart from the social, political, and distributional objectives, a land reform should contribute to economic development by increasing productivity. Not all land reforms have done so, and to counter the apparent preference for commercial agricultural enterprises in Brazil, the potential gains in productivity from newly created family farms need to be clearly demonstrated.

Table 8-3 summarizes the results of the land reform simulation for the agricultural sector as a whole. The gains in output are far short of what might be expected: Crop output rises by 13.3 percent, and gross output by 14.6 percent. Though livestock output might have been expected to decline, it increases by almost 20 percent because the production of the estate subsector is much more livestock-intense than that of existing small farms. This reflects the demand limitations, which result in a 5.3 percent decline in the overall price index. The gains in gross output arise from additions to the production of food crops for family consumption on the modules and additions to marketed production, the modules being more efficient than the existing estate sector. Much of the increase in crop output is of rice, beans, manioc, and corn, which the module farms, like family farms, grow mainly for on-farm consumption, but the production of other crops does not decline. This suggests that a land reform will not have a detrimental effect on the production of export crops and that the production of consumables, both crop and animal products, will increase.

The additional value of subsistence production is relatively small: Cr$572 million, or 28 percent of the increase in gross output of Cr$2,032 million. In the sense that the model "forces" family farms to produce a minimum consumption bundle, and the land reform simulation increases the number of these farms, the consumption gains from this source are somewhat artificial. There is, however, no reason to assume that module farms would not produce at least this amount of food crops for their own consumption. The remaining increase in output is "pure" in the sense that it arises from the reallocation of labor to land and the resultant decline in production costs. This increase is still greater than could be brought about by most of the traditional interventions reported in Table 7-7, the exceptions being those combining demand shifts with technical progress (5) and also with wage subsidies (7).

The employment gains from a land reform are more substantial than the output gains. Overall labor use rises by 15.7 percent, more than under any of the alternatives considered in Chapter 7 (even those that most favor labor—demand shifts and wage subsidies). More important, peak-month employment rises by more than 1 million workers.

The gains to consumers from a land reform are difficult to measure because the size and characteristics of the consuming population relying on the markets change as families on the newly formed modules produce their own food. The price decline of about 5 percent, however, indicates that all consumers would benefit. This follows, in part, from the output increases of about 15 percent in food crops and livestock products. The number of families who are assured of being able to produce and consume the minimum food crop "bundle" rises from 667,995 in the base case to 1,420,696 under the land reform, an increase of 113 percent. A land reform, then, is likely to benefit all Northeast consumers substantially, though to varying degrees, and ensure adequate consumption for an additional 750,000 families.

More livestock is produced under land reform than under any other intervention considered, but land in general is used much more intensively. Underutilized land falls from 7.08 million hectares in the base case to 3.90 million under the land reform—a far greater decline than under any other intervention. This is due partly to the increase in crop production and partly to the modules' tendency to use cultivated pasture, which is more labor-intensive and land-saving, whereas livestock maintenance on the estates in the base case was based mostly on native pasture.

Although the aggregate effect of a land reform would not be large, the micro effects are striking, as shown by a comparison of the output and employment of the large farm subsector before and after redistribution (see Table 8-4). Note that all other things, particularly the land endowments by quality, stock of tree crops, and so on, are identical. In this light, the potential increases are more convincing. For the entire subsector, crop output more than doubled, and gross output and employment nearly doubled. Whereas this subsector accounted for 22.1 percent of Northeast output in the base case, its share rose to 37.4 percent, slightly more than the 34.5 percent of the land these properties comprise. Thus, because of the land reform, the subsector's performance rose from far below average to become one of the most productive.

Table 8-4. *Performance of the Estate Subsector before and after Redistribution*

Zone	Crop output[a]			Livestock output[a]			Gross output[a]			Labor use[b]		
	Estates	Modules	Per-centage change	Estates	Modules	Per-centage change	Estates	Modules	Per-centage change	Estates	Modules	Per-centage change
West	480.19	740.02	+ 54	106.65	139.13	+ 30	586.85	879.15	+ 50	169.29	265.80	+ 57
Sertao	432.16	653.27	+ 51	201.90	540.51	+168	634.51	1,193.79	+ 88	150.70	290.99	+ 93
Southeast	4.44	848.85	+ ∞	306.94	232.60	− 24	311.38	1,081.46	+247	70.30	199.32	+183
East	289.28	445.26	+ 54	31.33	49.24	+ 57	320.61	494.51	+ 54	46.06	79.55	+ 72
Agreste	389.24	686.04	+ 76	173.43	289.17	+ 67	562.66	975.22	+ 73	173.08	262.88	+ 52
Northeast	1,595.76	3,373.46	+111	830.25	1,250.67	+ 52	2,416.02	4,624.12	+ 91	609.42	1,098.55	+ 80

Note: This table concerns only the estate subsector; it thus gives a more favorable impression than the net results for the agricultural sector as a whole that appear in Table 8-1.
a. In thousands of cruzeiros at constant prices.
b. In thousands of man-years.

The employment gains are also striking; the subsector, after redistribution, provided full employment (300 days a year) for nearly an additional half-million. Recall that under the 20 percent wage subsidy experiment employment increased by less than 30,000 on the large farms.

Table 8-4 also suggests the areas that might be prime prospects for a land reform. Cline considered the Zona da Mata (roughly corresponding to our East zone) as having priority, and INCRA included parts of the Sertao as well as the East. Their considerations, however, were highly influenced by the degree of social tension prevailing, whereas ours are only in terms of output and employment effects. Under these criteria, the Southeast, comprising most of the state of Bahia, is potentially the most profitable area, followed by the Sertao. The East is, in fact, below the Northeast-wide average gains in output and employment. The vast potential gains (of 50 percent or more) in output and employment in *all* zones, however, indicate that none should be ignored.

The most impressive gains from the land reform simulation are distributional. If we consider family incomes of US$456 (the bottom of ENDEF's third income class) to be at least acceptable,[11] all of the 790,000 module farms fall into this category. Presumably, the beneficiaries of the module farms would be temporary and permanent workers' families as well as sharecroppers' families—the vast majority of whom are earning substantially less than this figure. The land reform could thus raise the incomes of as many as 40 percent of these families to acceptable levels.

The 1978 base case showed only 680,000 families or farms earning incomes greater than US$456 from agriculture. In the land reform simulation, this figure nearly doubles to 1.32 million, for a net gain of 640,000. Although this gain is not impressive in view of the extent of poverty among nonlandowning families, it is impressive when compared with what could be accomplished through interventions other than land reform; none of the policies or packages of policies described in the previous chapter raised the number of families earning more than US$456 by as many as 100,000.

Potential Beneficiaries

Because there are about 2 million nonlandowning families depending on agriculture, there can be no shortage of beneficiaries for the approximately 700,000 module farms considered in this experiment. Most of the family heads probably meet INCRA's basic criteria (aged 21, sane, and of good

11. See the incomes discussion in the appendix to Chapter 3.

background or demonstrating the potential for rehabilitation). Given the technological level, minimal contacts with markets for both inputs and outputs, and simple practices observed for perhaps centuries, we discount the contention that a land reform would fail because of managerial short-comings and illiteracy. If, however, managerial experience were to be a criterion for selection, the roughly 250,000 existing sharecroppers and roughly 1 million permanent workers, who are often moradores operating their own family plots for food crops, would be the best candidates. If such a criterion were exclusively applied, however, it would limit the effect of the reform on income distribution, because those with the lowest income levels are temporary workers.

Estimates of Cost

Probably the most difficult aspect of evaluating a land reform is to estimate its cost.[12] In the early 1970s, Cline used an estimate of US$2,500 as the nonrecoverable cost per module,[13] which SUDENE later updated to US$2,722 to take account of inflation. A 1978 unpublished SUDENE study places the figure at US$5,000 per module, of which US$3,000 for prepara-tory land work and installations would be "recoverable." None of these sources provides a detailed breakdown of the costs involved, but they suggest rough orders of magnitude.

Each of the several costs of land reform has to be analyzed differently. First, there may be anticipatory costs: If a landowner feels that appropria-tion is imminent, he may alter the operation of his fazenda, possibly evicting sharecroppers and workers whom he may view as potential ben-eficiaries, causing real losses in employment and output and in his own income. In view of the long debate on the subject in Brazil, such costs have almost certainly been incurred, and they will be minimized only by deci-sive action one way or the other. Second, there are the transactional costs of legal services, surveying, title registration, and the like. Third, transfer payments will normally be made to compensate landowners. Whether this compensation comes from public coffers or from the beneficiaries makes little difference except in its distributional impact. Fourth, there are the investment costs of outfitting new farms with structures, equipment, ani-

12. All dollar figures in this section have been converted from cruzeiros at the spring 1974 exchange rate of Cr$6.40 = US$1.00.

13. In World Bank, "Rural Development Issues and Options in Northeast Brazil," report no. 665a-BR (Washington, D.C., June 23, 1975; restricted circulation).

Table 8-5. *Estimated Partial Costs of Establishing Land Reform Modules*
(1973 U.S. dollars)

Average value per module	West	Sertao	South-east	East	Agreste	Northeast average[a]
Land	1,781	1,756	4,766	7,193	3,685	3,073
Structures	1,504	1,636	2,494	3,864	2,087	1,995
Equipment	138	121	117	245	107	128
Animals	1,959	1,304	931	1,562	1,699	1,453
Total nonland value	3,601	3,061	3,542	5,671	3,892	3,576
Total value	5,382	4,817	8,308	12,864	7,527	6,649

a. Weighted by potential number of modules in each zone (see Table 8-1).
Source: SUDENE/World Bank survey.

mals, working capital, and facilities (mainly access roads) which enable them to purchase inputs and market their products. Finally, there are the costs of extension services, credit provision, and other administrative services, depending on how much the government is involved in the operation of the modules.

The SUDENE/World Bank survey data permit estimates of some of these costs. Table 8-5 reports the average value of land (a proxy for the cost of acquisition) and of structures, equipment, and livestock, by zone, for farms about the size of the INCRA modules, in U.S. dollars to ease comparison with the estimates quoted above. The land values per module were calculated from survey data based largely on farmers' own judgments. To check these values, the marginal returns to land on all estates were averaged for each zone, with weights corresponding to the quantities of land of the various classes of productivity. This yielded for the Northeast an average annual net income of about US$240 per module. Because half or more of the land on existing estates is not under productive use, and adjustment is made for differences in the shadow prices, the value of this stream over twenty years, discounted at 10 percent, is slightly over US$2,000, or about two-thirds of the average declared land value.

The value of structures, equipment, and animals amounts to about US$3,500 per module. SUDENE considers the costs of equipping new farms to be recoverable, and the model results suggest that they should be, because annual net money income, after family consumption requirements have been met, averages about US$1,000 per module. Assuming, however, a 50 percent default rate and interest charges that are just sufficient to cover administrative charges and opportunity costs, the cost of installations to be publicly financed would average US$1,750 per module.

Recent World Bank estimates of the annual cost of recommended extension services average about US$120 per family farm in the Northeast. Over, say, five years, presumably a time sufficient to achieve the performance estimated in the model, this amounts to US$600 per farm, or less than US$500 if discounted at 10 percent.

These considerations appear to confirm Cline's figure of US$2,500 in the early 1970s as an average for the real, nonrecoverable cost per module. On this basis, the establishment of the 790,000 modules considered in our experiment would cost US$1,975 million.[14]

The additional gross output of US$318 million a year that could be produced in the Northeast if the estate subsector were reformed amounts to 16 percent of the land reform costs. Discounted at 10 percent, this stream of output increases would enable the land reform to break even in ten years. To the extent that the model overestimates the efficiency of the existing estates, this output gain is understated, and the reform is more attractive.

Alternative Development Strategies in Conjunction with a Land Reform

Despite these benefits, a land reform alone could not solve the problems of the rural Northeast. In this section we therefore examine the possible effects of a land reform combined with the instruments described in the previous chapter.

Table 8-6 shows that if the estate sector were reformed the output of the Northeast could be raised by up to 35 percent and employment by almost 30 percent, depending on the combination of instruments. These are much larger gains than could be achieved by the interventions alone. The different strategies are difficult to evaluate without a social preference function, but a comparison of the results in this table with those in Table 7-7 shows that the traditional policy interventions—particularly the promotion of technical progress and measures to expand demand—would be more effective if the estate sector were reformed than they would be otherwise. Prices paid by consumers would always be lower, the incomes of all farmers higher, and total employment greater.

14. By 1976, PROTERRA funds amounted to roughly double this figure.

Table 8-6. *Alternative Development Strategies in Conjunction with a Land Reform*

Category	1978 base case (1)	(2)	(3)	(4)	(5)	(6)	(7)	(8)
Instrument[a]								
Technical progress			X			X		X
25 percent demand shift				X		X	X	X
20 percent wage subsidy					X		X	X
Land reform		X	X	X	X	X	X	X
Output[b]								
Crops	11,146	12,630	13,279	14,173	12,656	15,212	14,286	15,151
Livestock	2,813	3,361	3,727	3,003	3,474	3,396	3,118	3,561
Total	13,959	15,991	17,006	17,176	16,130	18,608	17,405	18,712
Output index	100.0	114.6	121.8	123.1	115.6	133.3	124.7	134.1
Price index	100.0	94.7	82.0	104.6	92.8	86.9	99.6	84.8
Income[c]								
Family farms	764	4,751	5,563	5,635	4,626	6,154	5,392	5,863
Other farms	6,994	5,780	5,884	6,162	5,777	6,281	6,096	6,324
Hired labor	2,634	1,462	543	1,525	1,696	798	1,864	1,316
Total	10,392	11,994	11,990	13,322	12,099	13,234	13,353	13,504
Employment[d]								
Farm family	1,222	2,215	2,274	2,464	2,099	2,448	2,309	2,196
Sharecroppers	630	587	0	576	587	99	576	6
Temporary workers	342	181	172	182	164	196	151	172
Permanent workers	427	51	43	96	223	46	346	525
Total	2,622	3,034	2,489	3,318	3,073	2,790	3,381	2,899
Peak month	3,178	4,274	3,952	4,148	4,401	3,999	4,315	4,478
Employment index	100.0	115.7	94.9	126.5	117.2	106.4	128.9	110.6

a. As defined in the text.
b. Thousands of cruzeiros at constant prices.
c. Money incomes in thousands of cruzeiros at model-exogenous prices.
d. Thousands of man-years, except peak month, which is thousands of men.

Two groups might, however, require special attention to prevent their incomes from falling to a poverty level as the result of a land reform. Existing medium-scale farmers, though they are better off than small-scale farmers and landless workers, could suffer a decline in income of up to 20 percent because of the price declines and because, in particular locales, only less skilled labor might be available for hire after a land reform (a possibility not recognized by the model but probably of some importance). Strategies to promote demand would reduce these income losses. Sharecroppers might also suffer unless they are among the direct beneficiaries of a land reform: Under the alternative programs considered, their employment fluctuates dramatically from 587,000 (slightly below the number in the 1978 base case) to zero.

Conclusions

The legislation, background information, and ample funding exist for a land reform like that simulated. The Land Statute, on almost all accounts, is precise, realistic, and to the point of the problems; the INCRA criteria for defining farm sizes and types are valid and consistent; and, even with allowance for inflation, existing PROTERRA funds are double our estimates of the probable cost. The analysis of farm performance has shown that there is little, if any, *economic* justification for the existence of most estates, given the vastly superior performance, by almost any economic criterion considered, of farms of module size or smaller. Furthermore, a reform involving 2.7 million families at a proposed cost of US$13,500 million was recently drafted in Brazil.[15]

Two central questions must, however, be borne in mind in any interpretation of the land reform simulations in this chapter. First, could a reform of the scale considered here actually be undertaken, given the political and administrative challenges it poses? Second, is a development program encompassing such a redistribution sufficient?

The administrative capacity to implement such a reform is at least as important as legislation and funding. To minimize disruption costs, any reform must be carried out swiftly and effectively. The bureaucratic nightmares associated with some of the resettlements attempted by the irrigation agency (DNOCS) are certainly not typical of current administrative capability in Brazil, but such examples emphasize the importance of administrative arrangements in any intervention. At a minimum, the administrative requirements for a land reform need not go much beyond measures to put the landless Northeasterner on the land. Farming techniques are simple and have been handed down from father to son for centuries. Though we do not dispute the need for extension services, research and dissemination of new varieties, a functioning credit network, and marketing facilities, we argue strongly that in the Northeast of Brazil such activities are subsidiary to the need to give better access to land to the multitude of available agricultural

15. As reported in "Agrarian Reform: A Time-Worn Subject Returns to the Headlines," *Veja*, December 7, 1977.

workers. Unless their access is extended, both human and land resources will continue to be underused, and the objectives of agricultural development will continue to be frustrated.

A land reform could increase production and employment and raise a significant number of people out of absolute poverty. But conditions in the rural Northeast leave the sufficiency of a land reform much in doubt. Even if a reform of the existing estate sector were supported by the successful stimulation of demand and technical progress and were accompanied by a subsidy on wages, more than 1 million families would remain without entrepreneurial access to land and near absolute poverty. It is clear that the full solution to the Northeast problem does not lie within the agricultural sector alone. But it is equally clear that a land reform holds the best prospects for directly improving productivity and the distribution of incomes within the rural Northeast.

9

The Northeast Problem and the Future of Brazilian Development

This study concludes in a quite sobering manner: The Northeast problem is probably more acute than previously imagined; it is not likely to disappear over time of its own accord; direct policy and project interventions are not likely to have much effect; thus, there is a need for sweeping structural change within the Northeast's agricultural sector. Yet even such a move will only partially alleviate the severe relative—and possibly absolute—poverty persisting in the region.

Because this study focused on a single sector in a single region and relied largely on a single cross-sectional farm survey, the above conclusions warrant further reflection and raise many questions. If Brazil can resume its "miracle" growth record, will the benefits eventually trickle down to the rural Northeast? Are there other, less politically sensitive solutions available? What should be the role of the agricultural Northeast in the future Brazilian economy? What are the likely ramifications if the Northeast problem is not solved?

Miracle Growth and the Rural Northeast

From the end of World War II to the early 1960s the Brazilian economy grew at rates envied by most of the developing world. This growth has been well documented and virtually unrefuted. Whereas most students would agree that the poor of Brazil have not experienced absolute declines in their welfare during the growth period, all indicators point to a decline in the income share of the poorest 40 percent of the population. Although two-thirds of the Brazilian poor are rural residents and half reside in the Northeast, the trickle-down argument is muted by the recent performance of the Brazilian economy in the 1970s and realistic forecasts for the 1980s.

Whereas the economy grew at rates averaging 10.1 percent from 1968 to 1974, the rate has slowed to an average of 6 percent since 1974.[1] With increasingly limited opportunities for import substitution, skyrocketing oil prices (Brazil is straitjacketed by its dependence on imports for 80 percent of its supply), increasingly tight external credit because of Brazil's massive outstanding foreign debt, and further curtailment of export markets as a result of trade limitations and lagging demand in the industrialized world, the growth prospects for Brazil in the 1980s are not optimistic. Thus, there are two serious doubts in the equation: Do benefits actually trickle down, and will there be sufficient growth from which the trickle may come?

Beyond the 1980s is another matter. Brazil's natural resource base provides good cause for longer-term optimism. The vast—and largely untapped—resources in the Amazon basin could well provide for another period of miracle growth. And, given the proximity of the Northeast, the army of available labor could easily be absorbed. But will this occur, given the growing sensitivities about the international ecological ramifications of the Amazon basin? When will this occur, and will the Northeasterner have acquired the education and skills to make him employable in such ventures?

Alternative Solutions

Certainly, alternative solutions are possible and, in some cases, feasible. A few of these options are discussed in this section.

Education and skill training to prepare workers for out-migration are probably the best possibilities for a longer-term solution in the absence of a structural reform. Land, natural resources (except oil), and unskilled labor are Brazil's most abundant resources. The shortage of an educated and skilled labor force has been, however, and will continue to be a critical constraint on the economy's growth. The underutilized human resources of the Northeast constitute a potential supply source. Can the Northeasterner be educated or trained to fill the need? Within a generation, the answer is probably no. Such a goal is not likely to be achieved in the near future. Decades of nutritional deficiencies, illiteracy rates of 75 percent, and sadly neglected educational infrastructures have culminated in a monumental socioeconomic challenge. That "there is a sense of urgency about education

1. Werner Baer, "The Brazilian Growth and Development Experience: 1964–1975," in *Brazil in the Seventies*, ed. Riordan Roett (Washington, D.C.: American Enterprise Institute for Public Policy Research, 1976), pp. 46–47; and World Bank data.

in Brazil" is recognized,[2] but how long will such a program take and how much national, human, and physical capital must be diverted to accomplish the goal? A human resource solution is, at best, decades away, and the national sacrifice of diverting skills and infrastructural investments from other, more pressing endeavors does not seem to be on the horizon.

A more favorable national policy toward agriculture could increase the incentives toward fuller utilization of land as well as increase employment. These strategies, in turn, would include devaluing the cruzeiro (to make the export crops more profitable), stabilizing inflation, providing investment incentives to agriculture, and intensifying research to develop new higher-yielding and more drought-resistant varieties. Of these various steps, the first two involve macroeconomic policies that would have sweeping effects on all sectors and regions. The narrow focus of this study does not warrant recommendations on such policies. It seems clear, however, that they will be addressed in terms of the wider goals of Brazilian developmental problems rather than in terms of the narrower Northeast problem alone.

The promotion of investment in agriculture is a multifaceted topic requiring a far more detailed analysis than is possible here. Agricultural investment in Brazil has been highly subsidized through loans with often negative real interest rates, but these policies have had mixed effects on both productivity and income distribution. In the Northeast, although subsidized investment has benefited the large-scale farmers, there is no evidence that it has increased productivity and resource utilization (particularly labor). The small-scale farmers and sharecroppers have probably benefited only from public investment in infrastructure. To recommend increased investment, therefore, raises the question of which type of investment is desired—labor-saving in an area of surplus labor, or land-saving in an area of underutilized land? Leaving this question open, this study finds that the problem is concentrated in distortions in the markets for the two factors that are most abundant—land and labor—and not in agricultural capital.

Agricultural research has been advancing vigorously since the inception of EMBRAPA and promises to yield favorable results. The question, however, is still this: Will the gains be sufficient to alter behavior patterns so markedly that land will be more intensely utilized and labor more intensely employed, given the proclivity of large-scale farmers to react less than optimally to economic opportunities? The technical progress experiments reported in Chapter 7 indicate that this may not be the case because small-

2. Robert J. Havighurst and J. Roberto Moreira, *Society and Education in Brazil* (Pittsburgh, Pa.: University of Pittsburgh Press, 1965), p. 251.

and medium-scale farmers may increase production of the price-flexible crops, whereas large landowners may restrict land and labor use to roughly maintain current income levels. Those results depended on the assumption that the new seed varieties and technology would be adopted by all farmers in the region. Yet the reluctance of small-scale farmers and sharecroppers—whose decisions to adopt new varieties may be dominated by safety-first criteria and who do not have the access to credit or the desire to borrow for new technology—may severely limit the potential benefits of agricultural research. This reluctance, combined with the motivations of large land-owners, could well mean that successful agricultural research would bring income gains to the more progressive medium-scale farmers, consumption gains to consumers, and no gains at all in the welfare of the small-scale farmers. In short, agricultural research is strongly warranted, but it cannot be a panacea, given the structure of the agricultural economy of the Northeast.

Nonagricultural activities in the rural Northeast could also alleviate underemployment and poverty in the region. Certainly, the dispersion of the 34/18 investments in industry away from the coastal cities, accompanied by more labor-intensive criteria for the subsidies, could absorb much of the labor force and induce secondary, multiplier effects. Apart from the agricultural processing industries, however, what comparative advantage, from a macro view, lies in such a dispersion? The paucity of nonagricultural resources, the location of markets, and the inadequate transport system undoubtedly override the advantages of cheap labor. On economic grounds, dispersion of industry into the rural Northeast makes little sense; on distributional grounds, there are other means available that need not run counter to regional comparative advantage.

The possible solutions to the Northeast problem mentioned above could well transform the rural Northeast from an impoverished, largely illiterate, underproductive agricultural region into one that is economically diversified, self-sufficient in food production as well as in educated and skilled labor, and profitable in terms of foreign exchange. The lack of national commitment to do so, however, the many "ifs" involved, the decades of time and enormous amount of effort required, and, from a national point of view, the far more pressing developmental needs competing for the scarce capital and human resource skills make this a remote possibility.

There is no short-term solution. But there is a short-term problem. More than half the natural annual increase in the Northeast's population migrates to the cities of the Northeast, the Center-South, and Southeast. These migrants, or *retirantes*, are unskilled and unprepared for absorption into the economies of Belo Horizonte, Rio, and Sao Paulo and tax the already overburdened services of these cities. Leaving families behind, they are frustrated and unwanted. They find refuge in *favelas* (squatter settlements) and obtain menial employment at best. And then, with news of "rain in the Sertao," the retirantes often return to the Northeast.

Potential Role of the Rural Northeast

The nearly 1 million viable farming units and sharecropped plots clearly demonstrate that the agricultural Northeast does provide a standard of living of at least acceptable standards for those favored with land. The nearly 30 million hectares of underutilized land of similar if not superior quality on the estates indicate that nearly another million families could achieve comparable living standards. On egalitarian grounds alone, a land reform is strongly warranted and provides the best prospect for swift rises in the living standards of the most impoverished groups in the rural Northeast.

Egalitarian arguments, however, are not the chief determinants of policy in dynamic, resource-rich economies with virtually unlimited potential, especially when protagonists of the trickle-down theory are vociferous. Nor should egalitarian principles necessarily shape policy, unless political exigencies so dictate.

The solution to the Northeast problem needs to be considered in the context of the long-term development of Brazil. True, the Northeast problem has existed and intensified for over a century, but the coming decades will undoubtedly alter all the justifications, motivations, and apologies for past policies toward the Northeast. A new role for the rural Northeast must be found, and that role must be compatible with Brazilian developmental goals and, subsequently, contribute to them.

That role will not lie in the monocultural production of crops for export. Sugar no longer has a comparative advantage. Cacao and the oil palms suffer from limited markets. Cotton remains a good prospect, but its labor intensity makes it most attractive to family farms or to estates using sharecropped labor. Nor will the Northeast become a major livestock producer; natural pasture is too poor to support more head of cattle under current or envisaged practices, and more advanced production of cultivated grass for fodder raises questions about alternative uses of land—such as for food crops.

The green revolution has to this day barely touched the Northeast, as is the case with most semiarid tropical zones in the world. If varieties and techniques are found that are amenable to Northeastern conditions, it is doubtful whether Northeastern farmers would adopt them, given their risk-averse behavior and lack of funds for investment. Newly discovered methods would have to be promoted and subsidized to a far greater extent than hitherto evidenced in Brazil.

The role of the rural Northeast, for the foreseeable decades ahead, reduces to a simple, yet vitally important one: to increase the traditional foodstuff production of corn, beans, manioc, and rain-fed rice to supply the rural and urban population of the Northeast and, ultimately perhaps, permit some excess to be exported to the South; to continue present levels of production of cacao, cotton, and oil palm for domestic consumption and exportation; and, finally, to increase livestock production through more intensive management of pasture. These objectives can be achieved simply through the more rational allocation of labor to land by substantially increasing the number of family farms of the type defined by INCRA. And this move can be abetted by strengthening the infrastructure and advancing research on appropriate technologies.

These would be the direct benefits of a land reform. The indirect benefits, however, may be far more important to the economic and political stability of Brazil.

Even when the Brazilian economy was growing at an annual rate of 10 percent, it could not absorb the masses of migrants to its Center-South cities. Now that growth has slackened and opportunities for migrants returning to the Northeast have improved little if at all, the urban problem continues to grow more acute. According to a recent estimate, 1.2 million people live in the Rio favelas,[3] and probably far more live in the Sao Paulo favelas. Most have come from the Northeast. The reasons behind such migrations are complex but generally encompass economic motives: The realities of life in the rural Northeast make the uncertain yet potentially better life in the Center-South cities attractive enough that those who can move do so. Unless and until the migrants are fully prepared for productive lives in modern, urban Brazil, however, they would probably be better off remaining in the Northeast. To this end, the most effective incentive is the provision for sufficient, productive land.

A reduction of rural-urban migration is an economic, if secondary, benefit of land reform. A noneconomic benefit of potentially as great importance is the lessening of political tensions. Such tensions have dimin-

3. "Brazil's Outcast Shanty Dwellers Offered a Helping Hand at Last," *New York Times*, October 22, 1979, p. A4.

ished considerably since the 1950s and early 1960s, and in the 1970s were not widely publicized. Yet they are still manifested in a sense of frustration, though not necessarily as a potentially disruptive force.[4]

Land reforms in other countries have bought time during which development in other regions and political reform could begin to rectify the structural problems and make further calls for land reform redundant. Mexico is a prime example: The reform bought time and a measure of political stability, and as an additional benefit agricultural production increased.[5]

Whether Brazil needs to buy time for a Northeast solution, and whether rural-urban migration and its effects pose important problems, are questions for Brazilian policymakers to assess. This study has concentrated on the economic aspects of the problem, and the economics of a land reform in Northeast Brazil can be summarized very briefly.

Four percent of landowners own more than 50 percent of land in agricultural properties; only one out of four agriculturally dependent families owns the land it works. The smallest farms employ twenty-five times more labor per hectare on their land than do the largest farms and obtain vastly higher productivity levels. The smaller farms (less than fifty hectares), though only 10 percent of the agricultural land, produce over 25 percent of the region's sugar, cotton, and rice and 40 percent of the beans, corn, and manioc. Yet 2 million agriculturally dependent families own no land at all while an area of land the size of France is un- or underutilized.

---

4. "Osvaldo Galvao, a rancher in [Piaui] was asked if he was encouraged by the announcement last week from Brasilia [that the government was undertaking a US$330 million program of well drilling and small dam construction]. He pulled a used soft drink bottle from a rack, held it upside down over a counter and watched several drops form a rivulet. 'That's how much we'll get, the rest will stay in the south as it always has.' " "Brazil's Arid Northeast Skeptical as Help Is Promised Once Again," *New York Times*, September 21, 1979, p. A13.

5. Shlomo Eckstein, Gordon Donald, Douglas Horton, and Thomas Carroll, *Land Reform in Latin America: Bolivia, Chile, Mexico, Peru, and Venezuela*, World Bank Staff Working Paper no. 275 (Washington, D.C., April 1978), p. 72.

Introduction to the Appendixes

The four appendixes that follow describe how the survey was carried out, from the design of questionnaires and samples to the fieldwork and the organization, validation, and retrieval of the computerized data. They are by no means intended as a manual for agricultural surveys in general; they simply record the methodology for this study.

Although some members of the research team had strong backgrounds in statistics, they were all economists and, aside from one short-term consultant, none had more than a passing acquaintance with the mechanics of large surveys. In retrospect it appears that the team's complementarity of skills largely overcame its lack of experience in such endeavors. The Brazilian members included agricultural economists and agronomists with intimate knowledge of Northeastern agriculture, and computer programmers who could identify potential computational bottlenecks. The World Bank members had expertise in sampling theory, mathematical planning techniques, and procedures for organizing and manipulating data. Most of the team had studied problems of agricultural economics, and some had taken part in large agricultural-sector planning studies. This combination of skills meant that many potential pitfalls were avoided. On the advice of computer experts, for example, questionnaires could be designed to facilitate the computational organization of the data once collected; with the help of a logistics expert, the sample was designed to ensure that interviews could actually be conducted as planned.

Appendix A
Questionnaire Design

Though we had originally intended to use a questionnaire used in a 1972 pilot survey by SUDENE and the Institute of Economic and Social Planning (IPEA), Ministry of Planning,[1] we decided, for several reasons, to construct an original one instead. First, the IPEA/SUDENE questionnaire did not yield the detailed input–output information necessary to permit the use of linear programming techniques at the farm level. Second, we wished to use a precoded system, both for the names of crops, implements, and so on, and for the actual data themselves: To speed processing and eliminate the step of transferring the information from the questionnaire to coding sheets, the questionnaire itself had to be in the form of coding sheets so that it could be keypunched directly. Third, as we consulted other institutions that might have an interest in the survey, we found that the informational content of the IPEA/SUDENE questionnaire was inadequate.[2]

Design Criteria

The new questionnaire was designed to maximize the information obtained subject to constraints on ease of processing and cleaning, interviewee fatigue, and logistics. Other considerations related to the diversity of ecological factors, cropping patterns, tenure relations, and ease of training enumerators also had to be recognized. Some of these constraints affected the sample design and are discussed in Appendix B.

The general approach was to group the desired information into tables (for example, on land use, production, distribution, equipment), the columns of which corresponded to fields on an IBM data card and the rows of which corresponded to individual data cards. The tables were organized

1. IPEA was originally to have assisted SUDENE in a study of the "typical size of the unit of production in the Northeast," or "tamanho tipico." Staff shortages were largely responsible for its withdrawal.

2. Lee Bettis, consultant to the World Bank, assisted in drafting this section.

into a unified questionnaire by proceeding from the general to the specific. Thus, one of the first tables contains questions on land use, subdividing the farm into cropland of different types, pasture, and so on. A following table records the use of cropland by crop, showing the age and structure of perennial crops, gross output, and so on. Then data on the outputs are tabulated to show how they are distributed among consumption, sales, payment in kind to laborers, inventory changes, and so forth. This method of organization not only permits a logical sequence of questions but also allows information obtained at various times during the interview to be cross-checked. These cross-checks were deemed necessary to ensure the consistency and quality of the data.

Figure A-1 is a representative table from the questionnaire covering sources and uses of the land on the farm. The table columns correspond to IBM card format; the small numbers 1–80 are the columns in which the data are directly keypunched. Each row of the table, if not blank, would be punched on a different card. Each card has a unique identifying number in columns 78–80; for example, for every farm surveyed, card 002 will always be the one for "total area." Columns 72–77 contain codes for state, muni-cipio, and farm, so that each card from the entire survey will have a unique identifier to permit computerized sorting and provide insurance against card "shuffling."

The items across the top, numbered in parentheses, are sources and modes of administration of each of the categories of land that are defined in the rows. Column (1) is the size of the property as given by the INCRA cadastral survey from which the farms in the SUDENE/World Bank survey were identified. If other properties belonging to the same owner were close by and were managed by the same person, they would appear in column (2). Columns (3) and (4) are for parcels rented or squatted upon, respective-ly, if, again, they are part of the same entrepreneurial unit.

The administration of land is divided into "direct," "sharecropper," "morador," and "rented out."[3] The farm is defined as the sum of the land under the first three types of administration, and this definition is used consistently throughout the study. A within-card consistency check is built into the table because total area under the sources, (1) + (2) + (3) + (4), must equal that under the administration types, (5) + (6) + (7) + (8).

Rows 2 through 11 allocate the total land area in row 1 to the possible uses. Here, across-card consistency checks are possible because the sum of rows 2–11 must equal row 1. A later table on crop-specific data provides a

---

3. Moradores are permanent workers who reside on the farm and are often allocated small plots on which their families plant subsistence crops.

Figure A-1. Representative Table from Questionnaire I

	Sources of land				*Administration of land*							
	Area of this property (1)	Area of other properties (2)	Area rented in (3)	Other occupied areas (4)	Directly admin-istered (5)	By share-croppers (6)	By moradores (7)	Rented out (8)				
	1 2 3 4 5 6 7 8	9 10 11 12 13 14 15	16 17 18 19 20 21 22	23 24 25 26 27 28 29	30 31 32 33 34 35 36	37 38 39 40 41 42 43	44 45 46 47 48 49 50	51 52 53 54 55 56 57	72 73 74 75 76 77	78	79	80
1. Total area										0	0	2
2. Single crops										0	0	3
3. Concortiated crops										0	0	4
4. Planted pasture										0	0	5
5. Native pasture										0	0	6
6. Forest										0	0	7
7. Cultivated timber										0	0	8
8. Area with structures										0	0	9
9. Fallow										0	1	0
10. Unutilized (but usable)										0	1	1
11. Unusable										0	1	2
12. Estimated value					X X X X X X X	X X X X X X X	X X X X X X X			0	1	3

check across tables, because the total area in crops identified there must equal the sum of rows 2, 3, and 4 in the table shown as Figure A-1.

Field Tests

Field tests were carried out by members of the World Bank, SUDENE, and the Federal University of Pernambuco in the state of Pernambuco, which has areas representative of the three major physiographic zones of the Northeast—the Zona da Mata, Agreste, and Sertao—and all the types of farms likely to be encountered, ranging from minifundia to large sugar plantations, and including all known tenurial types.

The most significant change in the questionnaire dictated by the field tests was a substantial reduction in its size, as the first version, it was found, could take up to eight hours to apply! Some tables were eliminated and others combined. These first field tests also pointed out the need to enlarge and make more precise the activity and other codes and to sharpen the definition of terms used.

Though doing this reduced enumeration time itself, the questionnaire still needed an average of four hours for each interviewee. We adopted, as a rule of thumb, a limit of two hours for the interview, both to prevent interviewee fatigue, and thus possible distortions, and to permit each enumerator at least two interviews a day.

Hence, the questionnaire was divided into two parts that could be applied independently but could be linked through overlapping tables. On the assumption that both parts were applied to identically drawn random samples from the same stratified universe, this overlap allowed the two parts to be linked later. The questionnaire was divided according to the use that was to be made of the data: The elements of a farm-level programming model can conveniently be divided into (1) the objective function and vector of resource constraints and (2) the technology matrix. Furthermore, we assumed that, for a given population of farms, the various data related to the objective function (output and input prices, transportation costs, and so on) and resource constraints (land of various types, equipment credit) would show greater differences among farms than would the technology data relating outputs to inputs. This assumption appears entirely plausible in the context of the Northeast, where technology is virtually all of a fixed proportion (man/hoe). It permits a much smaller number of questionnaire II (technology-oriented) than of questionnaire I to achieve a given level of statistical significance.[4]

4. For a precedent for this type of sample division, see United Nations, Food and Agriculture Organization, *Coffee in Latin America*, parts I and II (Rome, 1960).

Questionnaire Content

Questionnaire I contains questions on the identification and location of the farm, land tenure, off-farm income, production incentives, hired labor supply, and prices. Responses to these questions assist in establishing the setting within which the farm operates. The information from questionnaire I would also allow the construction of individual farm budgets, though this did not form part of the study.

Table 0 (zero) of questionnaire I provides information on the interviewer's travel time and mode of transportation to the farm and the duration of the interview. These data permitted cost and productivity analysis of the survey itself. The last table, Table 14, is a census of sharecroppers from which to select units to survey separately later (see Appendix B).

Table 2 deals with transactions in farmland in 1972 and 1973. It includes purchases, sales, and rentals in terms of area and value. This table is useful for further characterizing the farm setting and for checking the internal consistency of the responses.

Table 2A provides information on the land tenure system and distribution of the total farm area among broad categories of use, measured in area and value. This table gives the interviewer an immediate overview of the type of farm he confronts and compels him to be consistent about the total area of the farm throughout the later tables.

Table 3 contains data for estimating the stock of fixed capital including houses, barns, pens, roads, and dams; it captures the size, useful remaining life, market value, and annual service flow of each structure.

Table 4 provides information on the stock of farm machinery and equipment and the annual flow of services from it. Together, Tables 3 and 4 provide the data for calculating the amount and value of capital owned and rented by the farm.

Table 5 details information about land use according to cropping patterns and type of administration, that is, whether the farm is managed directly by the owner or by sharecroppers and hired laborers. Individual crops and consortiums (interplantings) are specified with great accuracy. This table provides the basis for several tables in questionnaire II and is thus of critical importance to the survey.

Table 6 records the disposition of the crops harvested in 1973 (which were specified in Table 5) showing the quantities used for family consumption, nonwage payment, feed, processing, and those retained as stocks. The table also indicates the quantity and market value along with unit price per kilogram of each crop marketed in 1973.

Table 7 contains data about the stock of livestock and poultry on the farm, actual livestock transactions during 1973, and all other possible disposition alternatives. Both quantity and value measures according to the breed and age of the animals are specified. It was difficult to obtain accurate information for all parts of this table because of the primitive nature of livestock markets in the Northeast. The aim was to collect the minimum essential information required by the model without overtaxing the interviewee's ability to respond or jeopardizing the completion of the table.

Table 8 records the quantity and value of agricultural commodities processed on the farm, such as flour, meat, and milk and other dairy products, and their disposition, as in Table 6 for crops. The table also records the amount of processed products sharecroppers produced and delivered to the owner.

Tables 9, 10, and 11 cover the sources and uses of labor in detail. Table 9 begins with a census of all persons occupied at least one day of the year on the farm, in any of eighteen categories of labor. It also provides the number of days worked on the farm and off and the monthly pattern of off-farm work. Remuneration, both monetary and in kind, is also recorded. Table 10 gives a monthly breakdown of the number of workers and man-days worked for several types of temporary workers and sharecroppers. Table 11 relates the cropping pattern recorded in Table 5 to the use of labor for crops and maintenance of pasture. For each cropping activity, the number of man-days employed is obtained for subactivities: preparing soil, planting, cultivating, fertilizing and applying insecticides and pesticides, irrigating, harvesting, and transporting to market.

Table 12 lists each specific input (for example, fertilizer, seeds, pesticides, forage, veterinary services) used on the farm during the previous year, showing the quantity produced on the farm, the quantity obtained from elsewhere, and its price, if purchased. It also records whether the use of the particular input had increased, decreased, or remained the same over the previous year. These input data are recorded only in gross terms at this stage; Table 19 in questionnaire II identifies them by activity.

Table 13 collects detailed information about the sources and value of credit used for farm production, according to activity and the term and length of the loan, and for loans used for operating expenses or for investment, according to the type of loan.

To summarize, the thirteen questionnaire I tables on the farm's production and exchange relations can be grouped under six headings:

—land tenure system and land use (2, 2A, 5)
—improvements, machinery, equipment, and animals (3, 4, 7)
—crop production and on-farm processing of livestock and crop products (5, 6, 8)
—labor and other inputs (9, 10, 12)
—financial capital (13)
—technical coefficients (11).

The first group describes in quantitative terms the relations among the various production agents, as revealed by the allocation of farmland among them. The second group records information on fixed capital. Together, the first two groups provide estimates for the constraint vector of the linear programming model. The third group quantifies the various production activities to be represented in the model. The fourth group covers the sources and uses of labor, which is probably the crucial element of the model and of the entire project. The information on labor was used to define the monthly requirements for labor, from which we determined the extent of seasonal unemployment. Information collected on the use and costs of fertilizers, pesticides, and so forth were combined with the gross revenue coefficients of the objective function to calculate net revenue. The information on financial capital recorded by the fifth group was used for several purposes; for the linear programming model it shows the equity limits and the areas of investment for financial capital (credit) prevailing in the Northeast. The information from Table 11 about input–output coefficients for the main production activities was used in the definition of the criterion used in the imputation of a more detailed technology to the farm.

Questionnaire II is designed to collect the information necessary to define the input–output matrix of coefficients for all production activities conceivable on a farm in the Northeast. It records very detailed data on yields, on inputs such as labor, fertilizer, seeds, machinery, equipment, and fuels, and on other operating costs, including interest on outstanding loans. Some tables are common to both questionnaires: 0, 2A, 5, 7, 9, 12, and 14, which appears as Table 23 in questionnaire II. They were used in the questionnaire II sample to delineate the structural context within which the individual activities are undertaken, and to provide the main elements for imputing a matrix of techniques to each farm in the first sample.

Tables 15 through 20 of questionnaire II collect data on specific activities for use in building up the technical coefficients. Table 15 deals with the labor, machinery, and equipment requirements of individual crop and pasture activities. The number of man-days supplied by different categories of workers and the pieces of equipment used in each month for each activity are specified for broad categories of a production activity, for example, preparing soil, planting, and harvesting.

Table 16 asks for information on the production of livestock and poultry on the farm for each month of 1973, including the number of work animals, cattle, and cows pastured and fed silage and the quantity of feed consumed by each animal. Questions are also asked concerning the quantity of swine, sheep, goats, and fowl slaughtered annually.

Table 17 records the labor requirements for each month in 1973 for processing agricultural commodities. Labor is disaggregated by category in Tables 15 and 9.

Table 18 collects data on the monthly labor requirements (also disaggregated by category of workers) for constructing and maintaining fixed capital on the farm.

Table 19 complements Tables 15 and 16 with data on the use of production inputs other than labor, crop, and livestock activity. Inputs include seeds, feed, fertilizer, veterinary medicine, fuel, and other operating expenditures.

Table 20 asks for information on the number of hectares used and the total output of each crop per activity from land of high, medium, and low productivity. Information on land quality, vital for a well-specified linear programming model, was sought in the following way: First, a pedologist studied soil quality in the sampled municipios; second, each farmer was asked to classify the land on his own farm according to his perception of its profitability by crop or consortium. By merging the results from the two sources, soil classes could then be delineated within each sampled area.

Tables 21 and 21A contain data on marketing and storage activities for each product (raw or processed), showing the quantity sold, price, form of payment received, and mode of transportation and distance to each type of buyer (whether landowner, intermediary, cooperative, processing plant, or final consumer) and also, for each product, the amount stored in owned or rented quarters, the type of storage structure, the storage period, average loss from storage, and sales price.

Finally, Table 22 furnishes information on water availability and quality and its influence on production. Questions are asked about the rainy months in 1973 in the area; whether there was a dry spell or flooding and which crops suffered most; what sources of water were used; in which months they were dry; how much land was lowland, hillside, and highland; and which crops did best on these types of land.

Appendix B
Sampling Procedures

Several critical factors had to be considered in designing the sample: The Northeast is a very large area (1.548 million square kilometers), and transportation and communications can often be quite difficult; ecological conditions and agricultural production vary widely, as do farm sizes and tenurial systems; and, because there were two questionnaires, two samples were needed.

To reduce logistical problems, we sampled clusters of farms scattered throughout the region. Our primary sampling units were the administrative subdivisions called municipios or counties, of which there are 1,365 in the Northeast. There were two broad choices for the selection of municipios: purposive sampling and stratified random sampling. Several past surveys in Brazil have employed the former method, selecting "typical" municipios on the basis of available data, intuition, and the judgment of field experts.[1] This technique is likely to introduce biases into the analysis, however. It will tend, in particular, to select larger primary units, as near as possible to the observers' concept of the "average," with a much smaller proportion of extreme cases than would be obtained in a random selection. Another shortcoming of purposive or other nonrandom sampling methods is that no statistical theory exists for measuring the reliability of their results.[2]

Because of these shortcomings, we adopted a stratified random sampling procedure that determines the strata state by state. In this procedure the primary units (municipios, or clusters of farms), are sampled in two stages: First, the primary units are selected by weighted random sampling in a two-way stratification; second, the units are selected by weighted random sampling in a one-way stratification. Subunits (farms) are then selected from each of the selected primary units by stratified random sampling.

1. For example, recent surveys coordinated by the Ministry of Agriculture and IPEA of the Ministry of Planning. See Ruy Miller Paiva and George F. Patrick, *Acesso a terra no Nordeste*, Colecao Relatorios de Pesquisa (Rio de Janeiro: IPEA/INPES; processed).
2. See Morris Hansen, William Hurwitz, and William G. Meadow, *Sample Survey Methods and Theory*, vol. 1 (New York: John Wiley and Sons, 1953), pp. 71–73.

In the first stage of the sample, we divided the 1,365 municipios of the Northeast into strata according to (1) their ecological characteristics, using the 114 ecological microregions of the Northeast defined by IBGE, the Instituto Brasileiro de Geografia e Estatistica, and (2) their production characteristics, by considering the types of crops (or livestock) that are their main sources of agricultural revenue. A weight was then assigned to each municipio to reflect its economic size or importance as an agricultural producing unit. Using this ecological/production pattern classification and the weights, we selected a sample of municipios at random. The number of municipios selected in each state depended on: the number of ecological/production pattern types represented in that state (we required the sample to include at least one municipio of each type in each state); our enumeration capacity; and the extent to which average farm size varied among the municipios of that state. The first-stage sample of municipios that resulted was too large for our enumeration capacity, and thus a second-stage random sample was drawn, stratified only by ecological microregion, not by production pattern, again using weights corresponding to economic size.

Having selected the municipios, we identified a preliminary sample of farms—"preliminary" because several modifications were made once the early results had been evaluated. The available data consisted of a cadastral survey of agricultural properties undertaken by INCRA, the National Institute of Colonization and Agrarian Reform, in 1972 and estimates of the enumeration time of questionnaires I and II from the pretests. Farm size was taken as a proxy for the range of factors limiting farm performance—the principal consideration of questionnaire I—and we assumed, initially, that the variation in the technical coefficients—the principal consideration of questionnaire II—could be related proportionally to the variation in size. To stratify the sample of farms, establishments smaller than 500 hectares in each selected municipio were divided into five size classes,[3] all of which were equal to one another in total area. Establishments of 500 or more hectares were placed in a sixth stratum. For each state, an enumeration team was available for eight weeks. The problem was to allocate their total enumeration time among the municipios selected in that state; among the strata (farm size classes) within each municipio; and between questionnaires I and II.

The allocation rule that resulted for each state in sample S_{mqs} (where m denotes the municipio, q the questionnaire, and s the stratum) depended on: the relative enumeration time needed for questionnaires I and II; the

3. Up to 9.9 hectares; 10–49.9 hectares; 50–99.9 hectares; 100–199.9 hectares; 200–499.9 hectares.

variance of farm size within each size class in each municipio; the number of municipios selected; and the total enumeration time available. A random sample for each state was drawn with this rule, together with a backup sample of equal size, to be used for replacing farms that, though recorded by the cadastral survey, could not be located or did not exist, and for extending the sample in cases where the estimates of enumeration time were found to have been too high. Thus, the actual sample could be greater or less than S_{mqs}, depending on the actual time spent in traveling, locating farms, and conducting interviews. The size of the actual sample in each state also depended on the estimated differences in the degrees of variance in the two groups of items being investigated by questionnaires I and II. As explained below, these differences determined the appropriate ratio between the sample size for questionnaire I and that for questionnaire II, and they were estimated with progressively greater accuracy as completed questionnaires were analyzed.

To summarize, the procedure followed used the general rule that sampling should be concentrated where the sampling unit is larger, where the sampling unit is more variable internally, and where the sampling is cheaper in the sampling unit.

Selection of Municipios

For the first-stage selection of primary sampling units, we hypothesized that the variances of the random characteristics of interest to the study are determined by two basic factors: ecological conditions (climate, soil, latitude, altitude, and so on) and the orientation of production. Ecological differences would be responsible for the variance between groups of farms that are not contiguous. Differences in production patterns would be responsible for the variance within such groups. Stratification according to both factors would then ensure that the sample of farm clusters would reflect both the ecological and the agricultural diversity of the universe, that is, the state.

A two-way stratification[4] of municipios based on these two factors was made using the microregions defined in physiographic terms by IBGE[5] and

4. For a discussion of two-way stratification, see William G. Cochran, *Sampling Techniques* (New York: John Wiley and Sons, 1963), pp. 126–28.

5. Instituto Brasileiro de Geografia e Estatistica, *Dados preliminares gerais do censo agropecuario, VIII: Recenseamento geral, 1970* (Rio de Janeiro, 1972). Our subareas do not correspond exactly to the 1972 census-defined microregions; in some cases we aggregated these microregions, in others the definition was altered in the final, published census.

Table B-1. *Production Patterns*

Monocultures
  A. Arroz (rice)
  B. Algodao (cotton)
  C. Cana de acucar (sugarcane)
  D. Coco (coconut)

Consortiums
  E. Mandioca, arroz, milho (manioc, rice, corn)
  F. Algodao, arroz, mandioca (cotton, rice, manioc)
  G. Algodao, arroz, milho (cotton, rice, corn)
  H. Algodao, arroz, feijao (cotton, rice, beans)
  I. Algodao, feijao, milho (cotton, beans, corn)
  J. Algodao, feijao, banana (cotton, beans, banana)
  K. Algodao, feijao, mandioca (cotton, beans, manioc)
  L. Feijao, mandioca, milho (beans, manioc, corn)
  M. Outros (other, mixed cropping)
  N. Pecuaria (livestock)

---

an unpublished set of SUDENE data on the main agricultural activities at the municipio level for 1964, because no more recent data were available at this level of disaggregation.

The municipios were classified according to the following production patterns, listed in detail in Table B-1:

—*monoculture*, where a single crop was the municipio's main source of agricultural revenue

—*consortium*, where a single consortium of intercropped products was the main source of agricultural revenue

—*livestock*, where livestock was the main source of agricultural revenue

—*other*, where there was a diverse production pattern in which no single activity yielded more than 50 percent of the municipio's revenue.

Because the municipios are administrative units, they differ significantly in their importance as agricultural producing units. To take account of this, we applied a technique suggested by Hansen, Hurwitz, and Meadow, whereby the municipios are given a probability of selection Z_i that is proportional to their degree of importance as agricultural producing units.[6] In determining these probabilities, we faced two problems: First, the Z_i were not readily definable and, second, since the purpose of the survey was to seek information on many different variables, it was necessary to consider various possible measures of economic importance in selecting the

---

6. Hansen, Hurwitz, and Meadow, *Methods and Theory*.

units to be sampled. For cases in which size Z_i is some aspect of the physical size of the unit, Cochran suggests using the measure of size that is most nearly proportional to the unit totals of the principal items of the survey.[7] We can thus assign to each municipio within each ecological/production pattern group a probability weight that is proportional to an index of a group of variables related to the principal variables of the survey. Preliminary data from the 1970 census were used to make the following selection of variables, where i indicates the municipio and j the stratum (ecological/production pattern group): Q_{ij} = population; H_{ij} = area; P_{ij} = employment; and F_{ij} = number of farms. The weight of the ith municipio in the jth stratum is:

(B.1)
$$W_{ij} = \tfrac{1}{4}\left(\frac{P_{ij}}{\bar{Q}} + \frac{H_{ij}}{\bar{H}} + \frac{P_{ij}}{\bar{P}} + \frac{F_{ij}}{\bar{F}} \right),$$

where the bars indicate statewide means. Then the probability of drawing the kth municipio in the jth stratum is defined as:

$$P_{kj} = \frac{W_{kj}}{\displaystyle\sum_{k=1}^{M_j} W_{kj}},$$

where M is the total number of municipios in the jth stratum.

The first-stage sample that resulted from this procedure consisted of one municipio from each ecological/production pattern group. It was much too large for our enumeration capacity. In reducing the sample, we decided that it was important to maintain coverage of all the microregions within each state but that the differences in production patterns within microregions were less important.[8] A second-stage random sample was thus carried out and yielded one municipio per microregion per state. Any excess enumeration time that permitted more municipios than this to be sampled was allocated to municipios in those zones that showed the highest variance in certain key variables that were to be sampled. Because we had no previous data about which were the key variables, available proxies were taken from the preliminary 1970 census data: establishment area, employ-

---

7. Cochran, *Sampling Techniques.*

8. The relative gains from stratification by zone, calculated in terms of Hansen's analysis, (Hansen, Hurwitz, and Meadow, *Methods and Theory*, pp. 200–01), proved to be substantial and are reported in Gary P. Kutcher and Pasquale L. Scandizzo, "Northeast Brazil Regional Studies Project: Sampling Procedures" (World Bank, Development Research Center, 1974; processed).

ment per establishment, and farm density (number of establishments per square kilometer).[9] From the microregion that showed the highest total variance of all these measures, a second municipio was selected.[10] This selection procedure was repeated, using the next highest variance, until the expected enumeration time was fully accounted for. The derivation of the probability weights used in the procedure is described in the last section of this appendix; the municipios finally selected are shown in Table B-2.

Selection of Farms

The framework established for the selection of farms thus ensured that all the ecological microregions of the Northeast would be represented by at least one cluster of farms and that those microregions in which agricultural activities are more diverse would be represented by more than one cluster of farms, in proportion to their degree of diversity. The farm sampling problem was then to allocate the fixed amount of enumeration time among the clusters of farms (municipios); farms of different size classes within the clusters; and the two questionnaires. We consider the last of these items first.

Of the two broad groups of variables of interest in the survey, questionnaire I covered the limiting factors on farm performance or, in a linear programming framework, the parameters of the farm's objective function and its constraint vector. Questionnaire II covered the technical coefficients and technological relations, or the matrix elements in linear programming terminology. We assumed that the information relative to the two groups of variables can be conveniently summarized by two proxy variables y_1 and y_2. These two variables may be an aggregate index of the variables in the groups, or they may simply be highly correlated with them. To give an example, for the first group a variable of this kind would be the total area of the farm because one would expect a close association between area and the endowment of most of the other limiting factors. For the second group, a possible choice is an index of the diversity of production or land use on the farm.

9. The Census Bureau defines an agricultural establishment as an unbroken parcel of land under a single management.

10. Total variance is defined as $W' \Omega W$, where Ω is the variance/covariance matrix of the four variables considered, and W is a vector of normalizing weights, taken in this case to be equal to the inverse of the means of the same variables.

Table B-2. *Selected Municipios, by State*

Alagoas (CIMN)	*Babia (DCKIMN)*	*Ceara (BIJKGMN)*
1. Coruripe (1)	1. Santana (1)	1. Araripe (1)
2. Cha Preta (2)	2. Sento Se (2)	2. Brejo Santo (2)
3. S. Jose da Leje (2)	3. Ibitiara (3)	3. Independencia (3)
4. Junqueiro (3)	4. Tapiramuta (4)	4. Jaguaretama (4)
5. Sao Sebastiao (4)	5. Itambe (5)	5. Itapipoca (5)
6. Traipu (5)	6. Condeuba (5)	6. Acarau (5)
7. Agua Branca (6)	7. Senhor do Bonfim (6)	7. Aquiraz (5)
	8. Barro Preto (7)	8. Itapiuna (6)
	9. Jequie (8)	9. Ipu (6)
		10. Mucambo (6)
		11. Tiangua (6)
		12. Poranga (6)

Maranbao (AEFGMN)	*Paraiba (BIMN)*	*Pernambuco (CBILMN)*
1. Godofredo Viana (1)	1. Rio Tinto (1)	1. Jaboatao (1)
2. Pinheiro (2)	2. Pilar (2)	2. Limoeiro (2)
3. S. Benedito do Rio Preto (3)	3. Areia (3)	3. Sertania (2)
4. Coroata (4)	4. Campina Grande (4)	4. Aguas Belas (3)
5. Sambaiba (5)	5. Frei Martinho (5)	5. Tabira (4)
6. Barra do Corda (6)	6. Uirauna (6)	6. Cabrobo (5)
7. Imperatriz (7)		7. Mirandiba (6)
8. Moncao (8)		8. Serrita (7)

Piaui (BFHIGMN)	*Rio Grande do Norte (BKIMN)*	*Sergipe (DCKIMN)*
1. Parnaiba (1)	1. Ceara-Mirim (1)	1. Porto da Folha (1)
2. Buriti dos Lopes (1)	2. Santo Antonio (2)	2. Aquidaba (1)
3. Aroazes (2)	3. Acu (3)	3. Propria (2)
4. Luzilandia (3)	4. Pedro Avelino (3)	4. Pedrinhas (3)
5. Capitao de Campos (4)	5. Areia Branca (3)	5. Araua (3)
6. Altos (5)	6. Caico (4)	6. Malha dos Bois (4)
7. Canto do Buriti (6)	7. Florania (4)	7. Frei Paulo (5)
8. Sao Joao do Piaui (6)	8. Apodi (5)	8. Itabaiana (5)
9. Jerumenha (7)	9. Sao Miguel (6)	
10. Santa Luz (7)	10. Alexandria (6)	

Note: The letters in parentheses refer to the production patterns (see Table B-1) in each state. The numbers in parentheses refer to the microregion that each municipio represents. Microregions represented by more than one municipio are those that exhibited the greatest heterogeneity, as explained in the text.

We assumed that the objective of the data collection within each state was to minimize the variance of the average measure of y_1 and y_2, subject to the statewide constraint on our enumeration capacity. This objective may be expressed as:

$$(B.2) \quad \min V(\bar{y}_1 + \bar{y}_2) = \sum_{i=1}^{M} \sum_{b=1}^{L_i} W_i Z_{ib} \left[\frac{{}_1S_{ib}^2}{n_{ib}} - \frac{{}_1S_{ib}^2}{N_{ib}} + \frac{{}_2S_{ib}^2}{m_{ib}} - \frac{{}_2S_{ib}^2}{N_{ib}} \right],$$

subject to
$$\sum_{i=1}^{M} \sum_{b=1}^{L_i} ({}_1c_{ib}\, n_{ib} + {}_2c_{ib}\, m_{ib}) = C,$$

where W_i = a weight inversely related to the probability of selection of the ith municipio

N_{ib} = number of farms in the bth size class of the ith municipio

L = total number of farms in the municipio

$N_i = \sum_{b=1}^{B_i} N_{ib}$, where B_i = the number of farm size classes in the ith municipio

$Z_{ib} = N_{ib}/N_i$

${}_1S_{ib}^2$ = relative variance[11] of y_j in the bth size class of the ith municipio, $j = 1, 2$

n_{ib} = sample size (number of farms to be selected) in the bth size class of the ith municipio for the variables of group 1

m_{ib} = the same variables of group 2

M = total number of municipios in the state

${}_1c_{ib}$ = cost (= time) of applying the questionnaire, relative to the group of variables represented by y_1, bth size class, ith municipio

${}_2c_{ib}$ = the same for y_2.

Solving equation (B.2) with the usual Lagrangian techniques yields the following expressions for the optimal sample size in the bth farm size class of the ith municipio:

$$(B.3) \quad n_{ib}^* = \frac{\sqrt{g_{ib}}\, {}_1S_{ib}/\sqrt{{}_1c_{ib}}}{\sum_{i=1}^{M} \sum_{b=1}^{B_i} \sqrt{g_{ib}}\, {}_1S_{ib}/\sqrt{{}_1c_{ib}}}\, n^*, \quad \begin{array}{l} i = 1, 2, \ldots, M \\ b = 1, 2, \ldots, B_i \end{array}$$

11. In order to make the minimization in equation (B.2) meaningful, the two variables y_1 and y_2 or their variances have to be normalized so that their differences are independent of the unit of measure. This normalization was performed by using estimates of the mean of each variable.

$$(B.4) \quad m_{ib}^* = \frac{\sqrt{g_{ib}}\, {}_2S_{ib}/\sqrt{{}_2c_{ib}}}{\sum\limits_{i=1}^{M}\sum\limits_{b=1}^{L_i}\sqrt{g_{ib}}\, {}_2S_{ib}/\sqrt{{}_2c_{ib}}} m^*, \qquad \begin{array}{l} i = 1, 2, \ldots, M \\ b = 1, 2, \ldots, L_i \end{array}$$

$$(B.5) \quad m^* = \frac{\sum\limits_{i=1}^{M}\sum\limits_{b=1}^{B_i}\sqrt{g_{ib}}\, {}_2S_{ib}/\sqrt{{}_2c_{ib}}}{\sum\limits_{i=1}^{M}\sum\limits_{b=1}^{L_i}\sqrt{g_{ib}}\, {}_1S_{ib}/\sqrt{c_{ib}}} n^*,$$

where $g_{ib} = W_i Z_{ib}$; n_{ib}^* and m_{ib}^* represent the optimal allocation of the sample for each municipio and farm size class; and n^* and m^* the optimal overall sample size for a given state.

To illustrate some of the implications of this analysis, consider its application to the state of Pernambuco, for which, as the first state to be surveyed, only minimal information was available on the values of the parameters. For Pernambuco there were sixteen people in the interviewing team, each available for only forty-eight days. Their employment during this period did not involve any variable cost; the limiting factor was time. During the pretest it had been established that questionnaire I took an average of about 0.65 day and questionnaire II roughly one day to apply. Although the variance of the variables in group 2 was actually expected to be smaller than the variance of the variables of group 1, for lack of direct information we first assumed it to be equal, that is, that ${}_1S_{ib} = {}_2S_{ib}$ for every i and b or, dropping the other subscripts, that $S_1 = S_2$. Under these assumptions, equation (B.5) becomes simply

$$(B.6) \quad m^* = \frac{\sqrt{t_1}}{\sqrt{t_2}} n^* = 0.8n^*,$$

where t_1 and t_2 indicate the time taken to apply questionnaires I and II. The cost equation can be written as:

$$(B.7) \quad t_1 n + t_2 m = 0.6n + m = 768.$$

Solving equations (B.6) and (B.7) for Pernambuco gave the following overall sample sizes for questionnaires I and II: $n^* = 561$, $m^* = 449$.

A general expression for the optimal size of the two samples, n^* and m^*, as a function of S_2/S_1 (the ratio between the degrees of variance they are to measure) can be written as:

$$(B.8) \quad n^* = \frac{768}{0.8\dfrac{S_2}{S_1} + 0.65}; \quad m^* = 768 - \frac{499.2}{0.8\dfrac{S_2}{S_1} + 0.65}.$$

Table B-3. *Change in the Optimal Size of Two Samples, as a Function of the Ratio between the Degrees of Variance They Are to Measure*

S_2/S_1	n^*	m^*
0.20	948	152
0.30	864	207
0.50	731	293
0.60	679	327
0.70	634	356
0.80	596	381
0.90	560	404
1.00	530	424

The variation of n^* and m^* with S_2/S_1 is illustrated by Table B-3.

Thus, the number of observations to be allocated to the two samples for Pernambuco was first determined by guessing that the ratio S_2/S_1 was one. Consideration of the equations (B.8) and of the values in Table B-3 suggested that when S_2/S_1 is less than 0.7 changes in the ratio cause only minor variation in the sizes of the samples. Hence, in the initial phase of the survey, lacking quantitative information on the variance of the limiting factors, we used the sample allocation corresponding to $S_2/S_1 = 0.7$. On the basis of the early results from the first three of the nine states, S_2/S_1 was reduced to 0.6 for the second three states, and finally to 0.56 for the last three.

Let us now consider the problem of allocating a specified number of observations to the municipios and the farm size classes. The actual time needed to apply the questionnaires was thought likely to vary among the municipios and the different sizes of farms, but we were unable to predict how. Nonetheless, it was possible to calculate the differences in the variance of y_1 and y_2 (or a related variable, total area) by municipio and by farm size class using data from the INCRA cadastral survey. Consideration of equations (B.3) and (B.4) then suggested the following two-stage procedure.

First stage: Allocate n^* and m^* to the municipios under the assumption $c_{ib} = t_{ib}$, for all i, b, according to:

$$(B.9) \qquad n_{ib}^* = \frac{\sqrt{g_{ib}}\, _2\hat{S}_{ib}}{\sum\limits_{i=1}^{M} \sum\limits_{b=1}^{L_i} {}_1\hat{S}_{ib} \sqrt{g_{ib}}}\, n^*,$$

$$(B.10) \qquad m_{ib}^* = \frac{\sqrt{g_{ib}}\, _2\hat{S}_{ib}}{\sum\limits_{i=1}^{M} \sum\limits_{b=1}^{L_i} {}_2\hat{S}_{ib} \sqrt{g_{ib}}}\, m^*,$$

Table B-4. *SUDENE/World Bank Survey: Farm Sample Size*

State	Questionnaire I		Questionnaire II		I and II together		Total farms observed
	Pro-grammed	Realized	Pro-grammed	Realized	Pro-grammed	Realized	
Rio Grande do Norte	509	261	247	126	48	85	472
Paraiba	400	280	195	122	108	111	513
Pernambuco	583	328	283	176	98	80	584
Alagoas	399	409	137	143	82	96	648
Sergipe	442	283	154	105	94	97	485
Bahia	836	664	317	249	97	138	1,051
Piaui	783	571	297	210	149	160	941
Ceara	970	768	377	320	107	151	1,239
Maranhao	637	392	251	166	124	150	708
Maranhao (IPEI)[a]	—	118	—	5	—	162	285
Total	5,559	4,074	2,258	1,622	907	1,230	6,926

— Not applicable.

Note: Questionnaire I, 5,304; Questionnaire II, 2,852; total, 8,156. Overall percentage realized = 79.39 percent.

a. A special survey of squatters undertaken with the Institute of Economic and Social Planning for the state of Maranhao.

where $_k\hat{S}_{ib}$, $k = 1, 2$, is the estimate of $_kS_{ib}$ (the degree of variance in the group 1 or 2 variables in the size class and municipio in question) derived from the cadastral survey. From equations (B.9) and (B.10) one can derive the time to be spent by the enumerators in each municipio and size class of farm:

$$(B.11) \qquad \hat{T}_i = \frac{\sum\limits_{b=1}^{B_i} (0.6\, n_{ib}^* + m_{ib}^*)}{E_i},$$

where $\hat{T}_i$ is the estimate of the number of working days T_i to be spent in municipio i, size class b, by the enumerating team, and E_i is the number of interviewers (the size of the team) working in the same municipio.

Second stage: Once the allocation had been made and put into effect, there were three possible outcomes: (1) $T_i = \hat{T}_i$. In such cases the allocation was exact and no action needed to be taken. (2) $T_i < \hat{T}_i$. In such cases the time for the application of the questionnaire in municipio i had been overestimated. The enumerator was required to expand the sample randomly, maintaining the same proportion between n_i and m_i until the predetermined time was exhausted. (3) $T_i > \hat{T}_i$. In such cases the actual time needed was longer than had been estimated. The action was simply to accept the sample produced in the predetermined amount of time.

To summarize, the original sample was modified in the field according to differences between actual and estimated enumeration time, and revisions in the estimated variance ratio S_2/S_1 as early results were evaluated and, therefore, according to adjustments in the questionnaire I/questionnaire II sample ratio. Table B-4 compares the original allocation with the modified one that takes account of these factors.

Supplementary Samples

Three supplementary samples were drawn up: a sample of sharecroppers; a sample of farms assisted by ANCAR, the National Agricultural Extension and Credit Agency; and a sample of squatters in a large frontier area of Maranhao.

The cadastral survey on which the main sample was based was a survey of agricultural properties and does not contain information on subdivision into sharecropped plots, which is particularly common in the interior dry lands. Both questionnaires I and II obtained an inventory of sharecroppers (if any) on each property sampled, and this provided the universe for a field-determined sample of sharecroppers, using the following rules:

—After one-third of the enumeration time for a given municipio has elapsed, consider the census of sharecroppers thus far obtained: n_i^s, where i indicates the farm size class.

—Find the largest sharecropped plot (A_i^M) and the smallest (A_i^m) in each size class.

—Determine the sharecropper sample size m_i^s for each size class:

$$m_i^s = \frac{0.29(A_i^M - A_i^m)}{S_i} m_i,$$

where S_i is the standard deviation of establishment size, and m_i is the regularly drawn sample size for questionnaire II. The numerator of this expression corresponds to the estimate of the standard deviation of the size of sharecropped plots, on the assumption that the latter does not vary with the size of establishments.

—Select, at random, m_i^s sharecroppers from the n_i^s.

The above procedure thus uses the information obtained from a field inventory of sharecropping units to allocate the (previously determined) sample for questionnaire II between sharecroppers and proprietors. The procedure is based on the assumption that the size of sharecropped plots is uniformly distributed, because this is the simplest hypothesis when there is no previous information on the distribution.

The survey offers a unique opportunity to study, through cross-sectional analysis, the success of extension services provided through ANCAR. To ensure sufficient observations of establishments receiving special ANCAR assistance, a subsample was drawn in the field from ANCAR lists so that the percentage of ANCAR-assisted establishments sampled was the same as the percentage of all establishments sampled in the municipio. If, for example, the regularly drawn sample was 12 percent of the total number of establishments, then additional randomly drawn establishments from the ANCAR lists were sampled so that 12 percent of the ANCAR-assisted establishments were surveyed.

In a large area in western Maranhao, a transitional zone bordering on the Amazon, a large number of squatters were encountered. Because few of the parcels of land they operated had titles, the INCRA cadastral survey was not a satisfactory base from which to draw a sample of them. The Institute of Economic and Social Planning for the state of Maranhao (IPEI) was particularly interested in studying these squatters, so an agreement was made by which a separate sample could be drawn. Based on cartography possessed by IPEI, a grid was drawn over the area, and cells were drawn at random, which were employed to locate nonpropertied farmers. These cells were then combined with the property sample for those INCRA-registered properties to make a more complete sample.[12] The sample size is shown in the last row of Table B-4.

Notes on Sample Expansion

For those microregions in which more than one municipio was sampled, the extrapolation from the sample to the microregion required weights that corresponded to the probabilities of the municipios sampled being selected. These probabilities are derived below.

Probabilities of Municipio Selection

As explained earlier, for each state of the Northeast the sample of municipios was drawn up in two stages, and probabilities of selection, proportional to the municipios' economic size (that is, their importance as agricultural producing units) were computed after each draw of the sample. The stage 1 sample was stratified by ecological microregion and by production pattern; municipios were selected using a set of probability weights that corresponded to the municipios' economic size. At stage 1, the probability of the ith municipio being selected is given by:

$$(B.12) \qquad p_1^i = \frac{W_i}{\sum\limits_{i} W_i} \text{ for all } j,$$

where W_i is the economic size of municipio i, and N_j is the total number of municipios in the jth ecological/production pattern group.

In the second stage, the strata were constituted simply by microregions, production patterns being ignored, and the sample was reduced initially to one municipio per microregion per state. In each of the eight states where this sample size did not exhaust the enumeration time expected to be available, a second municipio was added in the microregion that exhibited the highest variance of three measures suggestive of economic size. This procedure was repeated, and the municipio exhibiting the next highest variance was selected, until the enumeration time for the state was fully accounted for. In this iterative process, the probabilities of municipio i

12. For a more complete description of the procedure, see Institute for Economic and Social Planning (IPEI), "Metodologia da amostragem por areas geograficas de unidades produtoras" and "Pesquisa por areas geograficas de unidades produtoras" (Sao Luis, Maranhao, 1974; processed).

being selected were derived as follows. The conditional probability that municipio i is selected in the first draw of stage 2, given that municipio i has already been selected in stage 1 and that the cth combination of $m - 1$ municipios[13] of the microregion in question was selected, is:

$$(\text{B.13}) \qquad p_{21}^{i/c,1} = \frac{W_i}{W_i + \sum\limits_{i \neq j}^{m-1} W_{jc}}.$$

The conditional probability that the ith municipio is selected in the first draw of stage 2 is:

$$(\text{B.14}) \qquad p_{21}^{i/1} = \sum_{c=1}^{C} \frac{W_i}{W_i + \sum\limits_{i \neq j}^{m-1} W_{jc}},$$

where C is the total number of possible combinations of municipios belonging to the microregion and the different production pattern groups.[14]

The joint probability of municipio i being selected at stage 1 and at the first draw of stage 2 can then be obtained as follows:

$$(\text{B.15}) \qquad p_{21}^{i} = p_{21}^{i/1} \left[\sum_{c=1}^{C} \left(\frac{W_i}{W_i + \sum\limits_{i \neq j}^{m-1} W_{jc}} \right) \prod_{j=1}^{m-1} p_1^{ic} \right],$$

where P_1^{ic} is the probability of selection of the ith municipio, in combination c, at stage 1.

The conditional probability for the ith unit at stage 2, draw 2, given that the kth municipio was selected at draw 1 is:

$$(\text{B.16}) \qquad p_{22}^{i/k} = \begin{cases} \dfrac{p_{22}^{i}}{1 - p_{21}^{k}} & \text{if } i \text{ and } k \text{ are not in the same microregion and in the same production pattern group;} \\ 0 & \text{otherwise.} \end{cases}$$

Therefore, the probability of being selected at stage 2, draw 2, is:

$$(\text{B.17}) \qquad p_{22}^{i} = \sum_{k=1}^{m-1} \frac{p_{22}^{i}}{1 - p_{21}^{k}} p_{21}^{k}.$$

Expression (B.17) is recursive and can be generalized for any draw r:

13. From stage 1 there will be M possible candidates for the selection of a sample of size m.
14. Note that $p_{ij}^1 = p_i^1 p_j^1$ for municipios belonging to different production groups or different regions or both, but $p_{ij}^1 = 0$ if i and j are in the same production group and also in the same microregion.

(B.18)
$$p_{2r}^i = \sum_{k=1}^{m-1} \frac{p_{2r-1}^i}{1 - p_{2r-1}^k} p_{2r-1}^k.$$

Therefore, the probability that the ith unit will be selected in both stages is:

(B.19)
$$\Pi_i = \sum_{g=1}^{m} p_{2g}^i.$$

For municipio i, the conditional probability of being selected, given that k is also in the sample, is:

(B.20)
$$\Pi_{i/k} = \begin{cases} \sum_{g=1}^{m} \dfrac{p_{2g}^i}{1 - p_{2g}^k} & \begin{array}{l} \textit{if } i \textit{ and } k \textit{ are not } \text{in the same microregion} \\ \text{and in the same production pattern group} \\ \text{(case 1);} \end{array} \\ = 0 & \text{otherwise (case 2).} \end{cases}$$

Therefore, the joint probability of selection of the ith and kth municipios is:

(B.21)
$$\Pi_{ik} = \begin{cases} \sum_{g=1}^{m} \dfrac{p_{2g}^i}{1 - p_{2g}^i} p_{2g}^i = \sum_{g=1}^{m} \dfrac{p_{2g}^k}{1 - p_{2g}^k} p_{2g}^k & \text{in case 1;} \\ = 0 & \text{in case 2.} \end{cases}$$

Table B-5 lists the overall probabilities of selection for the municipios in those microregions in which more than one municipio was selected in each state.

Weights for Sample Expansion

For certain variables in the survey it was desirable to obtain estimates over broader areas than the clusters sampled and also to estimate population totals for such variables as employment or output. To proceed with these estimates, we needed to determine a system of weights for the municipios sampled and to estimate the population of farms by strata.

For those microregions represented by only one municipio, n, the estimate for the microregion mean $\hat{Y}$ of a sampled variable y was simply $\hat{Y}_i$, the estimate of the mean for that municipio. Where more than one municipio was sampled in a microregion, we desired a system of weights w_i such that

(B.22)
$$\hat{Y} = \sum_{i=1}^{n} w_i \hat{Y}_i; \quad \sum_{i=1}^{n} w_i = 1,$$

where i is the index of the sampled municipios in that microregion. Our rationale for using a normalized system of weights is as follows. For subsampling units (farms) of unequal size and with unequal probabilities of

Table B-5. *Municipio Weights for Sample Expansion*

State	Micro-region	Municipio	Probability of selection[a]	Weight
Rio Grande	3	Acu	0.1333	0.756
do Norte	3	Pedro Avelino	0.2991	0.164
	3	Areia Branca	0.1945	0.080
	4	Caico	0.9640	0.093
	4	Florania	0.0531	0.907
	6	Sao Miguel	0.4257	0.327
	6	Alexandria	0.0984	0.673
Pernambuco	2	Limoeiro	0.0406	0.380
	2	Sertania	0.0312	0.620
Ceara	5	Acarau	0.5815	0.156
	5	Aquiraz	0.0456	0.760
	5	Itapipoca	0.9347	0.084
	6	Itapiuna	0.6219	0.007
	6	Ipu	1.0000	0.012
	6	Mucambo	1.0000	0.006
	6	Poranga	0.1369	0.028
	6	Tiangua	0.0164	0.947
Piaui	1	Parnaiba	1.0000	0.171
	1	Buriti dos Lopes	0.4815	0.829
	6	Canto do Buriti	0.5508	0.020
	6	Sao Joao do Piaui	0.0154	0.980
	7	Jerumenha	0.0909	0.805
	7	Santa Luz	0.1638	0.195
Alagoas	2	Cha Preta	0.0820	0.311
	2	Sao Jose da Laje	0.0519	0.689
Sergipe	1	Porto da Folha	0.2671	0.499
	1	Aquidaba	0.3114	0.501
	3	Pedrinhas	0.0072	0.822
	3	Araua	0.0723	0.178
	5	Frei Paulo	0.0327	0.598
	5	Itabaina	0.3550	0.402

a. These probabilities would not apply if more than one municipio were selected to represent a single production pattern within the given microregion.

selection (our situation), an unbiased estimate of the population microregion mean is:[15]

$$(B.23) \qquad \hat{\bar{Y}} = \frac{1}{nM_0} \sum_{i=1}^{n} \frac{M_i \hat{\bar{Y}}_i}{Z_i^1},$$

15. See Cochran, *Sampling Techniques*, pp. 261, 305.

where, in our case, M_i is the number of municipios in the microregion, and $Z'_i = Z_i/n$, where Z_i is the absolute probability of selection derived above.

Although this estimate of the microregion mean is unbiased, its variance may be very large. In terms of expression (B.23), a further related problem is that because, in general, $\Sigma^n_{i=1} M_i/nM_0 Z'_i \neq 1$, that is, the sum of the weights of the sample municipio means in the population mean is not unity, the estimate of $\bar{Y}$ will be outside the range of the municipio mean estimates $\hat{\bar{Y}}_j$. Let us consider now the alternative estimator:

$$(B.24) \qquad \bar{\bar{Y}} = \frac{1}{\displaystyle\sum_{i=1}^{n} \frac{M_i}{Z'_i}} \sum_{i=1}^{n} M_i \frac{\bar{Y}_i}{Z'_i} .$$

Indicating with t_i a random variable with a value of one if the ith municipio is in the sample and zero otherwise, we can write expression (B.24) as:

$$(B.25) \qquad \bar{\bar{Y}} = \frac{\displaystyle\sum_{i=1}^{N} t_i M_i \frac{\bar{Y}_i}{Z'_i}}{\displaystyle\sum_{i=1}^{N} t_i \frac{M_i}{Z'_i}} .$$

The probability limit of t_i will be equal to $Z_i = nZ'_i$, that is, to the absolute probability of selection of municipio i. Therefore, by the Slutsky theorem, $\bar{\bar{Y}}$ is a consistent estimator of $\bar{Y}$:

$$(B.26) \qquad \text{plim}\,\bar{\bar{Y}} = \frac{\text{plim} \displaystyle\sum_{i=1}^{n} t_i M_i \frac{\bar{Y}_i}{Z'_i}}{\text{plim} \displaystyle\sum_{i=1}^{n} t_i \frac{M_i}{Z'_i}} = \sum_{i=0}^{n} \frac{M_i}{M_0} \bar{Y}_i = \bar{Y}.$$

Estimating the Farm Population

The procedure described above can be used to estimate the average population of each stratum (farm size class) and municipio. To extrapolate these results to the entire Northeast, we need an estimate of the corresponding stratified division of the Northeast population. The most natural auxiliary variable for this purpose, given the type of survey conducted, is the number of farms. Once estimates have been made of the number of farms in each size class in the Northeast, it is a simple matter to obtain estimates for those size classes of any other farm level variable, by using ratio estimates as described by Cochran.[16]

16. Ibid., pp. 154–88.

The definition of "farm" used for this study—a parcel or group of close-lying parcels of land (not necessarily contiguous) *under the same management*—differs from the definition of agricultural "properties" used by INCRA for their cadastral survey, which we used to identify properties for our sample. INCRA had defined a property as an undivided parcel *under the same ownership*. The interviewers for our survey were instructed, upon arrival at a property, to discover the number of farms it comprised. (The property may not have been a farm at all, or it may have been parceled into two or more farms, or it may have been only part of a larger farm.)

For the ith sampled municipio, an estimate of the total number of farms in the kth size class is:

$$(B.27) \qquad \hat{M}_{ik}^F = b_{ik} M_{ik}^P,$$

where $\hat{M}_{ik}^F$ = estimate of number of farms, municipio i, size class k
M_{ik}^P = number of properties in the INCRA cadastral survey, municipio i, size class k
b_{ik} = ratio of actual sample size of farms to sample size of properties, municipio i, size class k.

For nonsampled municipios, we did not have the complete distribution of properties, only the total numbers. We first estimated the number of properties in each size class and municipio for a given microregion:

$$(B.28) \qquad \hat{M}_{ik}^P = \hat{a}_k M_i^P,$$

where
$$\hat{a}_k = \sum_{i=1}^{n} w_i\, a_{ik},$$
$$a_{ik} = M_{ik}^P / M_i^P,$$

then the estimated number of farms in size class k, municipio i, is:

$$(B.29) \qquad M_{ik}^F = \hat{b}_k \hat{M}_{ik}^P,$$

where
$$\hat{b}_k = \sum_{i=1}^{n} w_i b_{ik}.$$

Before the formulas above were used to calculate the total number of farms per size class in the Northeast, it was necessary to test whether the number of properties was consistent with estimates that could be made of average property size. We knew the total number of properties per municipio, M_i^P, and the total agricultural area of the ith municipio, A_i. The desirable consistency conditions of the estimates $\hat{M}_{ik}^P$ of the number of properties and $\hat{S}_{ik}$ of the average property size are:

$$(B.30) \qquad M_i = \sum_{k=1}^{L} \hat{M}_{ik},$$

$$(B.31) \qquad A_i = \sum_{k=1}^{L} \hat{M}_{ik}\, \hat{S}_{ik}.$$

Such consistency checks may fail either because the size distribution of properties (both within and across the size classes) differs among municipios in the same microregion or because the average farm size of a given size class differs among municipios. Other than in the last size class (more than 500 hectares), there is little room for variation in the farm sizes within the size classes, because each is bounded from above and below in a relatively narrow range. (The consistency of average property and farm sizes within the first five strata had been verified by casual inspection.) Therefore, we permitted a variation of 10 percent in the consistency requirement (B.31) to allow for minor differences in the sizes and sought an adjustment rule for those municipios that still did not satisfy the requirement.

A practical procedure is to seek an estimated distribution closest in an appropriate sense to that estimated in expression (B.28) but meeting the requirements (B.30) and (B.31). Using the least squares criterion, one could construct a quadratic programming problem to find a distribution of properties consistent with the a priori information, the $\overset{*}{M}{}_{ik}^{P}$.[17] Minimize

(B.32) $$\Sigma\,(\overset{*}{M}{}_k^P - \hat{M}_k^P)^2\,,$$

subject to

(B.33) $$\Sigma\,\overset{*}{M}{}_k^P = M^P\,,$$

(B.34) $$\Sigma\,\overset{*}{M}{}_k^P\,\hat{S}_k^P = A\,,$$

$$\overset{*}{M}{}_k^P \geq 0\,,$$

for all k. In our case, however, this procedure would have entailed solving up to 1,300 quadratic programming problems, a task that is simply out of the question. If, however, we ignore, for the moment, the nonnegativity constraints, we can convert (B.32)–(B.33) into a Lagrangian,

(B.35) $$L = \Sigma\,(\overset{*}{M}{}_k^P - \hat{M}_k^P)^2 - \lambda_1(\Sigma\overset{*}{M}{}_k^P - M^P) - \lambda_2(\Sigma\overset{*}{M}{}_k^P\hat{S}_k^P - A),$$

which has the partial derivatives:

(B.36) $$\frac{\partial L}{\partial M_k} = \partial\overset{*}{M}{}_k^P - \partial\hat{M}_k^P - \lambda_1 - \lambda_2\hat{S}_k = 0,$$

(B.37) $$\frac{\partial L}{\partial X_1} = \Sigma\overset{*}{M}{}_k^P - M^P = 0,$$

---

17. We have deleted the i subscript in what follows because any procedure must be repeated for each municipio that fails the consistency check.

(B.38) $\dfrac{\partial L}{\partial X_2} = \Sigma \overset{*}{M}{}_k^P \hat{S}_k - A = 0.$

Summing (B.28) over k and rearranging, we have

(B.39) $\lambda_1 = -\lambda_2 \dfrac{\Sigma S_k}{N},$

where N is the number of size classes.

Multiplying (B.28) by S_k, and summing over k, that is, multiplying the number of properties by the average property size, for all size classes, and rearranging, we have

(B.40) $$\lambda_2 = \dfrac{\hat{A} - A}{\dfrac{\Sigma \hat{S}_k}{N} - \hat{S}_k^2},$$

where $\hat{A} = \hat{M}_k^P \hat{S}_k^P$ (the estimated total agricultural area is equal to the estimated total number of properties multiplied by their average size). Thus,

(B.41) $\overset{*}{M}{}_k^P = \hat{M}_k^P + \lambda_1 + \lambda_2 \hat{S}_k.$[18]

In computational tests of this procedure, it was found that occasionally the $\overset{*}{M}{}_k^P$ would be negative for either the first stratum ($k = 1$) or the last ($k = 6$). In such cases, we simply set the negative number to zero and solved the problem again for the other strata. The estimated distribution of properties for all municipios in the Northeast grouped by regions is given in Chapter 2.

For nonsampled municipios, the distribution of farms was estimated from $\overset{*}{M}{}_{ik}^P$ and (B.27). Again, we used b_{ik} on a microregionwide basis with the weights defined above. The complete estimated distribution of farms is also shown in Chapter 2.

---

18. $\overset{*}{M}{}_k^P$ is a consistent estimate of M_k^P because:
   plim $\lambda_1 = 0$ (as $\to\infty$) and plim $\lambda_2 = (A - \hat{A})/\Sigma \hat{S}_k^2 = 0$, since $A = $ plim $\hat{A}$.
Notice that if $E\hat{A} = A$, the estimate is also unbiased.

Appendix C
The Fieldwork

Perhaps the ideal enumerator would be a person familiar with both the agronomy and the agricultural economics of the region being surveyed, possessing sufficient statistical training to understand the causes and consequences of biases in response, a personality conducive to conducting a good interview with a strange farmer, and the stamina to endure the hardships of traveling in a remote region. Instead of finding or attempting to train such people, we opted for a team approach, combining people with complementary skills.

Selection and Training of Enumerators

Each enumeration team comprised five to eight people, depending on the size of the sample of farms and municipios, and had members selected from the four principal Brazilian participating institutions: Federal University of Pernambuco; Northeast Development Superintendency (SUDENE); the National Agriculture Extension and Credit Agency (ANCAR) for each of the nine states; and the Agricultural Planning Commission (CEPA) for each of the nine states. The Federal University of Pernambuco, which was contracted by the World Bank, provided six master's level economics students who served as enumeration team supervisors.[1] SUDENE provided several agricultural economists and agronomists from its staff, who, together with the university supervisors, provided continuity to the teams. ANCAR and CEPA provided agronomists and planning coordinators to the teams in their respective states. Thus, part of the team was constant throughout the survey as the teams moved from state to state, and part of the team, from ANCAR and CEPA, changed with each state. Although this required continual training of new enumerators, the benefits of having persons with intimate knowledge of their own areas outweighed the training costs.[2]

1. The university also loaned the services of Professor Yony Sampaio to the project during the sample selection and enumeration stages.
2. Not only the diversity of ecological conditions and farming practices but other differences, such as units of measurement, made the inclusion of local specialists a necessity.

The training of the enumeration teams for the survey of the first state (Pernambuco) began immediately after the revisions to the questionnaire, suggested by the first field tests, had been completed and a training manual produced. This training manual contained a discussion of principles of enumeration and a description of the types of analysis to which the data would be applied. It described the logic of the questionnaire, giving a detailed description of each table and showing how the tables fitted together to permit a "flow" of information and simultaneously to allow the answers to be cross-checked. It provided a conversion table for those instances in which measurement units used locally differed from regionwide official units.

The training sessions began with three days of classroom study, followed by exercises in filling out questionnaires under simulated conditions in the classroom. Subsequently, small groups of enumerators under the supervision of the project leaders were sent to nearby farms to conduct interviews under real conditions. The results of these test applications were reviewed back in the classroom, and further instruction given where needed.

The Paraiba and Rio Grande do Norte training sessions followed the same pattern as those in Pernambuco, except that the SUDENE and university counterparts took over the training. During these sessions, the pattern of two class days, one and a half field days, and one-half class day was established. In retrospect, this much training was not sufficient for such a complicated questionnaire; the testing and cleaning procedures later revealed that much more intensive training would undoubtedly have saved many months of data cleaning. It also has to be noted that the real period of training lasted longer than these four days, because the first several days of the actual fieldwork were considered a further training period, but without the interviewers' knowledge. This allowed for observation of the interviewers' performance under realistic and exacting conditions, while there was still an opportunity to refine their techniques.

Finally, it has to be stressed that the training was continued in the field not only through the daily interaction between the supervisors and the enumerators but also through constant contact between the field teams and the research group based in Recife. As will be explained below, the extensive traveling of the coordinators allowed them to transfer experience from one team to another team, anticipating difficulties and proposing uniform solutions to most of the problems.

Organization and Evaluation of the Fieldwork

The actual field enumeration of the questionnaires was carried out state by state in three phases: Pernambuco, Rio Grande do Norte, and Paraiba in October–November 1973; Ceara, Piaui, and Maranhao in December 1973–January 1974; and Alagoas, Sergipe, and Bahia in February–March 1974. An average of eight municipios were sampled per state, and four enumeration teams worked approximately one month in each municipio. The state-by-state procedure enabled us to take full advantage of the cooperation of the state agricultural planning agencies, which provided some of the interviewers and coordinated state-specific aspects of the fieldwork. It also permitted intense supervision of the enumeration by the joint SUDENE/ANCAR/university team. Within a given state, phasing was necessitated by the seasonality of agricultural activities.

Clearly, with such an intricate organizational structure cutting across several institutions and such a large area (the state of Bahia alone is the size of France), problems could be expected. There were, of course, delays, arising from bureaucratic difficulties and in the printing of questionnaires. The fieldwork was only eleven days late in starting, however. This minimum delay can itself be considered a success, since the design of the project was finalized only in May, the full team formed in late July, the questionnaire finalized in August, and the sample of farms drawn in early September.

If we discount the initial frictions and the slight problems caused by changes in schedule in the first fifteen days, the experience of the fieldwork was clearly a success. Altogether, more than fifty people were in the field from the university, ANCAR, SUDENE, and CEPA, working together as a group with no bureaucratic or institutional problems in spite of different institutional backgrounds, wage differentials, strains of daily interactions, and hardships encountered in the field. The field teams also developed good relations with local people such as mayors and officials of city planning agencies, who showed a strong desire to work closely with state and federal agencies in the agricultural planning of the Northeast. The supervisors were invited to use local radio and television stations to publicize the survey and participate in debates of general interest.

The scheme of work adopted for the coordinators was such that each team was visited by at least one member of the central team each week. This permitted the training to continue in the field and helped to unify and accumulate the experience of interpretation, application, and analysis of the questionnaires. These frequent visits, together with the active presence of the supervisors, also gave the enumerators the incentive to work from sunrise to sundown and at night in revision of questionnaires.

In general the questionnaire proved to be both a convenient and a feasible base for the interview. The results of the pretest on the average length of the interview were, in general, confirmed during the fieldwork: Questionnaire I took between three and five hours, and questionnaire II did not exceed seven hours. Though the time needed for locating the farmers had often been underestimated, between 1.2 and 1.8 questionnaires were applied per interviewer per day.

After three or four days of fieldwork the enumerators and the supervisors were already sufficiently familiar with the questionnaire to be able to remember most of the codes, which made the interview less formal and more flexible. The inclusion of extension agents on the teams proved particularly fortunate, not only because they could translate the questions into terms familiar to the farmers and translate back the answers, but also because they were genuinely interested in using the knowledge obtained from the interviews in their fieldwork.

Almost all farmers reacted positively to being interviewed, and cases of diffidence or open suspicion were very rare. Especially in the Sertao, farmers are very articulate and enjoy the opportunity of talking about their activities. Although excessive enthusiasm on the part of the farmer may itself make for distortions in the data collected, it can be said that the most successful interviewers understood the need to let the questionnaire be the basis for a widely ranging discussion of the characteristics of the farm.

Farmers in drought areas where the crop seemed to be scarce were more friendly and forthcoming than farmers in areas that had had a good year. It would have been valuable to analyze this difference quantitatively, because it could lead to distortions. Bad-year farmers could have been hoping for material help from SUDENE (whose cars were well known); or they might have been looking only for sympathy.

The interviewers as well as the supervisors acquired familiarity and confidence in the questionnaire very rapidly. On certain critical topics, however, it was discovered that the interpretation of the question was a matter of opinion; no clear-cut solution was possible for this. One of the main purposes of the coordinators' traveling was to provide a unified interpretation for such points of the questionnaire. These interpretations were promptly incorporated into a second edition of the field manual developed for the enumerators.

Appendix D
Data Validation Procedures

In addition to the obvious error of estimate, there are several potential sources of error in a sample survey of the type described here, simply because a random sample was taken instead of a complete enumeration of the population of farms.[1] Among these sources of error are: failure to measure some of the units in the chosen sample; errors of measurement, because farmers' answers were biased or because they could not remember or did not have certain information; errors of measurement because enumerators were biased, or were unable to translate the questionnaire into terms meaningful to farmers; errors introduced in editing, coding, and tabulating the results. The survey team was well aware of these sources of error and sought every means to control them with the time and resources available.

In areas where transport infrastructure is primitive, it was sometimes impossible to include all the units in the sample as originally designed—some of the farms surveyed could be reached only by burro or canoe! The drawing of a backup sample from the identical population minimized the consequences of this problem. Table B-3 shows the degree to which the preselected sample was realized.

Biases on the part of respondents are in general very difficult to measure, and the state of the art is far from precise. At least enumerators who were well versed in the agricultural practices of the area (particularly the extension agents) could immediately recognize answers that were obviously incorrect. In addition, the members of each coordinated team jointly reviewed their results daily, which assisted in identifying nonsystematically biased responses.

The survey was not advertised to the farmers as having any specific objective (such as property valuation for tax purposes, or particular development projects), and they generally had no obvious reason to bias their

---

1. Vinh Le-Si assisted in drafting this section.

answers. An exception, though, arose on the subject of sharecroppers: Recently enacted labor and land tenure laws had placed restrictions on farms with sharecropper employment. Several obvious attempts to "hide" sharecroppers—for example, by defining them as renters—or to give inaccurate information were discovered.

Answers that required a subjective evaluation by the farmers, however, were a source of problems. In particular, the questions on value of land and structures proved very difficult, partly because the market for land is very weak in many areas. The inconsistency in these subjective answers shows up in the tabulated results.

For one item, farm size, an alternative check was possible. In conjunction with an overlapping partial soil survey, precise measurements of the farms were taken and showed that virtually all farmers had accurate information on the size of their farms.

The use of complementary enumeration teams, composed of individuals drawn from several institutions and different backgrounds, helped to control enumerator bias, at least in the aggregate. Again, the daily reviews in the field, in which the entire team was usually involved, made it possible to spot bias on the part of individual enumerators. Because the enumerator is identified on each questionnaire, it would be possible to check for biases by, for example, cross-sectional analysis of the questionnaires enumerated by extension agents and SUDENE analysts. Time constraints have not permitted such checks as of the time of writing.

As mentioned above, the cleaning process began in the field with daily review of the incoming questionnaires by the enumeration team supervisor and members of the Recife-based SUDENE/World Bank coordinating team. As quickly as possible, the questionnaires were returned to the Recife office where they were reviewed by another SUDENE team before being keypunched. This last review was primarily concerned with verifying the codes for crops, equipment, type of farm management, and so forth, and checking calculations made in the field. The questionnaires were then keypunched and loaded onto magnetic tape.

At this point it was possible to use the computer to help detect certain types of remaining errors. Two programs were developed, Critica and Consistencia, and each questionnaire was processed with both programs twice. Critica checked each card individually, searching for detectable keypunch error, incorrect or missing codes, missing information, and within-card consistency. Some examples of the latter checks are: that the areas shown under sources and under uses of farmland (from Table 2A of questionnaire I) are equal; that the volume of output distributed equals the volume produced (from questionnaire Table 6); that the total annual labor remuneration equals the number of days worked times the daily wage (or number of weeks times the weekly wage), plus remuneration in kind (from questionnaire Table 9). The first processing with Critica revealed errors, most of them in keypunching, in about 30 percent of the cards. After correcting them, a second pass was made to verify the corrections before proceeding to Consistencia.

The objective of Consistencia was to reveal errors in consistency among cards and tables. The questionnaire was designed to permit several ways of asking certain questions and hence to permit cross-checks among answers. Some examples of Consistencia checks are: that the area of crops and pasture enumerated in questionnaire Table 5 matches the area given in Table 2A; that the consumption, sales, and other types of distribution of all outputs match the production and purchases; that a new crop (less than one year of age) identified in Table 5 should have associated labor inputs for soil preparation and planting shown in Table 11 of the questionnaire; that certain inputs shown in questionnaire Table 12 (for example, gasoline and oil) should match certain types of equipment (for example, mechanized equipment); that the labor drawn from various sources, shown in questionnaire Tables 10, 11, and 15, should be consistent with the census of labor in Table 9; and that the sharecropping information (land in Table 2A, production in Table 5, and the sharecropper census in Table 14) be consistent across tables. Consistencia revealed actual or possible errors in another 25 percent of the questionnaires, each of which was resolved by the Recife reviewing team, and, again, a second pass was made to check corrections.

The large number of errors encountered by Critica and Consistencia perhaps reflected difficulties on the part of the enumerators in fully understanding the spirit of the consistency requirements of the questionnaire and also, perhaps, their difficulties with the precoding system. Undoubtedly, the training period was insufficient, and some conceptual difficulties remained with the enumerators in the field. Many of the errors in consistency could have been avoided if the training had been more comprehensive and if the enumerators had been informed of the actual checks Critica and Consistencia would later make. Such prior warning, however, would have destroyed our ability to make independent tests of the data and would probably have yielded poorer data quality (if the enumerator were more concerned with the various consistency requirements, his effort to obtain accuracy on specific answers might suffer).

The data cleaning process took about nine months (the last data were collected in April, and Consistencia corrections were completed in November). The reviewing team comprised twenty people on the average (many of them returning field supervisors), and about fifty-five hours of SUDENE's IBM 360/30 computer time was required.

During the final stages of testing with Critica and Consistencia, the researchers began examining statistics on items such as the distribution of prices and yields, and some technical coefficients of production for use in preliminary linear programming work. We found that certain types of errors still remained, particularly those concerned with measurement units. The unit of production, for example, for most crops was kilograms but was metric tons for sugarcane. Often the enumerator mistakenly used kilograms for sugar, and if he did this consistently throughout the questionnaire the error remained undetected. Similar errors often encountered concerned eggs, which should have been recorded in units of 1,000 eggs but were often given in units of eggs; forage inputs (kilograms instead of tons); and electricity (only the annual cost was asked, but watts were sometimes given as well, resulting in enormous numbers when watts and annual cost were multiplied).

Therefore, still another round of testing was needed. We called this Supertest, because it involved interfarm comparisons, whereas the previous tests were concerned with the questionnaires on the basis of individual farms. The strategy followed in Supertest was to calculate the distributions of various key variables and search for outliers from these distributions.[2] These key variables were prices, yields, gross output, gross labor input, purchased inputs for livestock, and other purchased inputs.

For those variables that are not likely to be highly correlated with farm size (prices, yields, ratio of livestock inputs to herd value, and so on) we simply calculated the means and standard deviations on a statewide basis and flagged those farms for which the variable was not within one standard deviation of the mean.

The output from the Supertest computer program displayed these flagged farms with the corresponding values of the variables considered, enabling an economist to examine the results at a glance and decide whether further examination of the questionnaire itself was warranted. A low level of output per hectare, for example, was easily explicable if labor per hectare was also low. If there was no such obvious reason, the questionnaire was

---

2. For a technical discussion of the strategy of detecting errors, see Philip Musgrove, "Detecting Errors in Economic Survey Data: Multivariate vs. Univariate Procedures," *Annals of Economic and Social Measurement*, vol. 3, no. 2 (1974), pp. 333–45; and Frank E. Grubbs, "Procedures for Detecting Outlying Observations in Samples," *Technometrics*, vol. 11, no. 1 (February 1969), pp. 1–21.

again reviewed. In some cases, no error was detected, as the values of other variables provided an explanation. Low values for both output per hectare and output per man, for example, accompanied by a high input of labor per hectare may be perfectly plausible if the agricultural year surveyed on a particular farm was devoted largely to the establishment of new long-cycle crops; high output ratios accompanied by low labor inputs could be the result of drawing down livestock inventories during the year. Supertest revealed that, once these apparent anomalies had been accounted for, about 7 percent of the questionnaires contained errors.

Virtually all these errors were due either to the use of incorrect units for recording physical products, prices, or labor use or to a misplacing of the coded columns of the questionnaire.[3]

3. That is, if the number 10 is to be placed in the IBM card field comprising columns 24–32, a 1 should be placed in column 31. If it is misplaced or mispunched in column 30, the computer will read 100.

Bibliography

The word "processed" describes works that are reproduced from typescript by mimeograph, xerography, or similar means; such works may not be cataloged or commonly available through libraries, or may be subject to restricted circulation.

"Agrarian Reform: A Time-worn Subject Returns to the Headlines." *Veja*, December 7, 1977.

Ahluwalia, Montek S., John H. Duloy, Graham Pyatt, and T. N. Srinivasan. "Who Benefits from Economic Growth? An Examination of Fields' Reexamination for Brazil." *American Economic Review*, vol. 70, no. 1 (March 1980), pp. 242–45.

Andrade, Manuel Correia de. *A terra e o homen no Nordeste*. Sao Paulo: Editora Brasiliense, 1964.

Baer, Werner. "The Brazilian Growth and Development Experience: 1964–1975." In *Brazil in the Seventies*. Edited by Riordan Roett. Washington, D.C.: American Enterprise Institute for Public Policy Research, 1976.

Baer, Werner, and Isaac Kerstenetzky. "The Brazilian Economy." In *Brazil in the Sixties*. Edited by Riordan Roett. Nashville, Tenn.: Vanderbilt University Press, 1972.

Berry, R. Albert, and William R. Cline. *Agrarian Structure and Productivity in Developing Countries*. Baltimore, Md: Johns Hopkins University Press, 1979.

Bolch, B. W., and C. J. Huang. *Multivariate Statistical Methods for Business and Economics*. Englewood Cliffs, N.J.: Prentice-Hall International, 1974.

"Brazil's Arid Northeast Skeptical as Help Is Promised Once Again." *New York Times*, September 21, 1979, p. A13.

"Brazil's Outcast Shanty Dwellers Offered a Helping Hand at Last." *New York Times*, October 22, 1972, p. A4.

Britton, D. K., and Berkeley Hill. *Size and Efficiency in Farming*. Lexington, Mass.: Saxon House Studies/Lexington Books, 1976.

Buckwell, A. E., and P. B. R. Hazell. "Implications for Aggregation Bias for the Construction of Static and Dynamic Linear Programming Supply Models." *Journal of Agricultural Economics*, vol. 23, no. 2 (1972), pp. 119–34.

Candler, Wilfred V. "A Demonstration Model for the Dairy Industry of La Laguna." In *The Book of CHAC: Programming Studies for Mexican Agriculture*. Edited by Roger D. Norton and Leopoldo Solis M. Baltimore, Md.: Johns Hopkins University Press, forthcoming.

Castro de Rezende, Gervasio. "Plantation Systems, Land Tenure, and Labor Supply: An Historical Analysis of the Brazilian Case with a Contemporary Study of the Cacao Regions of Bahia, Brazil." Ph.D. dissertation. Madison: University of Wisconsin, 1976.

Castro, Josue de. *Death in the Northeast*. New York: Random House, 1969.

Cavalcanti de Albuquerque, Roberto, and Clovis de Vasconcelos Cavalcanti. "Regional Development Policies in Brazil: Precedents and Prospects." Seminar on Regional Development/Brazil, European Economic Community. Brasilia, October 17, 1972.

Cehelsky, Marta. *Land Reform in Brazil: The Management of Social Change*. Boulder, Colo.: Westview Press, 1979.

Chenery, Hollis B. "Development Policies for Southern Italy." *Quarterly Journal of Economics*, vol. 76 (November 1962), pp. 515–47.

Chow, G. S. "Tests of Equality between Sets of Coefficients in Two Linear Regressions." *Econometrica*, vol. 28, no. 3 (July 1960), pp. 591–605.

Cirne Lima, Luis Fernando. *Jornal do Brasil*, November 20, 1977.

Cline, William R. *Economic Consequences of a Land Reform in Brazil*. Amsterdam: North-Holland Publishing Company, 1970.

Cochran, William G. *Sampling Techniques*. New York: John Wiley and Sons, 1963.

Comite Interamericano de Desarrollo (CIDA). *Land Tenure Conditions and Socioeconomic Development of the Agricultural Sector, Brazil*. Washington, D.C.: Pan American Union, 1964.

Conjuntura economica (Rio de Janeiro), vol. 31, no. 7 (July 1977).

Day, Richard H. "On Aggregating Linear Programming Models of Production." *Journal of Farm Economics*, vol. 45 (November 1963), pp. 797–813.

De Azevedo, Fernando. *Brazilian Culture: An Introduction to the Study of Culture in Brazil*. Translated by William Rex Crawford. New York: Macmillan Company, 1950.

Dillon, John L., and Pasquale L. Scandizzo. "Risk Attitudes of Subsistence Farmers in Northeast Brazil: A Sampling Approach." *American Journal of Agricultural Economics*, vol. 6, no. 3 (August 1978), pp. 425–35.

Duloy, John H., and Roger D. Norton. "CHAC: A Programming Model of Mexican Agriculture." In *Multi-level Planning: Case Studies in Mexico*. Edited by Louis M. Goreux and Alan S. Manne. Amsterdam: North-Holland Publishing Company, 1973.

———. "Prices and Incomes in Linear Programming Models." *American Journal of Agricultural Economics*, vol. 57 (November 1975), pp. 591–600.

Eckstein, Shlomo, Gordon Donald, Douglas Horton, and Thomas Carroll. *Land Reform in Latin America: Bolivia, Chile, Mexico, Peru, and Venezuela*. World Bank Staff Working Paper no. 275. Washington, D.C.: World Bank, April 1978.

Egbert, Alvin C., and Hyung M. Kim. "Analysis of Aggregation Errors in Linear Programming Planning Models." *American Journal of Agricultural Economics*, vol. 57, no. 2 (May 1975), pp. 292–301.

————. *A Development Model for the Agricultural Sector of Portugal.* World Bank Staff Occasional Paper no. 20. Baltimore, Md.: Johns Hopkins University Press, 1975.

El-Tobgy, H. A. *Contemporary Egyptian Agriculture.* Beirut: Ford Foundation, 1974.

Estudo Nacional da Despesa Familiar. *Consumo alimentar antropometria, dados preliminares.* Regiao V. Rio de Janeiro: FIBGE, 1977.

————. *Despesas das familias, dados preliminares.* Regiao V. Rio de Janeiro: FIBGE, 1978.

Feder, Gershon, and P. L. Scandizzo. "A Two-Region Multisectoral Model for Brazil." Washington, D.C.: World Bank, Development Research Center, 1977. Processed.

Fields, Gary. "Who Benefits from Economic Development? A Re-examination of Brazilian Growth in the 1960s." *American Economic Review*, vol. 67 (September 1977), pp. 570–82.

Fishlow, Albert. "Brazilian Size Distribution of Income." *American Economic Review*, vol. 62, no. 2 (May 1972), pp. 391–402.

Forman, Shepard. *The Brazilian Peasantry.* New York: Columbia University Press, 1975.

Freyre, Gilberto. *The Masters and the Slaves: A Study in the Development of Brazilian Civilization.* New York: Alfred Knopf, 1946; abridged ed., 1964.

Fundacao Getulio Vargas. *Precos pagos pelos agricultores.* Rio de Janeiro, 1972.

Furtado, Celso. *The Economic Growth of Brazil: A Survey from Colonial to Modern Times.* Translated by Ricardo W. de Aguiar and Eric Charles Drysdale. Berkeley: University of California Press, 1963.

Goodman, David. "Industrial Development in the Brazilian Northeast: An Interim Assessment of the Tax Credit Scheme of Article 34/18." In *Brazil in the Sixties.* Edited by Riordan Roett. Nashville, Tenn.: Vanderbilt University Press, 1972.

Goodman, David, and Roberto Cavalcanti. *Incentivos a industrializacao e desenvolvimento do Nordeste.* Rio de Janeiro: IPEA/INPES, 1974.

Goreux, Louis M., and Alan S. Manne, eds. *Multi-level Planning: Case Studies in Mexico.* Amsterdam: North-Holland Publishing Company, 1973.

Grubbs, Frank E. "Procedures for Detecting Outlying Observations in Samples." *Technometrics*, vol. 11, no. 1 (February 1969), pp. 1–21.

Grupo de Trabalho para o Desenvolvimento do Nordeste (GTDN). *Uma politica de desenvolvimento para o Nordeste.* Rio de Janeiro: Conselho de Desenvolvimento, 1959.

————. *Uma politica de desenvolvimento economico para o Nordeste,* 2d ed. Recife: SUDENE, 1967.

Hadley, George. *Non-Linear and Dynamic Programming.* Reading, Mass.: Addison-Wesley Publishing Co., 1964.

Hall, Anthony L. *Drought and Irrigation in North-East Brazil.* Cambridge, England: Cambridge University Press, 1978.

Hansen, Morris, William Hurwitz, and William G. Meadow. *Sample Survey Methods and Theory.* Vol. 1. New York: John Wiley and Sons, 1953.

Harris, John R., and Michael P. Todaro. "Migration, Unemployment, and Development: A Two-Sector Analysis." *American Economic Review*, vol. 60, no. 1 (March 1970), pp. 126–42.

Havighurst, Robert J., and J. Roberto Moreira. *Society and Education in Brazil.* Pittsburgh, Pa.: University of Pittsburgh Press, 1965.

Hazell, Peter B. R. "Farm Planning under Uncertainty." *American Journal of Agricultural Economics*, vol. 53 (February 1971), pp. 53–62.

Hazell, Peter B. R., and P. L. Scandizzo. "Competitive Demand Structures under Risk in Linear Programming Models." *American Journal of Agricultural Economics*, vol. 56 (May 1974), pp. 235–44.

Heady, Earl O., and John L. Dillon. *Agricultural Production Functions.* Ames: Iowa State University Press, 1960.

Hirschman, Alfred O. *Journeys toward Progress: Studies of Economic Policy-Making in Latin America.* New York: Twentieth Century Fund, 1963.

Houthakker, Hendrik S., and Lester D. Taylor. *Consumer Demand in the United States: Analyses and Projections.* Cambridge, Mass.: Harvard University Press, 1970.

Instituto Brasileiro de Geografia e Estatistica (IBGE). *Anuario estatistico do Brasil.* Rio de Janeiro, 1975, 1976.

———. *Censo demografico VIII: Recenseamento geral, 1970.* Vol. 1, nos. 5–10. Rio de Janeiro, 1972.

———. *Dados preliminares gerais do censo agropecuario VIII: Recenseamento geral, 1970.* Rio de Janeiro, 1972.

Institute of Economic and Social Planning (IPEI). "Metodologia da amostragem por areas geograficas de unidades produtoras." Sao Luis, Maranhao, 1974. Processed.

———. "Pesquisa por areas geograficas de unidades produtoras." Sao Luis, Maranhao, 1974. Processed.

International Trade Centre. *Cassava: Export Potential and Market Requirement.* Geneva: UNCTAD/GATT, 1977.

Johnson, Allen W. *Sharecroppers of the Sertao.* Stanford, Calif.: Stanford University Press, 1971.

Katzman, Martin T. *Cities and Frontiers in Brazil: Regional Dimensions of Economic Development.* Cambridge, Mass.: Harvard University Press, 1977.

Kutcher, Gary P. "Agricultural Planning at the Regional Level: A Programming Study of Mexico's Pacific Northwest." Ph.D. dissertation. College Park: University of Maryland, 1972.

Kutcher, Gary P., and Pasquale L. Scandizzo. "Northeast Brazil Regional Studies Project: Sampling Procedures." Washington, D.C.: World Bank, Development Research Center, 1974. Processed.

———. "A Partial Analysis of Sharetenancy Relationships in Northeast Brazil." *Journal of Development Economics*, vol. 3 (December 1976), pp. 343–54.

Lacerda de Melo, M. "Espacos geograficos e politica espacial: O caso do Nordeste." *Boletim economico*, vol. 5, no. 2 (July 1969/December 1971), pp. 7–139.

Langoni, Carlos Geraldo. *Distribuicao da renda e desenvolvimento economico do Brasil*. Rio de Janeiro: Editora Expressao e Cultura, 1973.

Leff, Nathaniel H. "Economic Development and Regional Inequality: Origins of the Brazilian Case." *Quarterly Journal of Economics*, vol. 86, no. 2 (May 1972), pp. 243–62.

Leuthold, Raymond M. "On the Use of Theil's Inequality Coefficients." *American Journal of Agricultural Economics*, vol. 57, no. 2 (May 1975), pp. 344–46.

Ludwig, Armin K., and Harry W. Taylor. *Brazil's New Agrarian Reform*. New York: Praeger, 1969.

Mellor, John W. *The Economics of Agricultural Development*. Ithaca, N.Y.: Cornell University Press, 1966.

Miller Paiva, Ruy. "Modernizacao e dualismo tecnologico na agricultura." *Pesquisa e planejamento economico*, vol. 1, no. 2 (December 1971), pp. 171–234.

Miller Paiva, Ruy, and George F. Patrick. *Acesso a terra no Nordeste*. Colecao Relatorios de Pesquisa. Rio de Janeiro: IPEA/INPES. Processed.

Miller, T. A. "Sufficient Conditions for Exact Aggregation in Linear Programming Models." *Agricultural Economics Research*, vol. 18 (1966), pp. 52–57.

Musgrove, Philip. "Detecting Errors in Economics Survey Data: Multivariate vs. Univariate Procedures." *Annals of Economic and Social Measurement*, vol. 3, no. 2 (1974), pp. 333–45.

Nakajima, Chihiro. "Subsistence and Commercial Farms: Some Theoretical Models of Subjective Equilibrium." In *Subsistence Agriculture and Economic Development*. Edited by C. R. Wharton, Jr. Chicago: Aldine, 1970.

Nicholls, William H. "Paiva e o dualismo tecnologico na agricultura: um comentario." *Pesquisa e planejamento economico*, vol. 3, no. 1 (March 1973), pp. 15–50.

———. "The Brazilian Agricultural Economy: Recent Performance and Policy." In *Brazil in the Sixties*. Edited by Riordan Roett. Nashville, Tenn.: Vanderbilt University Press, 1972.

Nugent, Jeffrey B. "Linear Programming Models for National Planning: Demonstration of a Testing Procedure." *Econometrica*, vol. 38, no. 6 (November 1970), pp. 831–55.

"O feijao e o sonho," *Veja*, March 2, 1977.

Page, Joseph A. *The Revolution That Never Was: Northeast Brazil, 1955–64*. New York: Grossman Publishers, 1972.

Paris, Quirino, and G. C. Rausser. "Sufficient Conditions for Aggregation of Linear Programming Models." *American Journal of Agricultural Economics*, November 1973, pp. 659–66.

Patrick, George F. "Efeitos de programas alternativos do governo sobre a agricultura do Nordeste." *Pesquisa e planejamento economico*, no. 1 (February 1974), pp. 43–82.

Pfeffermann, Guy P., and Richard C. Webb. *The Distribution of Income in Brazil*. World Bank Staff Working Paper no. 356. Washington, D.C., September 1979.

Reboucas, D. E. "Interregional Effects of Economic Policies: Multisectoral General Equilibrium Estimates for Brasil." Ph.D. dissertation. Cambridge, Mass.: Harvard University, 1974.

Robock, Stefan H. *Brazil's Developing Northeast: A Study of Regional Planning and Foreign Aid*. Washington, D.C.: Brookings Institution, 1963.

Roett, Riordan, ed. *Brazil in the Sixties*. Nashville, Tenn.: Vanderbilt University Press, 1972.

Scandizzo, P. L., and T. Barbosa. "Substituicao e produtividade de fatores na agricultura Nordestina." *Pesquisa e planejamento economico*, vol. 7, no. 2 (August 1977), pp. 367–404.

Schuh, G. Edward. *The Agricultural Development of Brazil*. New York: Praeger, 1970.

———. "Modernizacao e dualismo tecnologico na agricultura: Alguns comentarios." *Pesquisa e planejamento economico*, vol. 3, no. 1 (March 1973), pp. 17–94.

Selowsky, Marcelo. *Who Benefits from Government Expenditure? A Case Study of Colombia*. New York: Oxford University Press, 1979.

Stigler, George J. *The Theory of Price*. Rev. ed. New York: Macmillan Company, 1952.

SUDENE. "The Brazilian Northeast and Its Institutions for Economic Development." Recife, 1961.

———. *Coeficientes tecnicos do Nordeste*. Recife, 1976.

———. *A economia agricola do Nordeste: Diagnostico parcial e perspectivas*. Recife, 1976.

United Nations, Food and Agriculture Organization. *Agricultural Commodity Projections, 1970–1980*. Vol. 2. Rome, 1971.

———. *Coffee in Latin America*. Rome, 1960.

Webb, Kempton E. *The Changing Face of Northeast Brazil*. New York: Columbia University Press, 1974.

World Bank. *Land Reform*. Sector Policy Paper. Washington, D.C., 1974.

———. "Rural Development Issues and Options in Northeast Brazil." Report no. 665a-BR. Washington, D.C., June 23, 1975. A restricted-circulation document.

———. *Rural Development*. Sector Policy Paper. Washington, D.C., February 1975.

———. *World Development Report, 1979*. New York: Oxford University Press, 1979.

Index

Agrarian reform, development and absence of, 191–94. *See also* Land reform

Agreste, 153; agricultural development and, 7; characteristics of, 35; family labor in, 91; farm size in, 49, 53; input costs in, 65; as physiographic zone, 22

Agricultural Planning Commissions (CEPA), 249

Agricultural production: capital and, 55; exchange rates and, 87–88; farm models and, 105, 145; farm size and, 97–100; input costs and, 63–67; model-simulated levels of, 152–55, 158; model overestimation of, 162, 163; model pattern of, 103; in Northeast, 24–25. *See also* Productivity

Agricultural sector: characteristics of, 89–94; early history of, 5–10; economic projection for, 170–73; family expenditures and, 74–77; as focus of SUDENE/World Bank survey, 4; global expenditures and, 79–81; monetary expenditures and, 77–79; output and, 60–63; production costs and, 63–67. *See also* Farmers; Farm size; Model of Northeastern agricultural sector

Article 34/18, 16

Bahia, 14; zone delineation and, 31, 34

Bank of the Northeast (BNB), 16; creation of, 13

Beans, 58, 117, 118, 178, 217, 218; demand intervention and, 189; farm family consumption and, 109. *See also* Crops

Brazil: early agricultural development in, 5–10; growth of, 3–4. *Se also* Model of Northeastern agricultural sector; Zones (Northeastern)

Brazilian Agricultural Research Company (EMBRAPA), 19, 176

Brazilian Institute for Agrarian Reform (IBRA), 15

Brazilian Land Statute of 1964, 29, 196–97, 210

Buckwell, A. E., 123, 125

Capital: agricultural, 53–57; in Northeast, 23–24; constraints at farm level, 166; farm models and, 107, 144; farm size and, 84–87

Cattle: beef production and, 60, 168; breeding of, 7–8; in farm models, 111–12; as income source, 54; inputs and, 65. *See also* Livestock

Cavalcanti, Clovis de Vasconcelos, 15, 17

Cavalcanti de Albuquerque, Roberto, 15, 17

Chenery, Hollis B., 63 n.10

Climate, 21; risk and, 110–11, 178, 179; settlement of Northeast and, 9. *See also* Drought

Cline, William R., 197, 205, 206, 208

Cacao, 59, 62, 87, 92, 104, 216, 217; farm incomes and, 69. *See also* Crops

Cochran, William G., 245

Coffee, 6, 87

Colonization: of Brazil, 5–7; land reform law and, 196; of western and northern Brazil, 14–15

Commercial farms, 95; farm models and, 122; market dependency and, 89–94. *See also* Family farms

Consistencia (data evaluation program), 254–56

Consumers, 173, 176, 177, 187; behavioral changes and, 170; demand intervention and, 189–90, 191; land reform and, 203; wage subsidies and, 182

Corn, 58, 117, 118, 178, 217, 218; farm family consumption and, 109. *See also* Crops

Costs, 163, 169; agricultural inputs and, 63–67; DRC coefficients and, 167–68; farm models and, 107; land reform, 206–08; of production, 25

Cotton, 13, 58, 59, 62, 88, 178, 193, 195, 216, 217, 218; farm models and, 108, 117–18; model-simulated production of, 153, 175; in the Sertao, 8, 113. *See also* Crops

Credit, 213; constraints at farm level and, 166; farm models and, 107

Critica (data evaluation program), 254–56

The full range of World Bank publications, both free and for sale, is described in the *Catalog of World Bank Publications;* the continuing research program is outlined in *World Bank Research Program: Abstracts of Current Studies.* Both booklets are updated annually; the most recent edition of each is available without charge from the Publications Unit, World Bank, 1818 H Street, N.W., Washington, D.C. 20433, U.S.A.

Gary P. Kutcher is an economist with the Development Research Center of the World Bank and is currently serving on the *World Development Report* core team.

Pasquale L. Scandizzo is a senior economist, formerly with the Development Research Center and now with the Agriculture and Rural Development Department of the World Bank.